# The Diabetic Bible

Dana Armstrong, RD, CDE
Allen Bennett King, MD, FACP, FACE, CDE

CONSULTANT
Gary Scheiner MS, CDE

Publications International, Ltd.

**Dana Armstrong, RD, CDE,** received her degree in nutrition and dietetics from the University of California, Davis, and the University of Nebraska Medical Center, Omaha. In private practice for over 25 years, she is the founder of Diabetes & Nutrition Support Services in Salinas, California. She has developed educational programs that have benefited more than 6,000 patients with diabetes, and she specializes in the use of insulin pumps and continuous glucose-sensing technology, as well as in a patient-centered approach to diabetes treatment. She speaks nationally on diabetes care and management to both diabetes professionals and people with diabetes, and she has authored two books and investigator-initiated studies in these areas. Having a child with diabetes, she combines her professional knowledge with personal experience and understanding.

**Allen Bennett King, MD, FACP, FACE, CDE,** received his degrees and training at the University of California, Berkeley; Creighton University Medical School; the University of Colorado; and Stanford University. He has authored more than 60 papers, book chapters, and books in medical science and speaks nationally on new advances in diabetes. Over his 30 years of practice, he has seen more than 10,000 patients with diabetes, some for more than 25 years. He is an associate clinical professor at the University of California, San Francisco, Natividad Medical Center and medical director of the Diabetes Care Center in Salinas, California.

**Gary Scheiner, MS, CDE,** is a certified diabetes educator and exercise physiologist who has successfully managed his own diabetes since 1985. He has received several awards for his diabetes teaching, and he delivers lectures worldwide for patients and health care professionals. His private practice, Integrated Diabetes Services (www.integrateddiabetes.com), features a team of diabetes educators that works with clients remotely on healthy lifestyles and intensive blood sugar control.

This book is for informational purposes and is not intended to provide medical advice. Neither the authors, editors, consultant, nor publisher take responsibility for any possible consequences from any treatment, procedure, exercise, dietary modification, action, or application of medication or preparation by any person reading or following the information in this book. The publication of this book does not constitute the practice of medicine, and this book does not attempt to replace your physician or other health care provider. Before undertaking any course of treatment, the authors, editors, consultant, and publisher advise the reader to check with a physician or other health care provider.

**Nutritional Analysis:** Linda R. Yoakam, MS, RD, LD

Every effort has been made to check the accuracy of the nutritional information that appears with each recipe. However, because numerous variables account for a wide range of values for certain foods, nutritive analyses in this book should be considered approximate.

**Photo credits:**

Brand X Pictures, Corbis, Image Source, iStockphoto, PhotoDisc, Shutterstock, Stockbyte, SuperStock, Thinkstock

All recipes and recipe photographs copyright © Publications International, Ltd.

**Pictured on the front cover** *(top to bottom):* Seared Roast Pork with Currant Cherry Salsa *(page 198)* and Crab Spinach Salad with Tarragon Dressing *(page 180).*

**Pictured on the back cover** *(top to bottom):* Teriyaki Salmon with Asian Slaw *(page 190),* Sassy Chicken & Peppers *(page 200),* and Flourless Chocolate Cake *(page 232).*

**Microwave Cooking:** Microwave ovens vary in wattage. Use the cooking times as guidelines and check for doneness before adding more time.

**Preparation/Cooking Times:** Preparation times are based on the approximate amount of time required to assemble the recipe before cooking, baking, chilling, or serving. These times include preparation steps such as measuring, chopping, and mixing. The fact that some preparation and cooking can be done simultaneously is taken into account. Preparation of optional ingredients and serving suggestions is not included.

# contents

# have you heard the good news?

You don't have to be a prisoner of diabetes, living a life of deprivation, sitting there waiting for complications to develop. By understanding diabetes, actively participating in your own care, using the management tools at your disposal, and expanding and improving the choices you make every day, you'll feel better and be healthier—and you'll have tighter control of your diabetes. You'll also lower your risk of diabetes complications. It takes dedication on your part; the right diabetes care team, with you as captain; and a treatment plan, developed especially for you, that evolves along with you. *The Diabetic Bible* is the perfect "how-to" book, always at hand to explain the who, what, why, when, and how of successful diabetes management.

The book's first section covers the basics: diabetes causes, types, and symptoms; how it begins and progresses; and what complications and other medical conditions are associated with it. You'll even learn about the growing incidence of diabetes in children and whether your family members may be at increased risk.

The second part covers the powerful tools at your disposal for managing

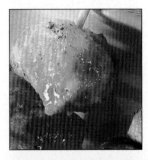

diabetes, from blood sugar testing and lifestyle changes to oral and injectable medications. And if you use insulin or certain classes of oral medications (sulfonylureas or meglitinides), the chapter on hypoglycemia (low blood sugar) is a must read.

In the third section, you'll discover that the strict diabetes diet of old has been replaced by options galore, and you can satisfy your appetite and please your taste buds as you tighten your control. You'll find useful dietary tips that can help you to improve your blood sugar, blood pressure, and blood cholesterol while shedding excess pounds.

The final surprise: more than 100 scrumptious diabetic recipes. Each recipe comes with nutritional information to help you predict how the dish will affect your blood sugar. Mix and match them to create flavorful, exciting meals that help you meet your goals. *The Diabetic Bible* makes it easy to say no to dieting and deprivation and yes to taking control of your diabetes and enjoying your life.

# educate yourself

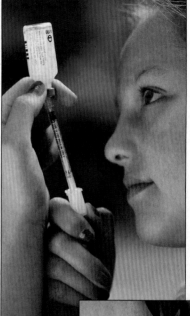

Whether you've only recently learned you have diabetes or you have been battling high blood glucose for years, it never hurts to remind yourself what all the fuss is about. Here, in the first part of this book, you'll rediscover what goes wrong when diabetes develops, why it happens (and why the "adult type" is starting to occur more often in children), and what you can do about it. You'll also explore which other health problems (including metabolic syndrome) often accompany diabetes, and what complications are likely to occur if you don't manage your diabetes properly. The more you know and understand about your diabetes, the better prepared and more motivated you will be to manage it effectively.

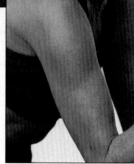

# what is diabetes, anyway?

To get the most from the latest advances and proven treatments in diabetes care, you need to understand just what it means to have diabetes. A good place to start is learning how the body uses fuel and how that process goes awry in diabetes.

## getting to know glucose

Even if you've only recently been diagnosed with diabetes, you've probably already heard the word *glucose*. It is an important player in the body and in diabetes. In your bloodstream, circulating to all your body parts, is sugar.

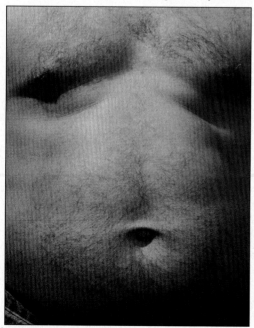

Most of the sugar in your bloodstream is the kind called glucose. Glucose's main job is to supply the body's cells with energy. Glucose is a quickly available fuel used by nearly all tissues in the body, and it's the only fuel your brain and nerves can use. The brain can survive without glucose for only a short time.

Therefore, your brain directs your body to protect your glucose level, making sure it does not fall too low. It does this by increasing the production of certain hormones. These hormones cause the liver to release its stored-up sugar into the bloodstream. So, when people talk about blood sugar, they are really talking about glucose.

The other fuel the body uses for energy is fat. Fat is stored in our fat cells and secreted into the bloodstream in a form called "triglycerides." When we consume (eat) more calories than we burn, the excess calories are stored in the form of fat. When we burn more than we consume, our fat stores are broken down for energy. Obviously, the more we store in our fat cells, the heavier we become. Nevertheless, glucose is the preferred fuel source for the majority of the body's cells and remains our primary source of energy.

## getting glucose where it needs to go

The glucose in your body comes from three major nutrients: fat, protein, and carbohydrate. About 10 percent of the fat and 50 percent of the protein you eat is eventually converted into glucose (the rest is used for other purposes or stored in the body's fat cells), but nearly 100 percent of the carbohydrate you eat is broken down into glucose. Chewing and swallowing begin the digestive process of breaking down starches and larger sugar molecules into glucose. The enzymes in your mouth and your intestines complete the breakdown. The glucose is then absorbed into the bloodstream and travels throughout the body. That's when the pancreas plays a vital role.

The pancreas is a fist-size organ just behind your stomach. One of its jobs is to make enzymes for food digestion. But the pancreas also plays another important role. It contains small groups of cells, the islets of Langerhans, that make hormones, which are released into your bloodstream. Some 80 percent of these islet cells are called "beta" cells that make two hormones: amylin and insulin. Amylin plays a secondary role in regulating appetite and the rate of digestion. Insulin plays a major role in allowing the body's cells to take in proteins, fatty acids, and glucose. Insulin is like a key that opens a door to the body's cells, so the nutrients needed by the cells can get inside. When a person who does not have diabetes eats any food, their blood glucose level rises. The beta cells detect this rise and release more insulin. The insulin goes to the liver, telling the liver to make less glucose. It also

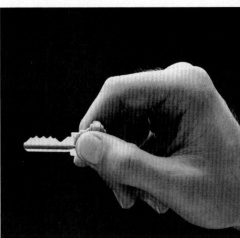

helps the liver, muscle, and fat cells to take up more glucose. This allows nutrients from the recently eaten food to enter and "feed" the body's cells, it keeps blood glucose from rising too high even after eating, and it allows the glucose level to return to a normal, healthy range quickly. When we go for many hours without eating, such as between meals or during sleep, the insulin levels fall, causing the liver to make more glucose to provide energy for the brain, heart, lungs, etc. until the next meal.

In a person with diabetes, this process doesn't work properly. Either the beta cells have lost the ability to produce insulin or the insulin does not do its job as well as it should. As a result, the amount of glucose in the blood rises and the body's cells become deprived of the fuel they need.

## detecting diabetes

In a person without diabetes, the body keeps the plasma glucose level (see "What's plasma?" on page 10) in the range of 60 to 99 milligrams per deciliter (mg/dl) between meals. After eating, the glucose level rises, based on the size and content of the meal, but does not exceed 139 mg/dl. It also quickly returns to the fasting, or

## What's plasma?

Throughout this book, when we refer to blood glucose level, we're referring to the plasma glucose level. The term plasma simply refers to the liquid part of the blood that remains after the blood cells have been removed. It's the portion of the blood that is tested during glucose tests in the laboratory or doctor's office. All blood glucose meters are calibrated to provide plasma glucose measurements, even though we call the results "blood glucose" measurements.

between-meal, range. In a person with diabetes, the blood glucose level rises abnormally high after eating, takes much longer to come down, and doesn't usually return to the normal range, even during periods of fasting. Therefore, to determine if you have diabetes, a doctor must test your blood glucose levels.

There are four different tests available to determine if you have diabetes. The most commonly used is a blood test in which your fasting plasma glucose is measured. A fasting test is done more than eight hours after you have had anything to eat or drink. When your fasting plasma glucose is more than 125 mg/dl on two consecutive occasions, diabetes is diagnosed. Another method is a random blood glucose test, which is done without regard to when you last ate. If your random glucose is 200 mg/dl or higher and you have symptoms of diabetes—frequent urination, excessive thirst, excessive hunger, weight loss, or fatigue—the diagnosis of diabetes is made. A third test is an oral glucose tolerance test. This test is done when a fasting plasma glucose shows a level close to normal but diabetes is suspected (because, for example, the above-mentioned symptoms are present). During an oral glucose tolerance test, your fasting blood is drawn and then you are asked to drink a liquid with a high glucose concentration over

a 15-minute period. During the remainder of the testing period, your blood is drawn at specified intervals. Diabetes is diagnosed if the blood sugar at the two-hour mark is 200 mg/dl or higher.

Another way to diagnose diabetes is through a blood test called hemoglobin A1c (or HbA1c). This single test estimates your average blood glucose level for the previous three months by measuring the percentage of red blood cells that have sugar stuck to them. A "normal" result is generally 4 to 5.9 percent. A result of more than 6.5 percent indicates diabetes.

You may have noticed that there's a gap between a glucose level that's considered normal and one that indicates diabetes. A normal fasting glucose level, for example, is less than 100 mg/dl, but only when the fasting glucose level rises above 125 mg/dl is a diagnosis of diabetes made.

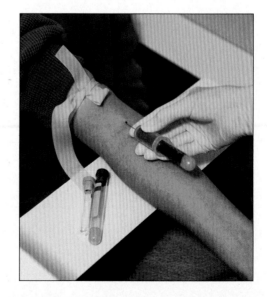

Likewise, at the end of a two-hour glucose tolerance test, a normal glucose level should be less than 140 mg/dl, and yet a diagnosis of diabetes isn't made unless the glucose level after those two hours is 200 mg/dl or higher. And an A1c below 6 percent is considered normal, but diabetes is not diagnosed until the A1c is above 6.5 percent. What about the range in between?

Glucose levels of 100 to 125 mg/dl when fasting and two-hour glucose levels of 140 to 199 mg/dl are not considered diabetes but are not normal, either. People with these levels are diagnosed as having impaired fasting glucose and impaired glucose tolerance, respectively. Although not yet considered to have diabetes, these people have a very high chance of developing diabetes within the next several years.

## different kinds of diabetes

Once the diagnosis is made, the next task is to determine what type of diabetes you have. There are three major types of diabetes: type 1 diabetes, type 2 diabetes, and gestational diabetes. Each type of diabetes requires a different treatment approach.

### type 1 diabetes

Type 1 diabetes affects about 5 percent of all people who have diabetes. It is sometimes referred to as juvenile diabetes, because there is a higher rate of diagnosis in children, but people of any age can develop type 1 diabetes. It may also be called insulin-dependent diabetes, because those with type 1 diabetes require insulin (via injections or an insulin pump) to not only control their blood glucose, but to stay alive. (As you will learn

## making the diagnosis

| type of test: | fasting blood glucose (fbg) | random blood glucose (rbg) | oral glucose tolerance | HbA1c |
|---|---|---|---|---|
| It is **diabetes** when: | FBG > 125 mg/dl on two consecutive blood tests | RBG ≥ 200 mg/dl plus diabetes symptoms | 2-hour glucose level ≥ 200 mg/dl | >6.5% |
| It is **impaired fasting glucose** when: | FBG ≥ 100 mg/dl and <126 mg/dl | | | |
| It is **impaired glucose tolerance** when: | | | 2-hour glucose level is ≥140 mg/dl and < 200 mg/dl | |
| It is **normal** when: | FBG <100 mg/dl | | < 140 mg/dl | <6.0% |

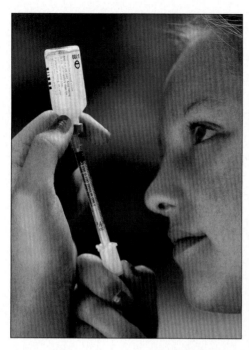

shortly, a small number of people with type 1 who are in the very earliest stages of the disease may not yet require insulin; eventually, however, they will need it.)

In type 1 diabetes, there is a chance of developing ketoacidosis because of the extreme lack of insulin in the body. The lack of enough insulin makes it hard for the body to use glucose for energy. If the body cannot get glucose from the blood, it breaks down fat to supply energy to the cells. One of the products of fat breakdown are ketoacids, or simply "ketones." In the absence of insulin, these acidic compounds accumulate in the blood and make the blood harmfully acidic. If not treated quickly, ketoacidosis can lead to coma and death.

Type 1 diabetes is an autoimmune disease. The immune system is responsible for recognizing foreign objects in our bodies and then attacking these foreign objects with antibodies. In type 1 diabetes, the immune system mistakenly believes that the beta cells of the pancreas do not belong there and mounts an attack on them. This destruction of beta cells can happen either very quickly or slowly over a long period of time. When enough beta cells are lost, the pancreas is unable to produce enough insulin and blood glucose levels begin to rise.

People with type 1 diabetes are born with an immune system that has a difficult time differentiating between the body's own cells and stuff that doesn't belong. What "triggers" the attack on the beta cells is not entirely understood. It could be a virus, exposure to a toxin, major stress, or something in our genetic makeup. Blood tests can be performed to determine a person's risk for developing type 1 diabetes. These tests detect the presence of certain antibodies that may attack the pancreas, certain enzymes, or insulin itself. However, the tests do not have 100 percent predictive value.

Your diabetes is most likely type 1 if you develop the disease before age 35, have a lean build, do not have a family history of diabetes, and require insulin. Additional tests may be done to confirm the diagnosis. These tests include measuring islet-cell antibodies (the antibodies directed toward destroying the islet cells), the C-peptide level (a measurement of the amount of insulin being made by the body), and urine ketones. A positive islet-cell antibody test, a low C-peptide level, or the presence of ketones in the urine all suggest a diagnosis of type 1 diabetes. If you have type 1 diabetes, you will probably require insulin to control your glucose. However, on occasion, a person in the earliest stages of type 1 may still have some beta cells left that secrete enough insulin so that insulin injections are not yet required. Other diabetes medications, changes in diet, and increased physical activity may be enough to control blood glucose temporarily. Still, because the immune system will continue to attack the beta cells, insulin will eventually become necessary.

**type 2 diabetes**

Type 2 diabetes is the most common form of diabetes. It is estimated that up to 90 percent of the people who have diabetes have type 2. The cause appears to be resistance to insulin's action compounded by a deficiency of insulin secretion. But how does one separate it from type 1 diabetes? Type 2 diabetes almost never causes ketoacidosis and shows no evidence of autoimmunity (in other words, there are no signs of antibodies attacking the islet cells). People with type 2 diabetes are usually over age 35, are overweight, and have a family history of type 2 diabetes. Distinguishing between type 1 and type 2 can be difficult, however, even for healthcare professionals. Indeed, it has been found that almost 5 percent of adults who are diagnosed with type 2 actually have type 1. Furthermore, type 2 diabetes is becoming increasingly frequent in children, so there can no longer be an automatic diagnosis of type 1 in children with diabetes.

Type 2 diabetes actually begins years before diagnosis, as an increasing resistance to insulin. This increasing resistance is the result of genetics, weight gain (especially abdominal fat), decreased activity, and aging. The major site of insulin resistance is the muscle tissue, which normally burns up the majority of the glucose in the bloodstream. When insulin has a

## What type of diabetes do I have?

| characteristics | type of diabetes | |
|---|---|---|
| | **1** | **2** |
| Age of onset | usually young | usually older |
| Need insulin | yes | maybe |
| Family history of diabetes | infrequent | usually |
| Big belly | no | usually |
| Ketones | potentially | rarely |

difficult time "opening doors" on the body's cells, the pancreas tries to compensate by making more and more insulin. For some people, the pancreas is eventually unable to keep up with the increased workload. Blood glucose levels rise above normal after meals, and fasting glucose levels begin to remain above normal, too. Ironically, very high glucose levels can damage the beta cells, a condition called glucose toxicity. This further accelerates the breakdown of the pancreas' ability to control blood sugar levels. When glucose rises high enough to produce symptoms (excessive thirst, frequent urination, wounds that don't heal, for example), or when a complication such as a heart attack, stroke, visual disturbance, infection, numbness, or serious gum disease is treated, the diagnosis of type 2 diabetes is often made.

### gestational diabetes

Gestational diabetes is diabetes that is diagnosed for the first time during pregnancy. It occurs in about 3 percent of all pregnancies. Gestational diabetes is diagnosed using a three-hour glucose tolerance test. If any two of the glucose readings during the test exceed the upper limits of normal, the diagnosis is made. Rarely are the glucose levels high enough to harm the mother. The problem is the mother's blood. Extra glucose flows to the developing baby, which then produces extra insulin. This, in turn, causes the baby to grow too quickly, resulting in a difficult labor and delivery.

Throughout the pregnancy, the mother's insulin resistance and glucose levels increase, right up to delivery. In 97 percent of cases, the mother's glucose levels promptly return to normal after the baby and placenta are delivered. Many women with gestational diabetes can control their glucose levels during pregnancy through diet and exercise. Some, however, require insulin to keep glucose levels within a healthy range for the fetus. Oral medications are not typically used during pregnancy because they have the potential to harm the fetus. One oral medication (metformin), however, is being used to help reduce the amount of insulin required to control blood glucose levels. Numerous studies have shown that use of metformin during pregnancy reduced the rate of miscarriage and fetal growth problems. What's more, metformin has not been shown to be harmful to babies. Still, metformin is not yet approved for use by the Food and Drug Administration (FDA), so your doctor will have to make the final call.

Women who have had gestational diabetes have a significantly greater chance of developing diabetes later in life. Studies have shown that weight control and increased physical activity reduce the risk of future diabetes by as much as 50 percent.

## who gets diabetes?

About 20 percent of Americans aged 40 to 75 have diabetes, and about half don't even know it. Certain ethnic groups have an even higher incidence of diabetes; these include African, Asian, and Hispanic Americans; Pacific Islanders; and Native Americans. Indeed, in some Native American tribes, eight of every ten tribe members have diabetes. Further, the prevalence of diabetes in the United States is increasing due to the aging of the population, the change in ethnic mix toward a greater percentage of susceptible people, increasing obesity, and decreasing physical activity. Type 2 diabetes is inherited as a dominant trait. If you have type 2 diabetes, each one of your children has about a 30 percent chance of developing it, too. People who have type 2 usually have a relative who has the disease. (There's more information on diabetes and heredity in the chapter "Children and Diabetes.")

## why control glucose?

When your blood glucose rises above 140 mg/dl, it begins to cause damage throughout your body, although you may not notice symptoms until it climbs above 180. When glucose levels are above 180, the kidneys start to "leak" sugar into the urine, causing increased urination; and, because you're losing more water through increased urination, you have increased thirst. Because your body's cells can't take in and use sufficient amounts of glucose, they become starved for fuel; you feel hungry and fatigued and become unusually sleepy, especially after meals. At high glucose levels, your white blood cells don't work as well, leaving you more vulnerable to infections. Wounds become slow to heal, and you are more likely to get bladder and yeast infections. If your glucose levels stay above normal for an extended period of time, it becomes toxic to your body, and severe damage begins to occur in your eyes, kidneys, feet, and heart. That's only a brief description of the changes that untreated diabetes can cause in your body (you'll find more details in "Diabetes Complications and Long-Term Concerns"). But you can take steps to forestall such frightening consequences of high blood glucose. Managing your diabetes wisely and well means that you will feel and perform better today and most likely avoid serious health problems down the road.

### Factors that increase your risk of developing type 2 diabetes

- You are overweight, especially if you have a lot of abdominal (tummy) fat.
- You get little or no exercise.
- You are 45 years of age or older.
- You are a woman who has given birth to a baby weighing more than nine pounds.
- You have a sister, brother, or parent who has diabetes.
- You are African, Hispanic, Asian, or Native American or are a Pacific Islander.

# taking command of your care

The right approach to diabetes treatment puts *you* in charge. Not your doctor. Not your spouse. *You.* You become the boss of your diabetes team, choosing the staff that best serves your needs, tracking your progress, and keeping your eyes on the ultimate goal—your health and well-being.

## assemble your staff

Getting the best treatment is not simply a matter of keeping your doctor's appointments and taking prescribed medications (although those *are* important). Diabetes affects many aspects of your life. And since nobody knows your life better than you do, you must

step into the role of the "general" of your diabetes care team. As the general, you'll want to surround yourself with knowledgeable, trustworthy, expert advisors—your diabetes care team—who can help you get the information, advice, treatments, and support you need to manage your diabetes effectively. This team may include your doctor, diabetes educator, and dietitian. Also onboard should be a pharmacist, dentist, mental-health professional, eye doctor, podiatrist (foot doctor), and cardiologist (heart specialist) as needed. As you go about assembling your team, remember that these people work for you. You are hiring them to help you learn about diabetes, understand how it affects you, and provide you with the tools that let you make your own informed health care decisions.

Your first task is to find a doctor. You'll not only want a physician who has skill and experience in diagnosing and treating diabetes, but also one who will support and work with you in becoming your own diabetes general. Together you and your doctor need to develop a good working relationship in

which there is mutual understanding, respect, and trust. You will need to feel comfortable talking with and asking questions of your doctor. If you are unable to develop such a relationship, you need to find another doctor.

Different physicians have different levels of expertise in treating diabetes. *Endocrinologists* typically have the most experience and skill in diabetes care. Internal medicine doctors (internists) usually treat a variety of chronic health conditions, diabetes being just one of them. General practitioners (family doctors) typically treat many short-term and long-term illnesses and have only a basic understanding of how to manage diabetes. Look for a physician who is board certified. This ensures that they receive continuing education and are updated on the latest treatment methods. To find a board-certified physician, visit the American Board of Medical Specialties' website, www.abms.org. Regardless of the type of physician you hire, he or she is ultimately responsible for screening for complications, prescribing the necessary tests and medications, intervening during a crisis, keeping you abreast of the latest developments in diabetes care, and making sure that you are maintaining control. If your physician is not meeting these minimum criteria, does not satisfactorily answer your questions, or does not support your pursuit of new technolo-

gies, management approaches, or other healthcare specialists, consider looking for someone else.

Education is by far the most important aspect of diabetes self-care. It involves learning how to take care of yourself and your diabetes, and it brings you into the decision-making process for your own health. So after you find a doctor, you'll need to add a diabetes educator to your team. The diabetes educator will provide you with information and one-on-one guidance. As with your doctor, the educator you choose should be someone you feel comfortable talking to and feel you can contact with questions about the practical details of diabetes care. Most often, a diabetes educator will also be a nurse, dietitian, or pharmacist by training. If possible, choose a certified diabetes educator, or CDE. A CDE is a trained health professional who is certified by the National Certification Board for Diabetes Educators to teach people with diabetes how to manage the disease. Your physician or health plan may be able to refer you to a certified diabetes educator, or you can locate a CDE in your area by visiting the CDE network at http://www.diabeteseducator.org/DiabetesEducation/Find.html.

With the help of your doctor and diabetes educator, you should be able to get additional referrals to a dentist, eye doctor, podiatrist, and cardiologist if needed. If you already have an established relationship with a dentist or eye doctor, be sure to discuss your diabetes diagnosis with them and perhaps even put them in touch with the other members of your team so that they can collaborate on your care.

## focus on taking control

Being diagnosed with diabetes and then being told to alter your life can spark some pretty intense emotions. It's natural to feel stressed, afraid, sad, or even angry at the news that you have this disease. But while such reactions may be normal, they can be harmful if you don't work through them and then refocus your energy into something positive—like taking care of yourself and your diabetes.

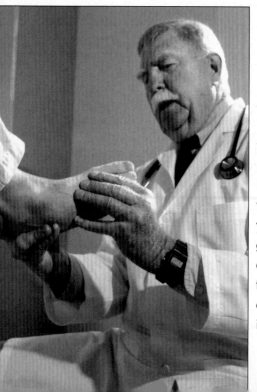

For some people, the stress of a diabetes diagnosis can turn into denial. Regularly checking your blood sugar becomes a constant reminder that you have diabetes. So, you skip the checks in an effort to pretend you don't really have the disease. To further the denial, you attribute your symptoms of high glucose levels, such as excessive thirst and fatigue, to some other cause, such as the hot weather or working long hours. Perhaps you cancel or simply don't show up for your medical appointments. Ignoring the fact that you have diabetes will not make it go away. People who live in denial about their diabetes die from their diabetes. And until that happens, you will live out your life in an ongoing droopy state.

Fear, too, is a common reaction to dealing with diabetes. Perhaps you know or have heard of someone who is suffering from multiple, crippling complications from diabetes or may have died from diabetes complications. While it makes sense to fear the complications of diabetes, you must not let that fear paralyze you. Instead, use the fear of diabetes complications as strong motivation for learning all you can about your disease and working hard to gain the best possible control of your glucose levels.

Feeling sad or helpless is yet another common reaction to a diabetes diagnosis; it can also occur in response to the stress of coping with the disease. If that blue feeling lasts more than a few days or really begins to interfere with your daily life or with taking care of your diabetes, it may be depression. Depression is a biochemical condition. It is not a defect in your character. Once this condition is treated with therapy or medications, your mood and functioning will improve. If you suspect that you may be experiencing depression, you should discuss it with your doctor. Your doctor may choose to prescribe a medication and/or refer you to a psychotherapist, psychologist, or psychiatrist.

## chart your own course

In terms of diabetes care, charting your own course is not just a figure of speech. As the general in charge of your diabetes care, you should create your own care chart. This way, you can have all the information about your diabetes care in one place, and you can take it with you each time you meet with a member of your diabetes care team. You'll find a list of the types of information your chart should contain in the box to the right. It is particularly crucial that your chart include a complete, accurate, and up-to-date list of all of your medications and the strength and dose of each. Include any vitamins, minerals, and natural products you take. You may be seeing more than one doctor, and it is important that each one knows what the other has prescribed for you and what over-the-counter products you take so that together you can avoid dangerous interactions. Note in your chart any side effects or unusual symptoms you experience that you suspect may be connected to your medications. This way you can inquire about them the next time you talk to your doctor. It's also very helpful to keep a running list of

questions you have about diabetes so that you can ask your team. Jot them down as they occur to you. Often, under the pressure of limited time or nervousness during the appointment, you can easily forget questions that otherwise seemed so clear just the day prior. If you aren't able to cover all of your questions during the visit, inform your doctor so that you can make another appointment and get answers to the remainder of your questions.

Take time to prepare for each visit before the appointment. Bring your chart as well as your blood glucose meter and any additional logsheets or record books (you'll learn more about meters and log books in upcoming chapters). Remember, you are the general in charge of your care. Take some time to make sure you have the personnel, focus, and resources at hand to accomplish your mission. That mission—taking care of your diabetes and yourself—really is a matter of life and death.

## What to include in your own medical chart:

- List of your medicines; their strengths; how, when, and why you take them; who prescribed them
- List of your medical conditions and dates of diagnosis, any drug allergies, all major medical events and surgeries
- List of all your doctors and health care professionals and their office and emergency phone numbers
- Laboratory test results, handouts, information sheets, and instructions given to you by your diabetes care team
- List of questions you have for your doctor or other diabetes care professional

# diabetes complications and long-term concerns

## Three keys to treating, delaying, or preventing complications

**EDUCATION**
Learn as much as you can about diabetes.

**EARLY DETECTION**
Learn the signs and symptoms of potential problems.

**REGULAR OFFICE VISITS**
Set up a schedule, and stick to it!

It can be hard to face each day knowing you have to check your blood glucose, watch what you eat, keep records, and all the rest. But keeping tight control of glucose and taking care of yourself now can help you avoid the long-term complications of diabetes.

## the bad news— and the good

People with diabetes are vulnerable to a variety of health problems, collectively called "diabetic complications." It usually takes many years before diabetic complications appear. However, because lots of people have type 2 diabetes for many years before it is diagnosed, complications may appear soon after diagnosis.

People with diabetes are more likely than other people to have a heart attack; stroke; eye problems that can lead to blindness; kidney disease; toe, foot, or leg amputations; frequent infections; periodontal disease; digestive disorders; frozen joints; and sexual dysfunction. All of these are more likely to occur if blood glucose levels have been high over many years. Fortunately, diabetes complications are no longer inevitable—unless you do not take good care of yourself and manage your diabetes. People with diabetes can live long, healthy, and productive lives. To do so challenges you and your diabetes care team to become intimately involved in recognizing, treating, and doing whatever it takes to prevent or delay the long-term complications of diabetes.

There are three keys to making this happen. First, you need to become educated. Learn the how, what, and why of complications. While these problems may be scary to think about, learning about them can help you to be proactive in preventing them. Second, understand the earliest signs and symptoms of the various complications. Have your exams and labwork completed on a timely basis, and keep track of the results. Any change, even when results are still in the normal range, may indicate that problems are developing. Third, see your diabetes care team regularly—at least every three months when you are feeling and doing well. But contact them immediately if you are having problems. Working together, you and your health professionals will form a strong prevention team.

## how do problems start?

When blood glucose levels exceed 140 mg/dl, the excess glucose becomes toxic to your body: blood thickens, plaque sticks to the walls of blood vessels, proteins in the bloodstream may not function properly, and nerves become inflamed. When glucose levels exceed 180 mg/dl, some of the excess glucose spills over into the urine, causing frequent urination and, consequently, increased thirst. This leads to dehydration, which causes muscle cramps and dizziness. Because glucose is having a hard time getting into the body's cells, you will probably feel fatigued and hungry, and you may begin to lose weight. In addition, the excess glucose impairs the ability of your white blood cells to fight off infections and heal wounds. Finally, your vision becomes blurry and you experience great fluctuations in your sight. This occurs because glucose has entered the lenses of your eyes, causing them to swell. This swelling changes the shape of your lenses and affects your vision. These changes in your body are generally recognized as the "early warning signs" of diabetes, and one or

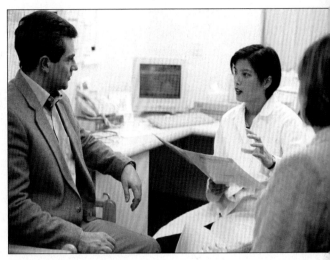

more of these may even have sent you to your doctor in the first place. Early on, all of these problems are completely reversible with the normalization of your glucose levels. It is only when your body is bathed in excess glucose over time that these problems continue and the long-term complications of diabetes develop.

## why do problems continue?

There are two significant events that take place when glucose remains above 140 mg/dl over extended periods of time. The first event is the formation of advanced glycated end products, also known as AGEs. The second is something called "oxidation." Have you ever looked at a freshly baked turkey and noticed how the skin has turned a golden brown and become stiff and crispy? Well, that is an example of glucose combining with protein, in an oven at 350 degrees Fahrenheit, to form advanced glycated end products. In the human body, glucose combines with protein in the same way but is baked at the lower temperature of 98.6 degrees Fahrenheit. The development of these "sugar-coated proteins" occurs in everyone, and they accumulate as we age. For people with diabetes, who have elevated glucose levels, these AGEs form at an accelerated rate. As the AGEs accumulate, the proteins thicken and affect the blood vessels of the kidneys, eyes, feet, and large blood vessels of the body, causing complications. The other event that occurs at an accelerated rate in diabetes is oxidation. Oxidation is the process that causes rust on cars. Similar damage occurs naturally in the human body. When your body breaks down glucose for energy, byproducts called free radicals are made. These free radicals increase the rate of oxidation, damaging cells and the tissues they form. It is as if your bloodstream and blood vessels are "rusting out." As this "rusting" continues, it damages the linings of your blood vessels and causes various tissues in your body to malfunction. If glucose levels are elevated, high numbers of free radicals are formed and more "rusting," or oxidation, occurs.

## Looking after your eyes

Ever wonder how your eyes "see"? You see an object when light is reflected off of it and directed back to your eye. The light enters your eye through a clear covering called the cornea. It passes through the lens, which focuses the light onto the retina, the light-sensing tissue at the back of the eye. The retina translates these visual signals into electrical impulses that are sent, by way of the optic nerve, to the brain so we can "see" the image. The retina is supplied with nutrients and oxygen by tiny blood vessels. If glucose levels are elevated, AGEs and oxidation cause the tiny blood vessels in the retina to thicken in some parts and weaken in others. This leads to the development of diabetic retinopathy, a disease of the blood vessels of the retina of the eye. As the tiny blood vessels in the retina become swollen, they may leak fluid into the center of the retina (an area called the "macula"), which may cause your sight to become blurred. This condition is called background retinopathy.

If the retinopathy progresses, the deterioration of your sight will progress as well. To try to supply the retina with nutrients and oxygen, many new, tiny blood vessels grow across the eye. This is called neovascularization. These vessels are very fragile and break easily, causing bleeding into the center of your eye, blocking vision and causing blindness. Scar tissue may also form near the retina, pulling it away from the back of the eye. This stage is called proliferative retinopathy. Treatment for diabetic retinopathy can help prevent loss of vision and can sometimes restore some lost vision or stop the progression of neovascularization. Thanks to modern medicine and laser technology, neovascularization can be treated. A laser beam can be focused on these fragile blood vessels, causing them to clot and stop bleeding. But this has to be done early in the course of the disease to be effective. While research is progressing on how to alter blood flow in the eyes to prevent the early changes of diabetic retinopathy, the best form of treatment is prevention. It is now well known that there are two essential things you can do to best safeguard your vision: Control your blood glucose levels and have regular eye exams.

Tight blood glucose control has a direct impact on the risk of developing complications of the eyes, as well as the kidneys, nerves, and heart. Two major research studies—the Diabetes Control and Complications Trial and the United Kingdom Prospect Diabetes Study—showed that every 1 percent reduction in the HbA1c is associated with approximately a 30 percent reduction in the risk of these complications. A 1 percent A1c reduction reflects an average blood sugar drop of approximately 30 mg/dl or 2 mmol/l.

Sound management of your diabetes and dilated eye examinations (at least once per year) to examine your retina can all but eliminate the severe forms of retinopathy that lead to loss of sight. What's more, for 95 percent of people with diabetes who are already affected by some abnormal blood-vessel growth, early screening and prompt treatment can prevent blindness. In addition to retinopathy, people with diabetes can have other eye problems that demand attention. Glaucoma, which is caused by too much pressure in the eye, occurs more often in people with diabetes. You may have no symptoms of glaucoma, but it can be diagnosed with a simple test that measures pressure in your eye. If detected, it should be treated promptly. When glaucoma is undetected or left untreated, blindness results—yet another reason to have regular eye exams by an eye doctor. Another common eye problem is a cataract, in which the lens of the eye becomes cloudy. Cataracts, like glaucoma, are more common in people with diabetes. The cloudy crystals in the lens of the eye are caused in part by AGEs. They can lead to poor night vision and, eventually, blindness if not treated. A cata-

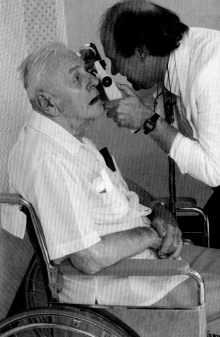

ract is treated by removing the lens and replacing it with an implant. Such surgery is done routinely at surgical centers, and most people can get right back to their usual routine within a day or two. The latest techniques in modern medicine can indeed help to prevent blindness caused by diabetes. But the key is to catch changes early; that's why regular screening is essential.

## keeping your kidneys fit

Your kidneys do many things, but the most important is getting rid of waste products from your blood by excreting them in urine and maintaining a proper mineral and fluid balance in your body. In this way, your kidneys are a bit like a filter, keeping the right

amounts of the good stuff in and getting rid of the things you don't need. There are a tremendous number of tiny blood vessels that feed the very small cavities in your kidneys, much like the many tiny blood vessels that feed the retinas in your eyes. The vessels in the kidneys have selective-size pores that allow certain molecules to fall into the cavities and be carried out with the urine while at the same time keeping needed molecules from leaving the body. As your glucose levels remain elevated, AGEs build

up in the walls of the blood vessels, causing the vessels to become abnormally leaky. In addition to AGEs, high blood pressure, nicotine, and certain other conditions can damage the small blood vessels of the kidneys. As a result, protein molecules start leaking through the pores in the blood vessels and end up in the urine.

In the early stages of kidney disease, albumin, the major protein in your blood, begins to leak through the damaged vessels and into the urine at an abnormal rate. This condition is called *proteinuria* (or in the earliest stages, *microalbuminuria*, since only small amounts of protein appear in the urine). Normally, less than 30 micrograms (a microgram, or mcg, is one-millionth of a gram) of albumin are found in your urine on any given day. Results greater than 30 mcg indicate some degree of kidney damage. As kidney disease progresses, the pores in the kidneys' blood vessels become larger and more protein is lost. When the protein loss reaches 1,000 milligrams, or 1 gram, each day, you may notice puffiness in your ankles due to fluid buildup (edema). As the kidneys become less effective at filtering, waste products slowly begin to collect in the blood; this buildup can be measured and is called your serum creatinine level. As the creatinine level increases, so do the levels of other waste products, causing you to become nauseated and fatigued. The waste buildup poisons the kidneys, harming their ability to make erythropoietin, a substance needed by your bone marrow to make oxygen-carrying red blood cells; you become anemic, which means your body's cells become starved for oxygen. At this point, your kidneys can no longer do their most basic job, and you require dialysis. Dialysis involves being hooked to a machine that removes the wastes from your blood.

Kidney disease and the slow deterioration of your body's filtering system do not need to happen. There are several things you can do to protect your kidneys and reduce the likelihood of kidney problems, prevent current problems from becoming worse, and even reverse problems that have started.

**get screened.** Maintaining kidney health starts with yearly screening for microalbumin. This test looks for small amounts of protein in the urine that cannot be detected by the usual "dipstick" test done during routine urinalysis. (Note, however, that infection, severe stress, heart failure, or strenuous exercise before the test can also increase levels of protein in your urine.) Should the results show increased microalbumin in your urine, treatment should begin to return this number to normal.

**tighten your control.** To keep your kidneys healthy or prevent problems from becoming worse, you need to

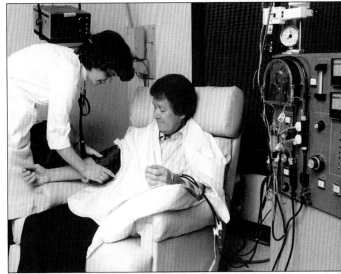

keep blood glucose tightly controlled. Kidney problems result from high blood glucose over a period of time, causing a buildup of AGEs. The closer to normal you keep your glucose levels, the better for your kidneys. With the guidance of your team, strive for an HbA1c (discussed in the chapter "HbA1c: Looking Back to Move Forward") of less than 7 percent, or less than 6 percent if that's possible without risking hypoglycemia (low blood glucose).

**keep your blood pressure in check.** It is important to maintain a normal blood pressure and to check it often. When blood pressure is high (above $130/80$ mm Hg), it slowly damages the kidneys. Have your pressure checked often, and learn how to monitor it at home. If it is consistently high, early treatment is important. Nicotine, salt, caffeine, and alcohol may raise blood pressure. By contrast, adding extra physical activity, managing stress, and losing weight can help lower your blood pressure.

## Take care of your kidneys

- Have a screening test done yearly for microalbumin.
- Improve your blood glucose control.
- Maintain a normal blood pressure.
- Avoid medications that can damage your kidneys.
- Avoid all forms of nicotine.
- Use preventive medications when needed.
- Lower your intake of protein if kidney problems develop.

**watch your meds.** Make sure you avoid medications that can damage your kidneys. When your doctor chooses a drug for you, such as an antibiotic for infection, confirm that it does not have the potential to harm your kidneys. Be aware that some over-the-counter drugs can cause problems, too. Excessive use of nonsteroidal anti-inflammatory drugs (NSAIDs), such as aspirin and ibuprofen, can cause damage to the kidneys. Large daily doses have been associated with kidney problems. If you need to treat ongoing pain or inflammation, talk to your doctor before using large doses of NSAIDs.

**say no to nicotine.** To maintain the health of your kidneys, you must avoid nicotine. Nicotine is found in all forms of tobacco. Nicotine is as harmful to the kidneys as untreated high blood pressure. Because nicotine is so addictive (more addictive than alcohol and narcotics), the best policy is never to start. If you already smoke or chew tobacco, ask your doctor about resources to help you quit.

**take an ACE or ARB.** To help slow or reverse kidney disease, it is recommended that prescription medications called angiotensin converting enzyme (ACE) inhibitors or angiotensin receptor blockers (ARBs) be used. Studies have shown that these classes of blood pressure medicines can slow kidney disease and protect the kidneys from further damage. In addition, they prevent damage to other blood vessels in the body. Whether or not you are already taking a medication for high blood pressure, speak with your doctor about using an ACE inhibitor or an ARB.

**go easy on protein.** There is no evidence to suggest that a high-protein diet damages healthy kidneys. However, once kidney disease is present, having large amounts of protein can aggravate kidney problems. When your kidney function begins to decrease, eating less protein generally helps to slow the process. The protein is an extra load for the kidneys to handle, particularly the nitrogen that results from the breakdown of proteins. For a diet prescription to maintain your kidney health, consult with a registered dietitian.

## taking care of your tootsies

Other than accidents, diabetes is the most common cause of limb loss in the United States. More than 50,000 amputations per year are linked directly to uncontrolled diabetes. Problems begin in your legs or feet due to peripheral neuropathy—nerves no longer providing adequate warning when there is a problem. Long-term high glucose damages the nerves, resulting in pain, numbness, or a tingling feeling in your feet and legs, all of which dull the sensitivity of your nerves and your ability to sense a potential problem with your feet. You may not notice a sore caused by a tight rubbing shoe or a blister from a new pair of shoes. The situation is made worse by changes in your blood vessels; those changes are caused by excess glucose, AGEs, and oxidation. Blood vessels become blocked, and your legs and feet do not receive enough blood. This can cause aching pains in your legs and feet, especially when walking, and sores that heal slowly. Minor foot injuries that are not noticed and left untreated can become severely infected and may require amputation.

Amputation is almost entirely avoidable and preventable. Proper foot care and regular visits to your diabetes care team can prevent foot and leg sores and ensure that any that do appear don't become infected. Proper foot care requires a combined effort by you and your doctor. You need to know what you can do to prevent problems and what to expect from your doctor as well. Self-care includes the inspection of your feet for sores, cuts, or signs of infection (redness, swelling, heat). Get a handheld mirror and examine your feet thoroughly every day. Feel all surfaces of your feet with your hands. Clean your feet daily and dry them well, especially between the toes, and keep them soft by using lotion after a bath or shower (except between the toes). Each time you buy shoes, have both the width and length of each foot measured to make sure your shoes fit

well and have enough space for your toes. Always wear shoes; never go barefoot, even in the home, where you can accidentally kick furniture or step on something sharp hidden in carpeting. Wear sandals or water socks at the beach, to protect your feet from burns and sharp objects in the sand.

And never, ever, do bathroom surgery on your feet. Leave corns, calluses, ingrown toenails, and thick, fungal nails to a podiatrist, who can do foot surgery, trim your nails (or teach you how to properly trim them at home), and prescribe medications for your feet when needed. See a podiatrist regularly if you have lost any sensation in your feet, if you cannot cut your own nails, or if you have a history of any foot problems. Be prepared to tell your doctor about any foot-care concerns. The doctor should check the pulses in both feet to see how well blood is circulating to them and should do a special test to check the sensation in your feet. If you have lost sensation, you are vulnerable to infections, sores, and, ultimately, foot loss. Studies have shown that you have a very good chance of avoiding further problems if you take good care of your feet, do not smoke, and keep both your blood pressure and diabetes under control.

# diabetes and metabolic syndrome

As they say, when it rains, it pours. Health problems are not usually isolated; they travel in packs. Type 2 diabetes is no different. If you have type 2 diabetes, you are likely to have a number of other conditions that, along with diabetes, contribute significantly to the risk of heart disease. These conditions include high blood pressure, central obesity (too much fat around the middle), abnormal cholesterol, and insulin resistance. Collectively, this cluster of health conditions is referred to as "metabolic syndrome."

## the discovery

In the mid-1970s, Dr. Gerald Reaven at Stanford University Medical Center described a condition that he coined "syndrome X." He noted a clustering of medical conditions that were associated with a very high rate of coronary artery disease (a common type of heart disease that affects the blood vessels that nourish the heart). These conditions included high blood pressure, glucose intolerance, and high levels of cholesterol and triglycerides in the blood; these, in turn, were associated with insulin resistance and, consequently, high insulin levels. Since the discovery of syndrome X, there has been a great deal of focus and many studies conducted to try to understand what causes it. Some of the resulting fingers of blame point to our ever-expanding waistlines.

## the belly connection

Each of us is here today because our ancestors had the genetics that allowed them to survive during times of frequent famine. Back then, if you had a fast metabolism, required a lot of food to maintain your weight, and lost weight readily when food was scarce, you didn't survive. Those who did survive the lean times passed on their genes, and that inheritance is still apparent today. These "thrifty" genes are still helping us conserve calories and are reluctant to let us lose fat stores. For those of us who live in this land of plenty—a land that's thankfully short on famine but also short on manual

labor—these same genes make it difficult to lose extra weight. To compound this effect, if you weighed less than six pounds when you were born, your body chemistry tends to favor conserving fat for the rest of your life. And, of course, there's no ignoring the fact that here in America, the older we get, the less active we tend to become, which means our fat stores just keep piling up. In fact, it is now estimated that more than 50 percent of all adult Americans are overweight, and as many as 30 percent are considered obese. In people whose fat stores accumulate primarily in the abdominal area, as opposed to the buttocks, hips, and thighs, a widening girth sets the stage for syndrome X (now referred to as metabolic syndrome).

## where the food goes

When you eat, your food is broken down in your small intestines into three basic nutrients—amino acids, glucose, and fatty acids. From your intestines, the nutrients enter the bloodstream, where they can be picked up and used by the cells that need them. The cells pluck amino acids from the bloodstream and use them to build a wide array of necessary proteins. In a pinch, the amino acids can also be broken down for energy; some can even be made into glucose. But because of protein's many other important and unique roles, the body generally uses

| The Food You Eat | | |
|---|---|---|
| **IS MADE UP OF** | | |
| Proteins | Carbohydrates | Fats |
| **WHICH ARE THEN BROKEN DOWN IN YOUR GUT INTO** | | |
| Amino Acids | Glucose | Fatty Acids |
| **WHICH ARE THEN USED BY THE BODY'S CELLS FOR BASIC FUNCTIONS, BURNED FOR ENERGY, OR, WHEN WE TAKE IN MORE ENERGY THAN WE NEED, STORED AS** | | |
| Protein (primarily as part of muscle tissue) | Glycogen (in the muscles) | Triglycerides (in fat cells deep in your abdomen and in surface fat cells found all over the body) |

amino acids for energy only when it cannot get enough from carbohydrate and fat. The body does not have a storage form of amino acids; if too many are taken in, the body will break them down, excrete parts of them, and turn the remnants over to be stored as glucose or fatty acids. So when other fuels are not available and the body is forced to call upon amino acids for energy, the body must divert them from their other uses or break down protein that is already in use elsewhere (such as in muscle tissue).

The glucose molecules released during digestion go to the liver (for storage in a form called glycogen) and to the other cells of the body, where they can be immediately broken down for energy. The liver maintains a store of glycogen, which it breaks down into glucose and shares with the brain and other metabolically active organs of the body between meals. Glucose is a readily available form of fuel, but because glucose molecules hold a lot of water and so are rather large, the body can only store a limited amount of them.

The fatty acids from a meal also enter the bloodstream and head toward the liver, where they are packaged and sent out to be used as energy by the body's active cells or stored in fat cells in the form of triglycerides. These dense packets of fat are the body's main form of stored energy. Triglycerides are stored in two primary places: inside the fat cells deep in the abdomen, called intra-abdominal fat, and in the surface fat cells all over the body. While the body needs some fat stores, trouble begins when far too much energy is taken in compared to the amounts expended, and fat stores grow too large.

## the battle ensues

When you continuously take in extra energy, more and more fatty acids are stored. As fat cells become larger, they have a harder time holding any more triglycerides—they're like a balloon that is blown up to its full capacity. Research has shown that fat cells secrete a hormone called leptin that causes insulin resistance, making it more difficult for insulin to

transport more fatty acids into the fat cells. As a result, the fatty acids begin to build up in the blood. In response to the buildup, the pancreas makes more insulin, trying valiantly to overcome this resistance to insulin and move the fatty acids into the fat cells. Not to be one-upped, the fat cells further increase their production of leptin. This battle increases the amount of free fatty acids and the levels of insulin in your bloodstream. That's bad news, because the fatty acids head back to your liver, where some are turned into triglycerides and stored in the liver, causing a "fatty liver," which often causes inflammation and scarring—and over time can lead to more advanced liver problems, including liver failure. Those that don't get stored in the liver are sent back into the bloodstream in the form of cholesterol to be transported to the body's cells. Eventually, the liver also puts up a wall of resistance to the insulin that is trying to push the fatty acids inside. Your liver, then, has become resistant to insulin, and your pancreas again tries to overcome it by making even more insulin. Fighting back, the liver's resistance increases, multiplying the amounts of fatty acids and insulin circulating in your blood.

Things go downhill from there. Remember that your body gets glucose from two sources: from the food you eat and, when you are fasting, from your liver. Insulin is responsible for limiting the glucose release from the liver. When your liver puts up the walls of resistance to keep out the fatty acids, it can no longer "see" the insulin in the blood, so it starts to pour out extra glucose, and blood glucose levels start to rise. To combat this increase in glucose, your ever-alert pancreas pours out even more insulin, further adding to the already increasing amounts of circulating insulin.

With the liver keeping out the fatty acids, they search out a new home—and they find your muscles. Unlike your glucose-dependent brain, your muscles can use either glucose or fatty acids for energy. Because fatty acids are now very abundant, your muscles start using less glucose for energy. Since your muscles are normally responsible for taking up more than 80 percent of the glucose in your blood, their switch to using fatty acids has a profound effect on your blood glucose levels.

As blood glucose levels rise, your pancreas tries in vain to lower those levels by further increasing insulin production, and your circulating insulin levels rise again. You've now entered an endless loop, with ever-increasing levels of circulating insulin, free fatty acids, and glucose, which now start to become toxic to your system.

## what do you mean "toxic"?

Let's start with the fatty acids. Since the excess fatty acids cannot be stored by the liver, they are made into triglycer-

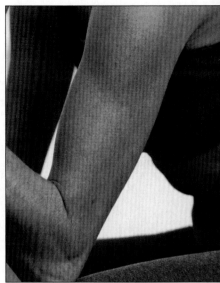

ides and released back into your bloodstream. In order to make these triglycerides, your body must rob parts from other fat molecules, most specifically, from your cholesterol molecules. One of the two main types of cholesterol molecules in your body is the high-density lipoprotein, or HDL, cholesterol. It is often called the "good" cholesterol because it removes fatty acids from your arteries. The other type of cholesterol molecule is the low-density lipoprotein, or LDL, cholesterol. LDL cholesterol is often referred to as "bad" cholesterol because it tends to deposit fat in the walls of your arteries. Unfortunately, it's the beneficial HDL molecules that take the biggest hit when the liver scavenges for parts in order to make triglycerides; the HDL level in the blood drops as a result. Parts of your LDL molecules are also used in the making of triglycerides; the effect, however, is not fewer LDL molecules but simply smaller ones. These small LDL molecules are too small to be picked out of the blood by the liver, so they tend to stay in the bloodstream, which allows them plenty of time to find a nice cozy weak spot on your artery walls where they can attach themselves. What you end up with, then, are high triglyceride levels, low levels of the beneficial HDL cholesterol, and a lot of small, artery-clogging LDL cholesterol molecules in your blood—all of which spell t-r-o-u-b-l-e for your arteries.

Your high insulin levels also cause the inside lining of your blood vessels to overproduce a substance called PAI-1 (pronounced "pie one"). PAI-1 is the main contributor to the clotting of blood. When PAI-1 levels are high, blood clots more readily, which increases the risk of heart attack and stroke. To make matters worse, the platelets, tiny cells in the blood that contribute to clotting, become sticky and form clots more readily when glucose levels are elevated.

During this whole process, the elevated amounts of glucose in your blood start their slow, destructive process, even though the blood glucose levels may not yet have risen into the diabetic range. As discussed in the previous chapter, free radicals and AGEs begin to accumulate, damaging the tiny blood vessels of the kidneys and eyes, and the large blood vessels that nourish the brain, heart, and lower extremeties. In more than half the people who are seen in the hospital for angina (chest pain caused by narrowing of the arteries leading to the heart) or a heart attack, their heart condition is caused by metabolic syndrome.

## do I have metabolic syndrome?

Most likely, yes. More than 90 percent of people with type 2 diabetes have characterstics consistent with metabolic syndrome, such as

**central obesity.** This refers specifically to the type of obesity marked by excess fat in the abdominal area as opposed to in the buttocks, hips, and thighs. This type of obesity more commonly occurs in men and in postmenopausal women, but it can occur in anyone. Women who have a waist measurement of more than 35 inches and men who have a waist of 40 inches or more are at greatly increased risk for heart disease.

**insulin resistance.** Whether you have glucose intolerance, prediabetes, or type 2 diabetes, you have at least some degree of insulin resistance.

**high blood pressure (hypertension).** High blood pressure (above $130/80$) is usually the result of atherosclerotic plaques caused by excess sugar, fatty acids, and triglycerides in the blood, accompanied by increased levels of circulating insulin.

**dyslipidemia.** Dyslipidemia means unhealthy levels of fats in the bloodstream: high levels of triglycerides, low levels of HDL cholesterol, and too many LDL cholesterol molecules.

## other conditions related to insulin resistance and high insulin levels

**acanthosis nigricans.** Acanthosis nigricans is a skin condition that causes a darkening and thickening of the skin of the neck and of the body folds, such as at the armpits, in the groin area, and underneath the breasts. The elevated levels of insulin in the body stimulate the growth of skin in these areas, and the resulting skin is darker.

**polycystic ovary syndrome (PCOS).** This is another condition that appears to be caused by insulin resistance and high levels of insulin. PCOS is characterized by infertility, lack of menstrual periods, and obesity. It occurs when elevated insulin levels stimulate a portion of the ovaries to overproduce male hormones, which throw off the menstrual cycle, cause acne, and increase hair growth.

**osteoporosis.** Osteoporosis is a bone condition defined by low bone mass, increased fragility, decreased bone quality, and an increased fracture risk. It is the most prevalent bone disease in the United States.

Large studies have confirmed that women with type 2 diabetes experience higher fracture rates in regions of the hip, humerus, and foot than do nondiabetic women. Bone loss has been observed to be greater in patients with poorly controlled diabetes than in those whose diabetes is in good control.

## what's the connection?

How is metabolic syndrome related to diabetes? That is a good question, and we as yet do not have a complete answer. Obviously, the continued demand on the pancreas's beta cells

to produce insulin puts a strain on these cells. As mentioned earlier, high glucose itself may also be toxic to the beta cells. And it is believed that genetics play a role. In any case, with increasing age, weight, and inactivity, the resistance to insulin increases, leading to higher and higher levels of insulin, free fatty acids, and glucose in the blood. During this "silent" period, before diabetes is diagnosed and treated, the body is exposed to harmful levels of these substances, causing high blood pressure and dyslipidemia. In 20 percent of the people who have metabolic syndrome, the beta cells gradually lose the ability to make insulin. Then, the first sign of diabetes appears: an abnormal increase in the blood glucose level after a meal.

At this stage, diabetes is usually only detected by an oral glucose tolerance test. If not diagnosed at this time, within five to ten years the elevated levels of glucose and free fatty acids lead to the further loss of insulin secretion by the pancreas. The pancreas just plain begins to burn out, overwhelmed by the demand for insulin. The increase in glucose levels then occurs in the fasting state—upon waking in the morning and before meals. Once the fasting glucose levels are more

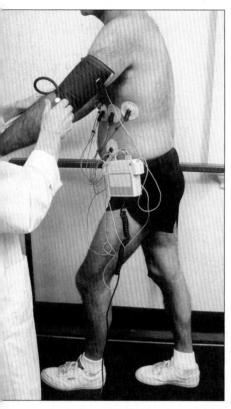

than 180 mg/dl, the symptoms of diabetes usually appear, sending the person to the doctor. At this point, a person may have had metabolic syndrome for more than ten years!

## a one-two (three-four?) punch to the arteries

Combining type 2 diabetes (or insulin resistance) with unhealthy levels of fats in the bloodstream contributes to atherosclerosis, also known as hardening of the arteries. Hardening of the arteries, in turn, produces high blood pressure, as blood vessel walls don't "flex" the way they should. High blood pressure makes the heart work extra hard to pump blood through all the blood vessels of the body. This is not like "exercising" the heart, which can make it more efficient. A heart that is constantly overworked by high blood pressure can actually become weaker and more susceptible to heart attack.

Cholesterol builds up in the artery walls because there is too much LDL cholesterol in the blood and too few HDL molecules taking it away. The LDL cholesterol becomes oxidized, which makes it more irritating to the artery and often leads to a localized inflammation of the artery wall. This irritation, as well as the accumulation of fat from

the LDL molecules, weakens the wall of the artery. The wall eventually cracks, causing an irregularity in the normally smooth lining of the blood vessel. The platelets and clotting factors in the blood, which are already "sticky" due to elevated glucose levels, see this wound and attach to it, which can lead to a sudden obstruction of one of the blood vessels.

If such an obstruction, or clot, occurs in the arteries feeding the heart (coronary arteries), it causes a sudden heart attack. If the obstruction develops more slowly, it is likely to cause angina (chest pain). A clot that occurs in the arteries to the brain, called the cerebral arteries, will cause either a transient ischemic attack (TIA)—if the obstruction clears quickly—or a stroke. In either case, there may be sudden onset of one-sided blindness, weakness, numbness, or an inability to speak.

If the obstruction occurs in the arteries of the kidney, there will be no immediate outward symptoms. However, the blood creatinine level, which is used to gauge kidney function, will gradually worsen. This indicates that damage has been done.

If this same type of obstruction suddenly occurs in an artery to the leg, it will bring on severe leg pain, and the leg will become cold. Many times, the obstruction of the leg artery occurs slowly; this is called claudication. The symptoms of claudication are calf, shin, or thigh pain on exertion that is relieved by rest. In a person who is not physically active, the only symptoms of claudication may be red or purple toes when the feet are dangled, loss of hair on the lower legs, thinning of the skin of the feet, or a foot ulcer.

Most people with metabolic syndrome and diabetes have atherosclerosis. For this reason, it is of great importance that you have regular screening tests and do what you can to minimize further blood vessel damage. Very often, the symptoms of heart problems may be vague, or they may not occur at all (see "'Silent' heart attack" at right). If you experience any discomfort in your chest, you should contact your doctor. An EKG, a painless test that measures electrical signals coming from your heart, can be done to detect a problem. Although an important tool, the EKG is not very sensitive or specific, so you may need to take an exercise stress test (in which your heart function is monitored as you walk on a treadmill). Depending on your risk factors and symptoms, your doctor may also order an angiogram, a test in which dye is injected into the blood vessels to visualize any narrowing or blockage.

Likewise, if you experience any symptoms of sudden and transient vision loss in one eye or temporary weakness on one side, contact your doctor at once. Your doctor can listen to the sounds of your blood flowing through the arteries in your neck (called the carotid arteries) to detect narrowing in these blood vessels. The doctor can then order tests of the carotid arteries to spot any obstructions.

Also, if you notice any symptoms of claudication, be sure to report them to your doctor so that the appropriate medical tests (called "Doppler" exams) can be done to detect any blockages.

## how can I treat metabolic syndrome?

Increasing your level of physical activity and changing your relationship with food are great places to start. These changes are usually inexpensive and are generally quite safe—and they are the cornerstones of treatment for both metabolic syndrome and diabetes. For some people, these changes are enough to decrease the levels of insulin resistance and diminish the signs of the syndrome. In addition, there are medications available for the treatment of the various components of metabolic syndrome:

**low-dose aspirin.** A 75 mg to 162 mg aspirin tablet, taken daily, is moderately effective in making the platelets in your blood less "sticky," so they are less likely to attach to rough spots in your arteries. This significantly counteracts the clot-forming tendencies

**"Silent" heart attack**

If the nerves that send pain impulses to the brain have been damaged by high blood sugar, a minor heart attack may cause no symptoms whatsoever.

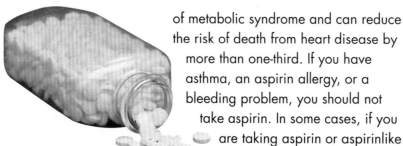

of metabolic syndrome and can reduce the risk of death from heart disease by more than one-third. If you have asthma, an aspirin allergy, or a bleeding problem, you should not take aspirin. In some cases, if you are taking aspirin or aspirinlike medications for chronic pain or arthritis, you may not need to take the additional low-dose aspirin for your heart. Before you consider taking a daily dose of aspirin, be sure to consult your doctor.

**statins.** Medications called statins have made managing dyslipidemia much easier. These medications have proven themselves to be very safe and yet powerful in lowering harmful LDL cholesterol and triglycerides, and increasing helpful HDL cholesterol. Common statin brands include Crestor, Lipitor, Loescol, Mevacor, Pravachol, and Zocor. All statins work the same way, by reducing the ability of your liver to make LDL cholesterol and by increasing your liver's uptake and destruction of the LDL cholesterol molecules in the blood. They are usually taken at bedtime and have few side effects. Liver irritation occurs in less than 1 percent of people treated with a statin, but it usually goes away when the drug is stopped. To monitor the liver, a blood test called ALT is performed 6 to 12 weeks after starting the drug and is repeated every year. You may also experience other side effects,

such as fatigue, insomnia, depression, headaches, rash, and intestinal upset, but they are very rare.

The goal in treating cholesterol is to get the LDL cholesterol level lower than 100 mg/dl and to raise the HDL cholesterol level above 40 mg/dl in men and above 50 mg/dl in women. The goal for triglycerides is a level below 150 mg/dl. If your LDL cholesterol is more than 100 mg/dl, talk to your doctor about trying a statin and see what effect it has on your LDL, HDL, and triglyceride levels. If this treatment is unsuccessful and if you also have multiple risk factors for heart disease or you already have heart disease, other medications such as fibrate or nicotinic acid may be needed.

**fibrates.** The fibrate medications available in the United States are Lopid and Tricor. They work to reduce triglycerides and raise the HDL cholesterol level but have little effect on LDL levels. Lopid appears to cause more stomach upset than Tricor does and has to be taken twice a day, while Tricor is taken only once a day—first thing in the morning when possible. Many doctors prescribe Tricor along with a statin to get more improvements in all lipid levels, although this combination carries a small risk of causing muscle damage.

**nicotinic acid.** Also known as niacin, nicotinic acid is considered to be the best medicine for raising HDL levels. It is a vitamin, but when used in high doses, it acts as a drug. Unfortunately, high doses of niacin can cause numerous side effects, including aggravation of peptic ulcers, gout, facial flushing for a few hours after taking the medication, hives, and other skin conditions. In addition, niacin causes an increase in insulin resistance, which is one problem that anyone with diabetes could do without!

**angiotensin converting enzyme (ACE) inhibitors.** High blood pressure can be extremely dangerous when combined with other aspects of metabolic syndrome. The increased pressure in the arteries accelerates coronary and cerebrovascular disease (disease in the vessels supplying the heart and the brain, respectively) and also aggravates small-blood-vessel disease in the kidneys and eyes. So your goal should be to get your blood pressure as low as possible without causing side effects, such as dizziness when you stand up. There are many medications that can help, including ACE inhibitors.

ACE inhibitors not only lower blood pressure, they also protect the lining of your blood vessels and reduce insulin resistance. In several recently reported studies, the incidence of diabetes in people who were at risk for developing it was 25 percent less in those receiving ACE inhibitors. Trials are ongoing to study whether ACE inhibitors should even be recommended as a prevention tool in those at high risk for developing diabetes. And, as mentioned earlier, ACE inhibitors offer special protection for kidneys in the early stages of kidney disease (microalbuminuria).

A common side effect of ACE inhibitors is a cough. Oddly enough, the cough is a good sign. By blocking a certain chemical reaction, ACE inhibitors allow the accumulation of a chemical in the blood that is very protective of the lining of your blood vessels. The cough means that you have this protection. Rare but serious side effects of ACE inhibitors include swelling of the mouth and tongue, and an elevation in the levels of potassium and creatinine in your blood. Blood tests will need to be done before starting these medications and should be repeated after a month of treatment and then periodically thereafter. Any swelling of the mouth and tongue should be reported to your physician immediately.

There are many ACE inhibitors available, including Accupril, Altace, Capoten, Mavik, Monopril, Prinivil, and Vasotec. They are usually taken once a day and are relatively inexpensive.

**angiotensin receptor blockers (ARBs).** ARBs can be used in place of ACE inhibitors in people who cannot tolerate the cough caused by ACE inhibitors. ARBs protect the arteries as well as ACE inhibitors do without causing a cough. Unfortunately, they are more expensive than ACE inhibitors.

And they may still cause the other side effects that are typical of ACE inhibitors, namely, the rise in potassium and creatinine levels. As a result, follow-up blood tests are required during ARB therapy as well. A partial list of brand-name ARBs includes Avapro, Cozaar, Diovan, Micardis, and Teveten.

**hydrochlorothiazides.** Hydrochlorothiazides are diuretics, or "water pills." In diabetes as well as in metabolic syndrome, hydrochlorothiazides are used in small doses to reduce blood pressure. When given in these small doses, however, it does not appear that their diuretic effect is what causes a decrease in blood pressure. Rather, the small doses seem to work by relaxing the small blood vessels. In larger doses (above 12.5 mg per day), hydrochlorothiazides cause an increase in insulin resistance and a reduction in insulin secretion by the pancreas. Other side effects, again generally found in doses above 12.5 mg per day, include loss of potassium, rashes, and cramps. There are literally hundreds of brands of hydrochlorothiazides on the market, and they are very inexpensive. They are taken once a day, in the morning.

**calcium channel blockers.** There are several groups of medications, called calcium channel blockers, that block the calcium channels in the muscles of the blood vessel walls and the heart, causing the blood vessels to relax, increasing the supply of oxygen-rich blood to the heart, and decreasing the heart's workload. Of the calcium channel blockers available, the vasodilating ones (the ones that relax and widen the blood vessels) may have the fewest side effects (generally only fluid retention and constipation) and are less expensive. They also have no negative effect on insulin resistance, which is a plus for people with diabetes. These medications include Norvasc and Plendil.

**beta blockers.** Beta blockers are an older group of medications that have both benefits and drawbacks. They act by limiting both the speed and power of heart contractions—important for those whose heart is weakened by limited blood flow. Beta blockers commonly used today are Inderal, Tenormin, and Toprol. Studies have shown beta blockers to be especially effective in treating people who have coronary disease, as these drugs have been shown to reduce the chance of dying from a heart attack. In addition, a large study conducted in England and reported in 1998 showed that Tenormin was as good as the ACE inhibitor Capoten in reducing disease of the large and small blood vessels in people with diabetes. The drawbacks to beta blockers are their side effects. They may cause nightmares, insomnia, and depression; they may block your ability to sense hypoglycemia; they may cause your hands to feel cold; and they may increase insulin resistance.

**combination medications.** It is also common for doctors to prescribe combinations of the above medications. For many people, successful blood pressure management occurs only with a combination of drugs. In addition, small doses of several drugs tend to cause fewer side effects than do large doses of just one. Indeed, some pharmaceutical companies have thoughtfully combined medications from different classes of drugs, such as an ACE inhibitor and a hydrochlorothiazide, into one pill. The ability to take a single pill, rather than having to remember and swallow several, can in itself be a benefit.

**coreg.** Other drugs for treating high blood pressure have also been introduced, and some have shown great promise. One in particular, Coreg, has properties of several of the drugs discussed; it can also lower insulin resistance and reduce the oxidation of blood that occurs in metabolic syndrome. It can, however, cause dizziness, and it is relatively expensive.

## what if my arteries are already narrowed?

Major advances have been made in unplugging heart arteries with balloons and lasers. When a sudden clot occurs, there are now powerful drugs that can dissolve the clot and keep the

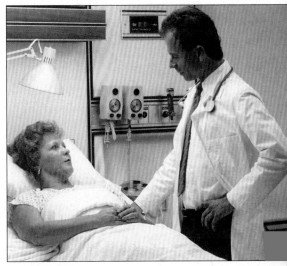

heart muscle from suffering irreparable damage. And surgery to bypass blocked arteries is safer and less traumatic than ever. In fact, you are generally up and about within a day or two after the surgery and home before the week is out. The same is true for surgery on your carotid arteries.

If a full stroke occurs, getting to emergency care very quickly can make all the difference. Medication is now available to dissolve the clot and open the carotid artery, although it must be given within the first few hours of the onset of the stroke. New medicines are also being developed to protect the brain or even to restore it after a stroke. Clots in leg arteries can now often be dissolved nonsurgically. And newer techniques allow for surgery on smaller and smaller arteries.

Still, the best medicine is prevention. Many of the complications of diabetes and metabolic syndrome can be prevented by following the treatment guidelines provided by your team and maintaining control of your diabetes. Ignoring or denying the fact that you need care is the greatest risk factor of all. Fortunately, it is the one over which you have the greatest control.

# children and diabetes

Diabetes is one of the most common chronic diseases in children, affecting more than 200,000 kids under age 20 in the United States. As the prevalence of childhood diabetes increases by more than 15,000 cases per year, the makeup has changed dramatically. Historically, almost all cases of childhood diabetes were diagnosed as type 1. But between the years 2002 and 2005, almost one-third of the young people age 10 to 19 who were diagnosed with diabetes were classified as having type 2.

Since type 2 diabetes is more common in certain racial and ethnic groups, children who are African American, Hispanic, Latino, or Native American; who are large for their age; and who have a family history of type 2 are at especially high risk for this type.

There is a third, rare form of diabetes seen in children called maturity-onset diabetes of the young (MODY), and it can occur in all ethnic groups. There are actually several varieties of MODY, all of which are caused by genetic defects that affect the insulin-producing cells. These defects are thought to be rare, and molecular diagnostic testing, currently available only in research laboratories, is required to diagnose MODY. The symptoms of MODY run the gamut from a mild increase in blood glucose to extremely high glucose levels and diabetic ketoacidosis. Treatments for MODY, therefore, range from diet and activity awareness to oral medications or insulin. Because it takes specialized testing to detect MODY, it often goes unrecognized, and most children with this form are treated as if they have either type 1 or type 2 diabetes.

## managing childhood diabetes

The child who is diagnosed with type 1 diabetes is insulin dependent and requires insulin to live. Since a child with type 1 diabetes produces little or no insulin, most oral diabetes medications are not effective and are not a treatment option. Very often, shortly after starting insulin injections, the child may experience a period of reduced insulin need called a "honeymoon period." During the honeymoon period, the remaining beta cells continue to produce insulin. Injected insulin doses may become very low, but it is important to continue the injections during this period because even low doses of insulin appear to help prolong this "honeymoon."

A child diagnosed with type 2 diabetes is generally born into a family with a history of type 2. When that predisposition is combined with factors such as weight gain and inactivity, the child develops type 2 diabetes in very much the same way that an adult does. And, unfortunately, just as in adults with the disease, it is common for a child with type 2 diabetes to be insulin resistant and to have high blood pressure, high cholesterol levels, and high triglyceride levels. So the child has an increased risk of heart disease and other diabetes complications early in life. As is the case with an adult who has the disease, the child with type 2 diabetes may need to take oral medication, insulin, or both to control their diabetes.

Regardless of the type of diabetes that a child has, the goal of effective diabetes management is to keep blood glucose levels as close to a "normal" range as safely possible in order to reduce the long- and short-term complications of diabetes and to promote normal growth and development. The target blood glucose range must be determined individually for each child.

## children are not small adults

Managing diabetes takes commitment and effort regardless of when it develops. But diabetes presents unique issues for children and teens. For example, the simple pleasures of childhood, such as going to birthday parties, school trips, or sleepovers, need careful planning for the child with diabetes. Participation in sports, peer pressure, growth, and pubertal hormones present additional challenges to maintaining optimal glucose control.

Every day, the child with diabetes will need to take insulin (or medication if type 2), check blood glucose several times, and monitor food intake and physical activity carefully. Depending on the child's age, these responsibilities may be assumed by the caregiver alone, shared between an older child and the caregiver, or shared between the child and caregiver.

For the parent or caregiver who is essentially playing the role of the child's pancreas, the responsibility can be daunting; it is a job that is impossible to do perfectly. And it is easy for the caregiver to become overwhelmed by the daily demands of determining exact insulin amounts, anticipating the

### Do as I do

One of the best ways to help a child who has, or is at risk for developing, type 2 diabetes is to make lifestyle improvement a family affair. Set a good example and involve everyone. Learn together about smarter eating and activity choices. Then explore them together. Tackle the produce section at the grocery store or farmers market. Give everyone a chance to pick a new fruit or vegetable for the whole family to try. Experiment with different colors, flavors, and textures. Explore some fresh herbs and spices in place of added salt and fat. Cut out the sugar-sweetened beverages, and eat out less. Next, get active together. Try doing some chores by hand or errands on foot. For fun, go on family bike rides or family walks. Spend a day at a local park or museum. You might even consider taking an activity-based family vacation. Go ahead, get creative. Then, get moving!

child's carbohydrate intake and activity levels, and preventing both hypoglycemia and high blood sugar levels. What's more, the stress of caring for a child with diabetes can aggravate any psychological, social, or financial problems that the family may already be experiencing. Because the diagnosis of diabetes changes a family and its dynamics forever, seeking and getting social and psychological support is essential for the well-being of all the family members.

As a child grows older and the daily responsibility of diabetes management shifts, the stress shifts as well. These years of transition, as the older child gradually learns self-management skills and develops personal judgment, are not often easy on the child or the family. The typical confusion and frustration that come with being a teenager can be aggravated by the stress of managing diabetes, even causing emotional and behavioral problems. Learning to cope with diabetes in adolescence is a big job, and reaching out to health professionals for additional support may help the teenager, the parents, and other family members.

The child's diabetes care team is an important resource and can often suggest care and treatment options that may help ease some of the difficulties. For example, a child who requires insulin daily may benefit from the use of an insulin pump (see the chapter "Using Insulin"). The pump not only improves control but helps restore some flexibility and spontaneity to the family's lifestyle and schedule. With the pump, gone are the schedules of meals, snacks, sleeping, exercise, and shots; there is also less risk of hypoglycemia. In addition, using the pump allows significantly more freedom in food choices and amounts.

Because so much of a child's life is spent in the classroom, it's also important to bring teachers and school officials into the loop as an added safety net. There are now laws to ensure that children with diabetes are treated fairly at school and that the child's medical needs are met. These laws apply to all public schools and most private schools and day care centers. All schools must have a written IEP (Individualized Educational Plan) for the child with diabetes. It must clearly state when the child needs to check blood sugar and take insulin, the timing of meals and snacks, the symptoms and treatment of high and low blood sugar, and the phone numbers for parents and other emergency contacts.

Yet another resource that can help ease the burden for the child and provide a break for the caregiver are the various camps for children with

| Type of diabetes | WHICH RELATIVE HAS DIABETES? | YOUR CHANCE OF GETTING DIABETES |
|---|---|---|
| Type 1 | Your brother, sister, son, or daughter | 10% |
| Type 1 | Your mother | 2% |
| Type 1 | Your father | 6% |
| Type 2 | Your brother or sister | 25% |
| Type 2 | Your mother or father | 12% |
| Type 2 | Your mother and father | 50% |
| Type 2 | Your identical twin | 90% |

diabetes. Camp provides a great opportunity for children and teenagers who have diabetes to get to know others who face the same challenges and to have fun in a safe environment while learning useful coping skills. An excellent resource for exploring diabetes camps in your area can be found at the Diabetes Education and Camping Association website: www.diabetescamps.org

Websites have the potential to offer support and information for young people with diabetes and their family members. To get started, try these sites: www.childrenwithdiabetes.com and www.parentingdiabetickids.com.

## it's nature and nurture: they both play a role

For the average American, the chance of developing type 1 diabetes is approximately 1 in 100 (1 percent). Meanwhile, 35 percent of U.S. adults (and 50 percent of adults age 65 or older) have pre-type 2 diabetes, and more than 2 million adults are diag-

nosed with type 2 every year. Having a family member with type 2 changes these odds, especially for type 2 diabetes (see the chart above). Type 2 seems to run in families much more often than does type 1.

While type 2 has a strong genetic link, it is also heavily influenced by lifestyle. In other words, a child or adult who doesn't have a family history of type 2 but who lives in an environment of inactivity and free-flowing calories can develop type 2 diabetes quite easily. Conversely— and fortunately— even a family history of diabetes doesn't condemn a child or adult to developing type 2 if healthy lifestyle habits are adopted.

# use your diabetes tool kit

**A diagnosis of diabetes** can be disheartening, but there is plenty of good news. These days, you have a well-stocked kit of diabetes tools available to help you keep your blood sugar under tight control and ward off the frightening complications associated with diabetes. You simply need to understand how to apply them to your best advantage and to commit yourself to using them faithfully. In this section, you will learn about these tools—blood sugar monitoring, HbA1c testing, healthy lifestyle habits, medications, and preparation for extreme circumstances—as well as how you and your diabetes care team can get the most from them.

# monitoring your glucose

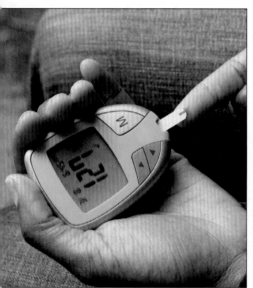

To achieve glucose levels that are as close to normal as possible, you need to monitor them regularly. Today, the meters available for glucose testing are small, fast, and relatively easy to use. Some require blood samples as small as one third of a *microliter,* allowing for pain-free alternate-site testing (drawing a tiny sample from the forearm or thigh). There are talking meters and large-display meters for the visually impaired, light-up meters for those who need to test at night, even meters with built-in food databases and record-keeping systems. What's more, continuous glucose monitors (CGMs) are now widely available and are often covered by health insurance. CGMs feature a tiny filament that is inserted just below the skin. A small radio transmitter is attached to the sensor and sends a signal to a handheld receiver. The receiver displays an estimate of the current glucose level every couple of minutes, along with trend graphs and alerts to let the user know when glu-

cose levels are heading outside of a desired range.

## to master, you must monitor

Blood glucose monitoring is a vital part of the diabetes management process, and frequent self-monitoring is a key to successful diabetes care. By checking your glucose, you get a precise measurement of what your blood glucose level is so you can adjust your food, medication, or activity level accordingly and with confidence. Knowing your glucose level also lets you see if your *previous* food, medication, or activity level brought your glucose to a desired range. It means far greater freedom to participate in any activities you choose and, therefore, far greater control over your life. The blood glucose values are like clues in a mystery novel. The more clues you have, the greater your ability to solve the mystery. Of course, the opposite can be true as well. The less you check, the fewer clues you have and the more your diabetes remains a mystery to both you and your diabetes care team.

Checking your blood glucose level is essential in managing diabetes because it is a critical factor in making treatment decisions. Research has shown that more frequent blood glucose checking is associated with an improved HbA1c level. And lowering the HbA1c will help reduce your risk for the many long-term complications discussed in the previous chapter.

Tight glucose control depends on frequent monitoring. Even for the person whose daily routine rarely changes, all kinds of things, such as stress, illness, unanticipated activity, alcohol, or medications, can throw off the balance, resulting in unpleasant and sometimes dangerous glucose fluctuations.

Checking your blood glucose on a regular basis allows you to know the ongoing status of your diabetes and will help you learn more about it and your body. Checking multiple times each day will give you even more information, helping you understand blood glucose patterns that occur when you eat certain foods and take specific medication doses, as well as how these are connected to your level of activity and stressors at home or work. Frequent checking also ensures that you can catch high or low levels quickly and respond to them with appropriate adjustments.

Your monitoring records can show how your personal glucose levels change in response to ordinary events, such as eating, menstruation, stress, and activity. Then, working together with your diabetes care team and through careful trial and adjustment, you can find out what works best for you—food, exercise, medications, or insulin—to keep your levels as close to normal as possible.

If you choose not to check your blood glucose levels, you cannot know whether your diabetes is really controlled. You never learn the relationship between what and how much you eat and your blood glucose levels. The lows that occur, say, after activity will remain a mystery, as will the high blood glucose levels that may be occurring after certain meals or first thing in the morning. It's like driving on a busy freeway with your eyes closed. Monitoring on a frequent basis allows you to control diabetes in the safest manner possible.

## Why would I want to know my blood glucose?

- To identify patterns in my blood glucose control
- To lead a more flexible life
- To reduce the risk of long-term diabetes complications
- To understand the impact of food, activity, and medications on my blood glucose
- To quickly identify either a high or low glucose level and treat the problem appropriately
- To figure out what may be causing my high or low blood glucose levels
- To perform at my best in my daily activities
- So my diabetes care team has to do less guessing when establishing a treatment plan for me
- To determine the effectiveness of my current diabetes treatment plan and identify when changes are needed
- To evaluate changes in my diabetes treatment plan and see if my glucose levels improve
- Because numbers are information, and with information I can better manage my diabetes
- Because knowing allows me to reach a level of freedom, security, and control that would otherwise be impossible
- To feel good
- To live healthy, well, and free from the complications of diabetes

## what meter is best for me?

Blood glucose monitoring systems are easier, faster, and more accurate than ever. Some meters give test results in as few as five seconds, and most store results for later recall or downloading to a computer. Meters include many features designed specifically to make self-monitoring convenient. All run on batteries, are small enough to fit in a purse or shirt pocket, and can be used almost anywhere. Most have an electronic memory, and more advanced models even contain built-in radio transmitters for sending the results to an insulin pump or computer. With so many options available, look at several models and discuss their advantages and disadvantages with your diabetes care team to determine the best model for you.

Today's meters use the newest electrochemical technology to measure glucose levels. Glucose in the blood causes a reaction on the test strip that produces a tiny electric current, and the meter detects and "reads" the current. All meters available in the U.S. have been tested for accuracy and approved for home use by the U.S. Food and Drug Administration (FDA).

As mentioned previously, all glucose meters report plasma glucose results. They simply take the value derived from a drop of whole blood and add 12 percent to the measured value. This plasma-calibrated value is equal to the reading that a laboratory might obtain, since all laboratory equipment is set up to measure the glucose that is present in a plasma sample of blood. When narrowing your choice of meters, and in order to get the most benefit from your monitoring, pick the meter that is covered by your health insurance plan and that you find easiest to use. This is crucial: You have to be able to perform the procedure properly to get reliable and accurate results. And you have to find a meter easy enough for you to use and maintain, or you'll be tempted to skip regular checking.

Meters themselves are usually relatively inexpensive. Many machines are available for free at pharmacies and clinics through special offers from manufacturers. Most manufacturers leave free sample meters at doctor's offices. Most also offer mail-in rebates after you buy the meter and trade-in rebates if you mail them your old meter. This way, if you don't like your original purchase, you can always trade it in for another at little or no cost. It is important to keep in mind, however, that you should never trade in your current meter based solely on the fact that the new one is free. Check to see if the new, free meter has all the features you feel are important, and also check with your diabetes care team to see if the trade would be a good deal for you.

| REQUIRED? | | FEATURES TO CONSIDER WHEN CHOOSING A METER |
|---|---|---|
| YES | NO | Does the speed of testing make a difference?<br>*(Meters can take anywhere from 5 seconds to 20 seconds to provide glucose results.)* |
| YES | NO | Do you want a meter that "beeps" to prompt you? |
| YES | NO | Do you want a silent meter? |
| YES | NO | Do you prefer individually wrapped test strips?<br>*(Some people find the foil-wrapped strips difficult to open, but such strips are less prone to spoilage if you use the meter in an area of high humidity.)* |
| YES | NO | Is "coding" required for each new package of test strips? Is the coding easy to perform? |
| YES | NO | Does the meter need to be cleaned? If so, is it an easy procedure? |
| YES | NO | Do you need a meter with a memory? How much memory? |
| YES | NO | Do you want the meter memory to give you the date and time of the glucose test in addition to the test result? |
| YES | NO | Do you want the meter memory to hold more than just glucose values (i.e., carbs, medication, exercise)? |
| YES | NO | Do you want a meter that allows you to check for ketones as well as glucose in a blood sample? |
| YES | NO | Do you want a meter that can download its memory to a computer? If so, is the meter's software compatible with your preferred computer system? |
| YES | NO | If your diabetes care team downloads your meter information at your visits, is the meter compatible with your team's system? |
| YES | NO | Will you be using the meter at high altitudes or in extreme temperatures? If so, are you able to use the meter under such varying conditions? |
| YES | NO | Do you have trouble getting a blood sample from your fingers? If so, does this meter require a very small sample of blood? |
| YES | NO | Would you prefer to use a test site other than your fingers, such as your arms or legs, to get a blood sample? If so, does this meter allow for it?<br>*(Meters that require .5 microliters of blood or less are best for alternative site testing)* |
| YES | NO | If you pay for your test strips yourself, are they affordable?<br>*(This will be your largest expense over the long haul. The difference between meter costs is small compared to the ongoing cost of the test strips.)* |
| YES | NO | Are the batteries easy to replace and convenient to find? |
| YES | NO | Do you want a meter that interfaces with your insulin pump or CGM? |
| YES | NO | Do you want to be able to label your readings as pre- vs. post-meal? |

If you have insurance, check with your provider about the coverage of diabetes supplies and which meters and supplies, if specified, are covered. Some health plans offer better coverage for certain meters' test strips, and less coverage for others. If you have Medicare, regulations in effect since July 1998 specify that Medicare will cover the costs of blood testing supplies for people with diabetes. Check with your local Medicare provider for details.

There are dozens of different meters available in the United States. Your choice of meter will depend, at least in part, on the individual features of the meters. Use the checklist on page 49 to help determine which features you prefer and/or require in your meter.

Entire chapters could be devoted to comparing all the meter systems available today. You could spend days, even weeks, traveling from pharmacy to pharmacy to see demonstrations of all the different meters. In general, no single store will have every meter available for you to evaluate.

Keeping all of this in mind, you might find it easiest to begin your search via the Internet or with a good, nonbiased reference guide. One of the best references is the buyer's guide published yearly in the December issue of the American Diabetes Association's *Diabetes Forecast* magazine. This buyer's guide can also be found on the American Diabetes Association's web-site at www.diabetes.org/diabetesforecast. All of the information is voluntarily supplied by the various product manufacturers. The American Diabetes Association does not review, endorse, or compare products but rather presents information about each category of products from those manufacturers who choose to provide it.

## when should I test?

A study published in the *British Journal of Medicine* showed that frequent blood glucose testing played a greater role in lowering blood glucose levels than did any medication, diet, or exercise plan. It showed that the more often a person tested blood glucose levels in a day, the better their blood glucose control was overall. And further research has shown that the better the glucose control overall, the lower the risk of long-term complications of diabetes.

So, the best time to test is . . . as often as possible! Most people find that the best times to check blood glucose levels are upon waking, just prior to meals and snacks, and before going to bed. You may also find it extremely helpful to check one to two hours after you eat to see the effect of food on your glucose levels. If you take insulin or oral medications that stimulate the pancreas to take more insulin (making you susceptible to hypoglycemia), it is also a good idea to check your glucose level before driving, exercising, using heavy equipment, or performing any high-risk tasks. By using your meter to check your blood glucose level at different times of the day, you begin collecting valuable information and keep yourself (and those around you) safe.

## what should my numbers be?

Your personal blood glucose goals will depend on your age, the type of diabetes you have and how long you've had it, any other health conditions you suffer from, your lifestyle, and your desired level of control. You should check with your diabetes care team to determine the best range of blood glucose levels for you.

The American Diabetes Association (ADA) has set the following as the standard of care for nonpregnant adults with diabetes:

- before-meal goals of 70–130 mg/dl
- less than 180 mg/dl at any time after a meal
- HbA1c < 7.0%

Finally, a word of caution. If your doctor does not ask you to do glucose testing or discourages the frequency of your testing, beware. You are not receiving appropriate care as recommended by the American Diabetes Association, the American Association of Clinical Endocrinologists, and the American Association of Diabetes Educators.

## am I doing this right?

Obtaining a drop of blood is sometimes the most difficult part of blood glucose testing. Meter manufacturers provide lancing devices that can be adjusted to varying depths, depending on individual need, which helps reduce the pain of monitoring and improves the chances of obtaining an adequate sample. Immediately before each check, make sure your hands are clean and free from anything that could influence your reading. When you wash your hands, use warm water. After drying, shake your hands below your waist and then squeeze, or milk, your test finger a few times before you lance a site. Make sure you use a new lancet before each test to ensure that it is clean and sharp. Place the lancing device firmly against the side of your fingertip, where there are fewer nerve endings, then push the release button on the lancing device. Squeeze gently from the base of your finger toward the tip until a drop of blood appears.

If you have ongoing problems obtaining an adequate blood sample, talk with your diabetes care team for suggestions. You may also want to explore using one of the alternate-site meters that allow you to obtain a blood sample from your arms or legs.

As previously discussed, blood glucose monitoring is a vital part of managing your diabetes. However, appropriate decisions regarding changes in your

## When to check more often

There are certain times when you may want to increase the frequency of your glucose checks, for example:

- Before and after exercise
- One, two, and three hours after eating when you want to know how a specific food affects your glucose levels
- When you start a new medication (especially a steroid), so you can closely monitor its effect
- During periods of stress, illness, or surgery
- If you become pregnant
- When you suspect your blood glucose level is high or low
- Any time there are changes to your daily routine or treatment program, such as in medication dose, meal plan, or activity level

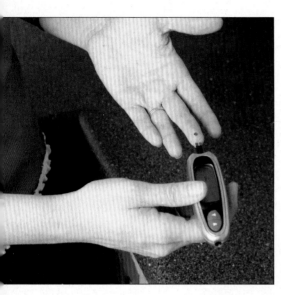

medications, eating, and level of activity can be made only if the results of your blood checks are accurate. According to an FDA-sponsored study, the main reasons for inaccurate readings were inadequate training in the use of meters and a misunderstanding of the manufacturer's instructions, lead-ing to errors in the operation of the meter.

The most common errors that were found among meter-users were:

- failure to follow the manufacturer's instructions
- inadequate amount and improper placement of blood on the test strip
- failure to "code" the meter
- the use of outdated test strips

Based on the FDA study, suggestions were made for reducing these errors. It was recommended that you:

- get professional training and guidance for the use of your particular meter
- make sure you are using test strips before their expiration date and are storing them appropriately
- ask your health care provider to check your technique
- follow the manufacturer's instructions carefully
- If your meter requires coding for each new package of test strips, be sure to do so

If you faithfully follow these suggestions but suspect that your meter values are incorrect, reread the manufacturer's instructions. Then run a test using the control solution provided by the meter company. If the results are not within the range printed on the test strip package, call the meter manufacturer's toll-free number, which is usually located on the back of the meter.

What if your meter readings don't match up well with your HbA1c? If the A1c is higher than expected, perhaps you need to check your after-meal blood glucose more often. You may be missing frequent spikes in your blood sugar that are raising the A1c. If the A1c is less than expected, perhaps you should check in the middle of the night to make sure your glucose is not dropping low while you are sleeping.

## what do I do with the numbers?

If you are putting in the time, money, and effort to test your blood glucose levels regularly, then you sure want something to come of your efforts. Try as you might, you will never be able to say for certain that you have complete control of your blood glucose levels. You will not be able to wake up one morning and confidently state that "All of my glucose levels will be exactly 120 today." You can, however, use the numbers that you get to help you confidently manage your diabetes.

To get the most out of your monitoring, you need a few pieces of information. First, make sure you know your target glucose levels, and figure out the best times to check so that you and your team can see how often you are within that range. Finally, write down your results, even if your meter has a memory and you or your team can download the data from your meter.

When you keep a written record, not only do you have the time, date, and glucose levels that the meter records, but you are also able to record essential, and sometimes critical, information. Record the type and dose of each diabetes medicine you take and the time you take it. (Do not fill out your record book ahead of time; your dose may change at some point or you may forget to take a dose. You want the record to accurately reflect what is happening to you.) Record changes in your routine that may be affecting your glucose levels. You will want to note any unusual events such as changes in mealtimes or the amount of food eaten, changes in activity, illness, or unusual stress. Also be sure to record any hypoglycemic events that occur.

With such detail, you and your team can identify glucose patterns and determine what causes your blood glucose fluctuations. You'll have enough information to manage your diabetes and develop a plan to get

| EXAMPLE OF CALCULATION TO FIGURE ACCEPTABLE RANGE WHEN COMPARING YOUR METER RESULT TO A LAB RESULT OF **231** | | | |
|---|---|---|---|
| **PLASMA-CALIBRATED METER** | | **WHOLE-BLOOD METER** | |
| $231 \times .20 = 46$ | Variance | $231 \div 1.12 = 206$ | Converted Result |
| $231 + 46 = 277$ | Acceptable High | $206 \times .20 = 41$ | Variance |
| $231 - 46 = 185$ | Acceptable Low | $206 + 41 = 247$ | Acceptable High |
| Acceptable Meter Range = $185 - 277$ | | $206 - 41 = 165$ | Acceptable Low |
| Which is $\pm 20\%$ of 231 | | Acceptable Meter Range = $165 - 247$ | |
| | | Which is $\pm 20\%$ of 206 | |

your blood glucose levels into your target range more often.

Keeping this written record is vital. Well-organized records can help you and your team determine the reasons for your out-of-range glucose values. Always have your professionals "think out loud" when they make changes in your treatment plan. Ask them what they saw in your record of glucose levels to prompt a change. How do they think the change will affect your future values? Make sure you understand their thinking and logic. In this way, with time and practice, you may be able to do the same type of analysis.

## meter choices today and tomorrow

The real excitement in blood glucose monitoring is about the development of continuous glucose monitors (CGMs). These devices have the potential to revolutionize the way we monitor blood glucose and, as a result, care for diabetes.

The three systems that are currently available (from Abbott, Medtronic, and

Dexcom) utilize a thin filament inserted just below the skin to sense glucose in the interstitial fluid (fluid between fat cells). The information from the sensor is transmitted via radio signals to a handheld receiver, which displays an estimate of the current glucose level. Trend graphs, direction arrows, and high/low alerts are also provided. All CGM systems require occasional calibration from fingerstick readings. The sensor values are generally within 10–15 percent of the fingerstick values.

Perhaps the most valuable aspect of CGM is the ability to detect *approaching* high or low glucose levels. Although they may not detect every high and low, CGMs will provide an early warning for the vast majority—and much earlier than most people can detect them on their own. The trend arrows/graphs also have considerable value. They give us the ability to forecast where the glucose is headed so that appropriate decisions can be made about food, activity, and insulin/medication.

The CGM receivers are downloadable for analyzing statistics and trends. Research has shown that those who use a CGM consistently tend to have fewer (and less severe) lows and improve-ments in their A1c. Those who don't use them consistently see little benefit.

Why would anyone *not* use CGM all the time? Well, they do have a few issues. Inserting the sensor can be a bit awkward and uncomfortable, and just having something stuck on the skin all the time bothers some people. There are occasional periods of inaccuracy and false alarms, and there is inherent "lag time" in any CGM system (its readings are about 10 minutes behind actual blood glucose values). And finally, there are costs: Even with insurance coverage, there are usually copays and deductibles that must be met.

It is difficult to know if CGM is right for you without trying it first. CGM companies all have a 30-day return policy, so there is little risk in trying it. Before dismissing the idea, remember this: When home blood glucose meters first came out, many people were skeptical about their value too!

If purchasing a system outright does not interest you, many endocrinologists' offices and diabetes treatment centers have clinical CGM systems that you wear for a short while and then return to the office for downloading to a computer and subsequent analysis. The information gained from proper analysis of CGM data can be quite valuable in revealing problem areas and fine-tuning your medical therapy.

# HbA1c: looking back to move forward

The blood glucose checks you perform at home provide incredibly valuable information. Each reading tells you what your glucose level is at a particular point in time, so that you can take steps immediately to bring a high or low level back under control. But there is yet another essential tool that you and your doctor can use to monitor your glucose levels and make decisions about your diabetes treatment. It's a laboratory test called the glycosylated hemoglobin (HbA1c, or simply "A1c") test, and it can help you and your doctor evaluate your level of glucose control over the previous eight to twelve weeks. Measuring the A1c does not replace the blood glucose checks you do at home. Rather, it adds to the information you and your doctor can use to manage your diabetes.

## what is the A1c?

Inside your red blood cells is a protein called hemoglobin that is responsible for carrying oxygen from your lungs to all the tissues in your body. Glucose that's circulating in your blood can

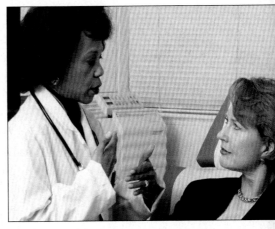

attach to, or glycate, the hemoglobin inside the red blood cell, forming glycohemo-globin. Once the glu-cose attaches to the hemoglobin, it stays there as long as the red blood cell lives, which is generally about two to three months. Red blood cells don't turn over, or die, all at once (otherwise, you'd be without oxygen until they could be replaced). Old ones are constantly dying, and new ones are constantly being made. You might say that, at any one time, your red blood cells are a mix of the very old, the middle aged, and the quite young, with more of them being on the younger side of their lives.

Normally, in someone who does not have diabetes, about 4 to 6 percent of the hemoglobin in their blood is coated with glucose. In the person with diabetes who has blood glucose levels that are higher than normal, more hemoglo-

### HbA1c Corresponding EAG Values

| A1c % | EAG (MG/DL) | EAG (MMOL) |
|---|---|---|
| 5% | 97 | 5.4 |
| 6% | 126 | 7.0 |
| 7% | 154 | 8.6 |
| 8% | 183 | 10.2 |
| 9% | 212 | 11.8 |
| 10% | 240 | 13.3 |
| 11% | 269 | 14.9 |
| 12% | 298 | 16.5 |
| 13% | 326 | 18.1 |
| 14% | 355 | 19.7 |

bin molecules have glucose attached. For the person with diabetes, as much as 20 percent (or more) of the hemoglobin molecules can become coated with glucose. The A1c test measures this percentage. And because some of the hemoglobin molecules are older and some newer, the test results provide a backward glance at the *average* glucose levels over the past two to three months. Looking at these numbers can help you and your doctor evaluate how well your current diabetes therapy is working and whether any adjustments need to be made to improve your blood glucose control.

It is recommended that people who have type 2 diabetes have an HbA1c test at least twice a year. Those with type 1 should have the HbA1c four times per year. More frequent testing is warranted in certain situations, such as when a new medication or treatment regimen is being tried or when blood glucose goals simply aren't being met.

The HbA1c value is not affected by a meal eaten right before the test, so there's no need to fast before you give blood for the test. However, certain blood abnormalities such as iron defi-

ciency anemia, and sickle-cell trait will affect the accuracy of HbA1c measurements. Donating blood can also produce an artificially low HbA1c result for the following couple of weeks.

Some healthcare providers have machines that can measure HbA1c in a few minutes from a fingerstick blood sample. Most laboratories use more sophisticated equipment that requires blood drawn from a vein. There are also single-use home-use HbA1c kits that can be purchased at pharmacies and through mail-order suppliers. While home-use kits are deemed reasonably accurate, they require strict compliance with the procedures that come with the kit.

## what does an HbA1c number mean?

In general, when evaluating an HbA1c test, each percent increase in the hemoglobin A1c reflects an increase in average blood glucose of approximately 30 mg/dl (1.7 mmol/l). So, if an HbA1c of 6 percent is equal to an average blood glucose level of 130 mg/dl (7 mmol/l), then 7 percent would be equal to approximately 160 mg/dl (8.7 mmol/l), 8 percent would equal 290 mg/dl (10.4 mmol/l), and so on. The American Diabetes Association recommends that the hemoglobin A1c be less than 7 percent for most people with diabetes; the American Association of Clinical Endocrinologists recommends an A1c of less than 6.5 percent. (Again, these recommendations should be individualized by you and your physician based on your potential benefits and risks). To calculate your "estimated average glucose" (eAG) based on your HbA1c, use one of the formulas below:

In mg/dl:

(A1c × 28.7) − 46.7 = estimated average glucose for the past 2–3 months

In mmol/l:

(A1c X 1.59) − 2.59 = estimated average glucose for the past 2–3 months

## why bother with home blood tests?

As previously mentioned, HbA1c testing is not a substitute for your own daily blood glucose monitoring. The HbA1c measures only the average glucose level over the past two to three months. It can provide you with an overall picture of how well you have been controlling your blood glucose over time, whether your current treatment plan is helping to maintain or improve your control, and whether a shift in your plan is needed. The HbA1c can't, however, tell you about the *quality* of your control. Are the readings frequently high and low, or are they generally stable? You can have a decent average with lots of highs and lows, but that doesn't mean that your control is where it should be.

The blood glucose monitoring you do at home gives you specific information about your glucose level at the time of the test. It allows you to take immediate action to keep your blood glucose from going way too high or way too low. Based on the reading, you may decide that you need a snack, for example, or more insulin. It's the overall effectiveness of these individual day-to-day decisions, which you make based on your daily blood testing, that is reflected in your HbA1c.

The two types of testing—at-home blood tests and HbA1c tests—also serve as cross-checks for one another. For example, say your record of blood glucose tests for the past couple of months indicates your levels have been in a range that reflects excellent control of diabetes. But the HbA1c test results you just received suggest a much poorer level of control over that same time period. It's possible that your blood glucose is going very high at times when you don't normally check, such as after meals or in the middle of the night. It is also possible that your meter is not working

## Relationship between HbA1c and average blood glucose

Your hemoglobin A1c value (HbA1c) is equal to an average blood glucose over the last two to three months. The American Diabetes Association recommends that your HbA1c value be less than 7 percent to reduce your long-term complications of diabetes. A level that is below 6 percent is an even better target to aim for.

Another formula you can use to determine your exact blood glucose average is:

$$(HbA1c \times 35) - 75 = \text{Average Blood Glucose}$$

| HbA1c % | AVERAGE BLOOD GLUCOSE (MG/DL) |
|---|---|
| 13.0% | 380 |
| 12.0% | 345 |
| 11.0% | 310 |
| 10.0% | 275 |
| 9.0% | 240 |
| 8.0% | 205 |
| 7.0% | 170 |
| 6.0% | 135 |
| 5.0% | 100 |

correctly or you are not using it properly. Without data from both of these tests, you might never have known there was something wrong. Getting to the bottom of these contradictory results may help you and your doctor identify a problem in your current treatment plan. Then you and your team can take steps to remedy the problem and improve your control.

If your HbA1c value does not seem to agree with the average of the values recorded by your blood glucose meter (some meters provide an average of your readings over a specified period of time; otherwise, simply add up all the readings as you've recorded them in your log and divide that by the total number of entries to get your average), you should ask yourself the following questions:

- Am I testing frequently enough? Checking four times a day and occasionally one hour after meals should indicate your average value.

- Have I been testing long enough? You need to take the average of at least six weeks' worth of blood glucose readings to get a valid comparison to the HbA1c.

- Is my meter accurate? Using a single blood sample, compare the readings from your meter against readings from your doctor's meter or from the lab (see the chapter "Monitoring Your Glucose" for more information on this procedure).

- Do I have a medical condition that may be affecting the accuracy of my HbA1c tests? There are some instances in which HbA1c testing can give you a false result: anemia caused by blood loss, pregnancy, renal (kidney) disease, and vitamin deficiencies. Rarely, the HbA1c value can be artificially high as a result of abnormalities in the hemoglobin itself; in such cases, HbA1c values can even reach levels above 50 percent.

If you've been testing long enough, if your meter's readings appear to be accurate, and if conditions that affect hemoglobin have been ruled out as possible factors, ask your doctor to redo your HbA1c test. If there is still a discrepancy, you will need to work with your diabetes care team to determine and correct the problem.

# eating for better control

Eating is essential to life, but we eat for many reasons: out of hunger or habit, for pleasure, even as a way of dealing with emotions. A diagnosis of diabetes can make the simple act of eating seem overwhelmingly complicated. With education and experimentation, however, you can turn eating into a powerful diabetes management tool.

## there is no diabetes diet anymore

When you learned you had diabetes, you may have assumed you'd have to go on a special, restrictive diet. Perhaps you'd heard of people with diabetes who had to give up every food they enjoyed or who stopped going to certain events or restaurants because there was nothing they could eat there. Well, cheer up. You don't need to follow a "diabetic diet" anymore.

A *diet* implies that you need to eat sparingly or according to strict prescribed rules. Diets also have a nasty habit of prohibiting rich, high-calorie, mouthwatering foods. Research shows that dieters often report overwhelming desires for the foods they're not supposed to eat on a diet and that they often give in to those cravings. Once

they give in, they are likely to overindulge. This diet/binge cycle is very common in those who frequently go on weight-loss diets. It leads not only to failed weight-loss attempts but to weight regain, yo-yo dieting, feelings of guilt, and constant food cravings.

The traditional diabetic diet was really no different than traditional weight-loss diets; indeed, it prescribed even greater food restrictions and pretty much dictated what foods were and were not allowed. Likewise, studies have shown that those following a traditional diabetic diet were no different than other dieters—they, too, eventually gave in to their desires and binged on "forbidden foods." For the person with diabetes, falling off the traditional diabetes diet wagon led not only to weight regain, guilt, and constant cravings but to something potentially more dangerous—poor diabetes control.

The actual problem with diets in general—and the source of the ongoing diet/binge cycle and constant food cravings—is that dieting is based on four flawed assumptions:

1. The first flawed assumption is that eating is always done in a continu-

ous state of awareness. For some people, however, eating comes close to being on the same level of consciousness as breathing. Have you ever found that you've polished off a whole box of crackers or cookies and don't even remember taking the first bite? Somehow eating, like breathing, just happened without any thought. That's not to say that for periods of time a person can't focus intently on a diet, following every rule and detail. It's just that, in time, the spell will be broken and the person will drift back to old eating habits.

2. A diet presumes that we eat only to provide our bodies with fuel. But many people have strong expectations to have certain foods at certain times and places. Diets rarely take into consideration birthday or holiday celebrations, complete with traditional foods and cultural associations. Nor do they take into account Dad's classic Sunday brunch extravaganza or Grandma's jar full of buttery homemade cookies. Only certain foods and food combinations will do at these times, otherwise it's just not the same.

3. Diets work on the belief that all of your emotional needs are met. Cravings for food and the need to eat may be responses to stresses in your life that need to be addressed. A diet discounts the need for comfort foods that calm and that are eaten in an attempt to soothe away life's troubles and turmoil. These foods have pleasurable tastes and textures and are used as rewards or to provide solace, a practice commonly begun in childhood and continued throughout life.

4. Diets operate on the idea that demand should equal supply. In other words, when a diet restricts certain foods, your desire or demand for them should not increase. However, just the opposite tends to be true. The deprivation of dieting sets you up to long for, think about, and plan your days around foods that you cannot or should not eat. It becomes a simple case of wanting what you can't have.

It's foolish and, in the end, self-defeating to deny the associations we have with food and the emotions certain foods evoke. Attempting to ignore these influences, which is what we try to do anytime we "go on a diet," sets us up for disordered eating behaviors, such as bingeing and overeating. By trying to totally avoid certain foods, people instead tend to overconsume them in the end. For you, the person with diabetes, this can lead to additional problems. You may skip glucose testing or not record results—you may even cancel medical appointments—because you figure you've "blown" your diet and testing your blood sugar would just remind you of your failure.

Rather than a restrictive diet, what you need is knowledge and information. You need to understand how food fuels and affects your body, especially your glucose levels, and then use that information, along with glucose monitoring, to choose a variety of foods—including the ones you enjoy most.

## how foods affect blood glucose

Your body needs adequate amounts of six essential nutrients to function normally. Three of these—water, vitamins, and minerals—provide no energy and do not affect blood glucose levels. The other three, carbohydrate, protein, and fat, provide your body with the energy it needs to work. (Protein also provides the building blocks for growth, and repair and maintenance of body parts.) This energy is measured in calories. Any food that contains calories can cause your blood glucose levels to rise. For your body to properly use these energy calories, it needs insulin. Whenever you eat, your food is digested and broken down or converted into your body's primary fuel source, glucose. While all energy nutrients are broken down into glucose, carbohydrates have

a more direct effect on blood glucose levels. Protein and fat have a slower, more indirect effect on those levels. Understanding this can help you predict how food will affect your glucose levels.

### carbohydrates
Commonly known as sugars and starches, carbohydrates are your body's main, and preferred, source of energy. They enter your bloodstream rapidly, are fairly predictable in the way they affect glucose, and generally are completely broken down within two to four hours. There are three types: simple carbohydrates, or sugars (such as table sugar and honey); digestible complex carbohydrates, or starches (in bread, pasta, and potatoes); and nondigestible complex carbohydrates, or fiber. Nearly 100 percent of the sugars and starches you eat break down into glucose; the speed at which they do so varies, but ultimately all the carbs you eat (except for the fiber) turn into blood glucose. Ironically, many starches raise the blood sugar faster than some sugars, so don't worry so much about the *type* of carbohydrate as much as the *amount*. We'll discuss this in greater detail later on.

There are two types of simple carbohydrates: monosaccharides and disac-

## TYPES OF CARBOHYDRATES

| NAME | TYPE | WHAT IT LOOKS LIKE | WHERE IT IS FOUND | SPEED IT RAISES BLOOD GLUCOSE |
|---|---|---|---|---|
| dextrose | simple disaccharide | two glucose units | many candies and hypoglycemia products | very fast |
| fructose | simple monosaccharide | single fructose unit | table sugar, fruit, molasses, and honey | moderate |
| galactose | simple monosaccharide | single galactose unit | milk and dairy products | slow |
| maltose (malt sugar) | simple disaccharide | two glucose units | produced during the breakdown of starch | super fast |
| sucrose (table sugar) | simple disaccharide | one glucose and one fructose unit hooked together | table sugar, fruit, vegetables, and grains | fast |
| lactose (milk sugar) | simple disaccharide | one glucose and one galactose unit hooked together | milk and dairy products | slow |
| starch | straight chain | long chains of glucose | potatoes, rice, bread, cereal | fast |
| starch | branched chain | units hooked together | legumes, pastas | very slow |
| fiber | complex polysaccharide | long chains of glucose units hooked together that the body's enzymes can't break down | fruits, vegetables, and legumes | very slow |

charides. Monosaccharides, such as glucose and fructose, are single sugar units. Disaccharides consist of two sugar units; for example, sucrose, or table sugar, is made of a glucose sugar hooked to a fructose sugar.

Digestible complex carbohydrates, or starches, are polysaccharides; they consist of many long chains of glucose units hooked together. Starches are found in grains, legumes, and potatoes. When starches are digested by your body, they are broken down into glucose, the simplest form of energy used by your body and your brain. The starch in a potato and the sugar in your sugar bowl, therefore, are really the same as far as your body is concerned. The body breaks down and utilizes the glucose from each in identical ways, and it has no way of knowing whether the energy originally came from a simple carbohydrate or a complex one.

However, people with diabetes often think, or have been taught, they cannot or should not have any simple carbohydrates, or sugar, in their diet. Sugar has traditionally been viewed as a forbidden or dangerous food for people with diabetes. After all, the blood "sugar" is high, so why complicate matters? Doctors and dietitians always assumed that since sugar was a simple carbohydrate, it must be more quickly digested and absorbed into the blood than more complex starches such as those in potatoes and breads. They further assumed that simple sugars would most likely cause a larger rise in blood glucose levels.

Well, doctors, dietitians, and all the food police were wrong! Multiple studies have shown that simple sugars don't increase your glucose levels any higher or faster than starches alone do. The American Diabetes Association's nutritional recommendations now say, "scientific evidence has shown that the use of sucrose as part of the meal plan does not impair blood glucose control in individuals with Type 1 or Type 2 diabetes." *It is now generally recognized that the total amount of carbohydrate in your diet, not the source of the carbohydrate, is what significantly influences your blood glucose levels.*

Fiber is different. Fiber is made up mostly of complex carbohydrates—so complex, in fact, that they cannot be broken down by enzymes in your body. There are two types of fiber, soluble and insoluble. Soluble fiber remains suspended in water, while insoluble fiber does not. Soluble fiber, found in oats, barley, cereals, apples, and citrus fruits, delays glucose absorption, lowers cholesterol, and decreases the speed at which food moves through your intestines. Insoluble fiber, found in all fruits, vegetables, legumes, and seeds, also delays glucose absorption and slows the breakdown of starch, but it increases the speed at which food moves through your intestines.

## protein

The second major nutrient needed by your body is protein. The protein in food (meats, poultry, fish, beans, dairy products, and eggs) is broken down into amino acids by your body; only about 50 percent of it is eventually changed into glucose. This is a long process, however: It takes about three to five hours after a meal for the protein you have eaten to start having any impact on your blood glucose. When carbohydrates are not available or are in short supply (as when you don't eat any carbs in a meal or skip a meal), amino acids can be made into glucose as a backup source of energy for the brain and other vital organs.

### fat

The third nutrient needed by your body is fat. Fat is used to maintain healthy skin and hair, to carry fat-soluble vitamins through your body, and as a major source of stored energy when you take in fewer calories than your body needs. Fats are changed by your body into fatty acids, which are an important source of energy for your muscles and heart. It generally takes about six to eight hours for the fat in food to be digested, and its components are released very slowly into your blood. In the end, only about 5 to 10 percent of the fat you eat is changed into glucose, so it has little direct impact on your blood glucose levels. Indirectly, however, fat does play a role in elevating blood glucose.

Fat blocks the action of insulin (fatty acids increase your insulin resistance) and increases the time it takes for food to travel through your intestines. So, for example, if you eat a dinner of fried chicken, mashed potatoes, gravy, and biscuits, it may not greatly affect your glucose reading before bed. During the night, however, when this fatty, slow-moving meal finally hits your system and the fat doesn't let your insulin work very well, your blood glucose level rises. In the morning, you awaken to a whopper of a blood glucose number.

### is alcohol a body fuel?

Alcohol is not a carbohydrate, protein, or fat. The body views it more as a toxin than an energy source. To your body, alcohol is a poison that needs to be broken down, detoxified, and removed from your blood as quickly as possible to prevent it from accumulating and destroying cells and organs.

When you drink, alcohol passes very quickly from your stomach and intestines into your blood without being broken down. Enzymes in your liver then do the job of breaking down the alcohol, but this process takes time. Your liver can only metabolize alcohol at a set rate, regardless of how much you have had to drink. For the average adult, it takes the liver approximately two hours to break down the alcohol in one drink. If you drink alcohol faster than it can be broken down, it moves through your bloodstream to other parts of your body until it can be metabolized. Your brain cells are affected by this excess, impairing brain function and causing intoxication.

Whether or not you have eaten and what you have eaten are two factors that influence how quickly alcohol is absorbed into your blood. Since alcohol can only be processed at a certain rate by your liver, slowing down the absorption time (how quickly alcohol appears in your blood) can be beneficial. How fast your stomach empties into your intestines is the main control for how quickly alcohol is absorbed. The higher the fat content of a meal, the slower the emptying and the longer the absorption process. A study found that people who drank alcohol after a meal that included fat, protein, and carbohydrate absorbed the alcohol about three times more slowly than when they drank the same amount on an empty stomach.

Aside from the intoxication alcohol can cause, the process of breaking down alcohol cuts ahead of other processes on the liver's agenda. Normally, if your blood glucose level starts to drop, your liver responds by changing stored energy into glucose. This glucose then helps you avoid or slow a low blood glucose reaction. However, since your body sees alcohol as a poison, it wants to clear it from your blood as quickly as possible. In fact, it is so busy processing the alcohol, it will not make or release as much glucose as usual until the alcohol is gone from your system.

The inability to produce sufficient amounts of glucose can put you at risk for a number of different problems,

including a severe hypoglycemic (low blood glucose) reaction (see the chapter "Fighting Hypoglycemia"). In addition, if you have consumed enough alcohol, your judgment may be impaired, decreasing or even erasing your ability to notice or recognize symptoms of hypoglycemia. To top it off, because the symptoms of hypoglycemia mimic intoxication, a low blood glucose reaction can easily be confused with drunkenness, possibly delaying emergency treatment even further should you become incoherent.

So, do you have to abstain from alcohol in order to control blood glucose? Can you have a beer with your pizza or a glass of wine with your spaghetti? There is no one right answer. You must discuss it with your diabetes care team. Your history of alcohol consumption needs to be reviewed, the medications you take need to be assessed for potential interactions with alcohol, and your diabetes control needs to be evaluated. Should you receive the okay, remember:

1. Drink only if your diabetes is under good control. Alcohol can make some diabetes problems, such as neuropathy, worse. Alcohol can accumulate in nerve cells, intensifying damage from high glucose

levels and worsening neuropathy. It also raises triglycerides, blood pressure, and risk of cataracts. If you have frequent hypoglycemia or a past history of severe hypoglycemia, alcohol may be too big a risk for you.

2. Drink in moderation. The breakdown of alcohol by your liver is a slow process, so the amount of alcohol you drink needs to be controlled to prevent intoxication. Moderation generally means no more than two drinks per day for men and no more than one per day for women. A single drink is defined as 12 ounces of beer, 5 ounces of wine, or 1½ ounces of distilled liquor. Remember, alcohol has no nutrients, only calories, most of which your body stores as fat.

3. Do not skip a meal or decrease your food intake when drinking. Have your drink with a meal or shortly after eating. Never drink on an empty stomach, and do not skip meals or substitute alcohol for your usual meal or snack.

4. Always carry a form of identification, preferably one that indicates you have diabetes. This lets people know that your erratic behavior or loss of consciousness may not be due to intoxication but rather to severe hypoglycemia.

5. Never drink alone. Inform those around you that you have diabetes, and teach them the signs and symptoms of hypoglycemia. This way, they will not confuse these symptoms of hypoglycemia with intoxication and ignore or delay treatment of a possible hypoglycemic reaction.

6. Remain sober. Since alcohol has a relaxing effect, it can impair your judgment. You need to eat your meals, take your medication, and test your blood sugar on schedule.

7. Test your blood glucose frequently. Learn how alcohol affects you by testing prior to drinking, after drinking, and the next day. Be sure to always test your blood glucose before going to sleep. And never give yourself extra insulin or take extra diabetes pills to treat a high blood glucose reading just before going to bed. You could become dangerously hypoglycemic as you sleep and never even notice it.

### what about sweeteners?

There are two types of sweeteners on the market today—those that have calories, called nutritive sweeteners, and those that have no calories, called nonnutritive sweeteners. Only the nutritive sweeteners affect blood glucose directly, but you'll still need to pay attention to the other ingredients in foods that use artificial sweeteners.

**nutritive sweeteners.** The simple carbohydrates sucrose and fructose are the most common nutritive sweeteners; both contribute calories and influence your blood glucose levels.

*Sugar alcohols,* also called polyols, contain calories and carbohydrates and are often used as substitute sweeteners, especially in candy. Although sugar and alcohol are forbidden ingredients, sugar alcohols are neither sugars nor alcoholic substances in the common sense of the term. (The scientific definition of alcohol is simply "a processed liquid.") Sugar alcohols are the commercially produced, processed liquids from sucrose, glucose, and starches (polysaccharides). They also occur naturally in plants such as fruits and berries. Common sugar alcohols include sorbitol, mannitol, maltitol, and xylitol.

Another sugar alcohol, called hydrogenated starch hydrolysate, is made by partially breaking down corn, wheat, or potato starch and then adding hydrogens, at a high temperature and under pressure, to the partially broken-down mixture. As a result, it contains higher quantities of hydrogenated polysaccharides as well as sorbitol, mannitol, maltitol, and xylitol. It is kind of the "complex carbohydrate" of the sugar alcohols, used in a variety of products, especially sugar-free candies, because it does not crystallize. It also blends well with flavors and can be used with low-calorie sweeteners.

As a group, sugar alcohols are not completely absorbed and used by your body, so they contribute fewer calories and carbohydrates than the same amount of other nutritive sweeteners, such as sucrose. For this reason, they are referred to as reduced-energy or low-energy sweeteners. But because they are not completely absorbed, they can produce unpleasant side effects, such as diarrhea, bloating, and gas, when consumed in excess.

**artificial sweeteners.** Artificial sweeteners are man-made, intensely sweet products most commonly used in reduced-calorie foods and beverages. They are termed nonnutritive sweeteners because they add very few, if any, calories and carbohydrates to foods. Because such a small amount of these sweeteners is needed to produce a "sweet" taste in foods, they are also referred to as high-intensity sweeteners. The major artificial sweeteners are NutraSweet (aspartame), Sweet One (acesulfame K), Splenda (sucralose), and Sweet'N Low (saccharin).

**"sugar-free" products.** How is it that a manufacturer can slap a big "Sugar Free" label on the front of a box of cookies even though the product contains sugar? The answers: "Quite simply" and "quite legally." All that the term "sugar free" means is that a product contains less than .5 gram of sugar in a serving—and "sugar" in this

## SWEETENERS

### nutritive (calorie-containing) sweeteners

| | |
|---|---|
| sucrose (white sugar) | It is very versatile in terms of use, readily available, and inexpensive. |
| glucose | This is what carbohydrates are turned into to circulate in the bloodstream. |
| fructose | It is sweeter than sucrose in cold liquids, but in warm liquids and solid foods, it is only as sweet as sucrose. It enhances fruit flavors. |
| honey | It is nutritionally similar to sucrose and is chemically formed from nectar by bees. It has a very distinctive flavor and a very high water content. |
| lactose | It is the sugar found in milk and is a disaccharide, made up of glucose and galactose linked together. It has a very low sweetness, which limits its uses, but it is often used in combination with intense sweeteners as a "filler." Lactose intolerance is common and occurs in people who lack the digestive enzyme lactase, which breaks apart the glucose and galactose units. |
| sorbitol, mannitol | They are sugar alcohols and are about half as sweet as sucrose, which limits their uses. They are incompletely absorbed by your body, so they add fewer calories and have less impact on blood sugar than ordinary carbohydrates. Because of incomplete digestion, they can cause diarrhea, gas, and bloating when used in large quantities. They are more expensive than sucrose. |
| xylitol, maltitol | They are sugar alcohols. Both are about as sweet as sucrose and so are more widely used, especially in candies and baked goods. They are incompletely absorbed, so they have fewer calories and raise the blood sugar less than ordinary carbohydrates. Large quantities may cause diarrhea, gas, and bloating. |
| hydrogenated starch hydrolysate | It's the "complex carbohydrate" of sugar alcohols. It's made of large chains of polysaccharides plus hydrogen put together under heat and pressure to form very stable, complex sugar alcohols. Widely used in candies and with low-calorie, nonnutritive sweeteners. |

### nonnutritive (calorie-free) sweeteners

| | |
|---|---|
| saccharin (Sweet'N Low) | It provides no energy. It is 200 to 700 times sweeter than sucrose but has a bitter, metallic aftertaste. |
| aspartame (NutraSweet) | It is made up of two amino acids linked together. The amino acids break apart when they are heated, and the sweetness deteriorates, so it can only be used in cold foods and drinks. It is 160 to 220 times sweeter than sucrose. It cannot be used by people with phenylketonuria. |
| acesulfame K (Sweet One) | It is an organic salt consisting of carbon, nitrogen, oxygen, hydrogen, sulphur, and potassium atoms. It is 200 times sweeter than sucrose and is heat stable. |
| sucralose (Splenda) | It is the only nonnutritive sweetener made from sugar. Through a special method, three hydrogen-oxygen groups on the sugar molecule are replaced with three chlorines. It is used as a sugar replacement and an additive in various desserts, confections, and nonalcoholic beverages. It is 600 times sweeter than sucrose. Its sweetening power is not reduced with heating. |

context is defined as sucrose. That's right. "Sugar free" simply means that table sugar or cane sugar is not in the item. The manufacturer can add fructose and any other nutritive sweetener and still call it "sugar free."

As a result, it is not unusual for a sugar-free product to actually contain more total carbohydrates than the regular version of the same product. For the person with diabetes, that means the sugar-free item will actually raise blood glucose more than the regular version of the food would. The same applies for many fat-free foods. They truly have less than .5 gram of fat per serving, but when the fat is removed, simple carbohydrates may be added instead. So some fat-free and some fat-free/sugar-free products actually have more carbohydrates and will raise blood glucose levels higher than the regular item would.

Also understand that a sugar-free food is not always calorie free, low in calories, or low in simple carbohydrates. Some foods may even have sugar listed on the label, even though they fit the legal definition of "sugar free." Milk is a good example. On the food label for milk, you will find that one serving contains 11 to 13 grams of sugar. Milk doesn't contain sucrose, or table sugar. It does, however, contain the naturally occurring simple carbohydrate (sugar) called lactose. The point is that because a product is labeled "sugar free" doesn't mean you can ignore its potential effect on your blood glucose levels.

**check that label!**
It's important to look closely at the nutrition label on a food to find the actual calorie and carbohydrate counts. As you look at any product, the middle part of the nutrition label contains information on carbohydrate, fat, protein, and other nutrients. This section has the greatest amount of information for the person with diabetes who is trying to analyze the connection between food and glucose levels.

On all U.S. labels, carbohydrates are measured in grams. As you've learned, gram for gram, all carbohydrates have the same effect on blood sugar levels. So use the food labels to compare foods in terms of their total carbohydrate as well as their fiber content. Make sure the serving sizes you are comparing are similar. Then choose the product that best fits into your carbohydrate goals (which you'll learn about shortly). In addition, monitoring your blood sugar before and after eating or drinking will help you to see a food's effect on your blood sugar.

## carbs are key
Okay, so now you have a basic understanding of how the nutrients in food affect your blood glucose. To successfully use this knowledge as part of your

| SOME OF THE FOODS THAT CONTAIN CARBOHYDRATE | | |
|---|---|---|
| rice | pasta | breads |
| cereals | fruits | juices |
| vegetables | milk & milk products | nuts |
| candy | cakes | pies |
| chips & pretzels | beans | popcorn |
| crackers | soda | pancakes & waffles |
| tortillas | cookies | jams & jellies |
| FOODS THAT DO NOT HAVE CARBOHYDRATE | | |
| meats and fats | | |

diabetes self-care, you need to make personal food choices that are compatible with your blood glucose goals and your tastes. Since carbohydrates obviously have the greatest direct effect on glucose levels, determining the amount of carbohydrates that your body can manage well is a cornerstone in your glucose management. It's simple, really. But before you begin, you should take a close look at your perceptions, preconceptions, and habits regarding food and eating; they can make eating much more complicated than need be. Adjusting them can allow you to enjoy the freedom that simplicity brings—and allow you to enjoy eating while you control your diabetes.

### don't stereotype your carbs

According to multiple studies, the amount of digestible carbohydrate in what you eat is more important than the type (sugar or starch) in terms of blood glucose. In other words, a carbohydrate is a carbohydrate. While a snack of one large, extra-chunky chocolate chip cookie may seem "bad" and a snack of three small sugar-free cookies may seem "good," your body can't tell the difference between them if both snacks have the same amount of digestible carbohydrate. Both will raise your glucose level the same amount.

You may be thinking, "No way." You may have preconceptions telling you that eating an extra-chunky cookie or a candy bar must raise your glucose levels higher than eating, say, a baked potato or even a few sugar-free cookies. Perhaps your experience seems to back you up. The culprit in this apparent discrepancy, though, is not the type of carbohydrate. Your preconceptions—and the total amount of carbohydrate you consume—are much more likely to blame.

Consider this: Generally, when, what, and why you eat has as much (or more) to do with habit or craving as it has to do with hunger. So while you may eat just one baked potato, you may be driven to eat an entire candy bar, not because you are still hungry after finishing half of it, but because it just tastes so good and perhaps it has been a long time since you've allowed yourself to have chocolate. You may even feel that, because it's been so long, you are entitled to two candy bars. So you end up eating more

candy—and more total carbohydrate. It's that larger amount of carbohydrate, not the source of the carbohydrate, that sends your glucose soaring.

The kind of deprivation that might drive you to eat a second candy bar can drive your eating in other ways as well. There's nothing that can heighten your desire for a food quite like being told you cannot have it. So, you have a nice lunch, followed by a sugar-free cookie—followed by three extra-chunky chocolate chip cookies. You figure you've eaten what you were supposed to eat, it's only fair that you get to eat what you really want in return. You then blame your elevated glucose levels on the extra-chunky cookies. While they are a contributor, they are not the problem. If you had ended your lunch with one of the extra-chunky cookies you wanted in the first place, your glucose level would have been lower in the end. It was your initial self-imposed deprivation that set you up to fail. It's this kind of restrictive thinking that makes some foods seem off-limits or more dangerous in terms of glucose control. And it's this kind of restrictive thinking that can make you feel deprived, triggering unhealthful eating behaviors that defeat the best intentions.

Deprivation can also lead to desperation, which leads to desperate measures. For example, perhaps you're always the last one in your household to go to bed, staying up well past the others because you're "just not tired yet." Or perhaps you decline dinner invitations and evenings out because you are "too tired"; you send everyone else out and stay home, alone. Now you can eat in peace, without anyone watching your intake. You're like an escaped convict, trying to outrun the food police and avoid being thrown back into deprivation jail.

These types of preconceptions and dysfunctional eating habits can also interfere with your dietary diabetes management. Food habits and eating patterns are developed over years and are often ingrained from childhood. You do something one way because that is just how it is done. You clean your plate because you shouldn't waste food. You eat every last bit of food because you paid for it or it is free. You eat because the label on your pill bottle says you must take it with food. You eat because the clock tells you it's time. These food-related habits have very little to do with hunger or your glucose levels, but they have become the rules that drive your eating.

To end this cycle of deprivation and dysfunctional eating and be able to truly use your food choices to help control your diabetes, you need to make all food equal and make no food off-limits. You need to convince yourself once and for all that there are no such things as good foods and bad foods.

## IT'S NOT WHAT YOU'RE EATING, IT'S HOW MUCH YOU'RE EATING

| 30 grams of carbohydrates | amount you would normally eat | amount of carbohydrates actually eaten |
|---|---|---|
| 1 baked potato | 2 potatoes | 60 |
| 1 regular-sized candy bar | 2 candy bars—one because you crave it and one because you've blown your diet anyway, so you might as well go for it | 60 |
| 2 pieces of whole-wheat toast | 3 pieces of toast—because the toaster holds two slices. In addition, you have to have the third piece because "there are children starving somewhere." | 45 |
| 1½ cups of a cereal | 3 cups—Who decided that ¾ of a cup of cereal was a serving size? In a country where we "super size" everything, small is sure to leave me hungry. | 60 |

There are merely foods that affect your blood glucose in different ways. This will eliminate your feelings of deprivation. If you know you can have candy whenever you want, the drive to eat it secretively will disappear. You'll be able to eat because you are hungry for a certain item, not because you'll never have it again.

Instead of eating because you want to or are supposed to, ask yourself instead if you are hungry. You have an internal wisdom that lets you know when you need to eat and when you need to stop. While this system has many triggers, one is your blood glucose level. When your blood glucose is on the low side, you become hungry; when it's normal, hunger is diminished. (If you find yourself having to eat when you're not hungry because you need to take your medication with food, discuss this fact with your diabetes care team.) Eliminating the deprivation and examining your habits will let you find the carbohydrate balance that allows you to maintain your glucose goals. And it will help you change your relationship with food for the better. It may even enhance your ability to battle other aspects of metabolic syndrome, such as overweight and high blood cholesterol.

**explore and experiment**

To gain a more detailed and concrete understanding of how to use food choices to control your blood sugar levels, you must pay attention to how individual foods act in your body. Approach this like a scientist, collecting data about blood glucose and types and amounts of foods, then drawing conclusions that are based on that data.

The first step is for you to eat absolutely normally. Have the foods you usually eat, in the amounts your normally have, as frequently as you usually have them. Check food labels to determine which foods contain carbohydrate, then keep a running tally of the total grams of carbohydrate you eat throughout the entire day. Take detailed, honest notes.

Along with taking these notes, you need to test your blood glucose levels. Testing allows you to see how well your insulin level (either from insulin you injected or that your body produced) matches your carbohydrate intake. No matter its source, insulin works with the food you eat. If you eat too much food for the insulin that is available, your glucose level will be too high; if you eat too little, your glucose level will be too low.

Test before you eat and then one, two, three, and four hours after the meal. As a general guideline, aim for a pre-meal glucose goal of 90–130 mg/dl; one hour after the meal, less than 180 mg/dl; two hours after the meal, less than 160 mg/dl; three hours after, less than 140; and at four hours, or prior to your next meal, back to 90–130 mg/dl. Just as you

know the number of miles per gallon (mpg) of gas you can travel in your car, you will gradually begin to figure out your body's cpm, or carbohydrates per meal—the "distance" your body can go each time you eat a certain amount of carbohydrates.

You may find that eating foods that contain only carbohydrates causes your blood glucose to rise rapidly or stay too high after the meal. Carbohydrates in combination with varying amounts of fat and/or protein will affect your blood glucose differently. In addition, you may discover that high-fat foods elevate your blood glucose levels as well.

It is important to know that any food has the ability to make blood sugar levels rise, but different types of food as well as different amounts will result in different blood sugar levels. You may find that overeating makes blood sugar

## FIGURE YOUR CPM (CARBS* PER MEAL) RATE

| What you ate (Specify the foods you ate and the amount of carbohydrates.) | blood glucose start 90–130 | 1 hour <180 | 2 hours <160 | 3 hours <140 | 4 hours 90–130 |
|---|---|---|---|---|---|
| | | | | | |
| | | | | | |
| | | | | | |
| | | | | | |

*Note: It is fine to use total carbohydrate values to figure your CPM. Subtracting out the amount of fiber, which does not raise blood glucose, from each food item can be complicated and time consuming; in addition, for many food items, the fiber content is not available or listed on the packaging. Whichever method you choose, it is probably best to be consistent, using either total carbs or total carbs minus fiber for your calculations.

levels increase rapidly and stay too high. Overeating may not allow insulin to do its job properly. If you listen to your body's hunger cues and respect the feeling of fullness, your blood glucose will rise more slowly and peak at a lower level. Insulin, in turn, will be able to do its job and keep blood sugars at a healthy level. This type of balanced eating helps control diabetes and helps you feel better.

As you experiment and test your blood glucose, try a wide variety of foods. Enjoy different types of carbohydrates, from pasta to potatoes, biscuits to green beans, and bread to blueberries. Eat a variety of proteins, from eggs to cheese and ground turkey to prime rib. Try various types of fats, from butter to margarine and sour cream to mayonnaise. Look for patterns in the ways various foods and food combinations affect your glucose.

Eating a wide variety of foods will also help ensure that you get the nutrients you need—not just the carbohydrate, protein, and fat but also the vitamins and minerals that are essential

to good health. In addition, the multitudes of tastes, textures, and colors will continue to enhance your eating pleasure and help prevent feelings of deprivation that can lead to bingeing and overeating.

## listen to your body

There truly is an alternative to diets, those externally imposed, dictatorial dietary restrictions that result in those overpowering cravings and abandonment of self-care. Work to understand the effect of foods on your blood glucose levels. Know that restricting foods creates "good" and "bad" food and that these terms imply guilt and assign emotional labels to food.

Learn how you use food for comfort and calming. When you catch yourself eating when you're not hungry, ask yourself why. What do you really need? Do you need a break from that project? Would a walk, a bath, or a call to a friend make you feel better? Do you have a craving because you've been trying to avoid a particular food? Listen to your body; it knows what it needs.

Part III of this book will help you expand your food horizons. With more foods to choose from, you'll find it easier to select foods that match your carbohydrate needs and please your taste buds. Part III also helps you choose foods that fit into your diabetes care plan *and* improve your health, helping you temper other risk factors such as high blood pressure and high blood cholesterol. So let food be both a joy and a remedy.

# moving toward better control

The three cornerstones in the treatment of diabetes are food, medications, and activity. Of these three, activity is often a first choice for the person who has diabetes. Moving toward a more physically active life is generally inexpensive, convenient, and easy and usually produces great rewards in terms of blood glucose control (due to improved insulin sensitivity) and a general feeling of well-being.

If you recall, whenever you actively use a muscle, you burn both fatty acids and glucose. During and after periods of activity, your falling glucose level is sensed by the beta cells in your pancreas, and they relax their output of insulin. This gives your beta cells a break from excessive insulin production. In addition, the lower insulin levels signal your liver to empty its glucose reserves (glycogen) into the blood to supply the muscles with needed energy. As physical activity continues, the liver converts amino acids, lactic acid, and fats into glucose to supply the muscles. If the activity continues long enough, even the body's fat cells get in the game. They compensate for the reduced fatty acid levels in your blood by converting their stored triglycerides into fatty acids.

When all of these steps are considered, it's easy to see why using your muscles is the perfect treatment for diabetes. It lowers blood glucose, lowers fatty acid levels in your blood, and reduces the workload of your pancreas. And, unless you are on a medication that can cause hypoglycemia, physical activity won't cause your blood glucose level to fall below normal the way some other diabetes treatments may.

## before you get going

Becoming more physically active is not completely without risks for people with diabetes. (On the other hand, remaining sedentary is no bargain, either; it does nothing to help your glucose control, your weight management, or your overall well-being.) To gain the benefits of increased physical activity and minimize potential risks, you need to

## Benefits of being more active

- Lower blood glucose
- Improved insulin sensitivity
- Lower blood pressure
- Lower blood fats
- Better cardiovascular (heart and lung) fitness
- Weight loss and/or maintenance
- Improved sense of well-being

understand and evaluate those risks up front and take steps to prevent problems before they occur.

### hypoglycemia

For people with diabetes who take insulin or medication that stimulates the pancreas to secrete more insulin (sulfonylureas like glyburide and glipizide, or meglitinides like repaglinide and nateglinide), hypoglycemia is a possibility during or after exercise. Whenever you are physically active, your muscles burn glucose. First, they gobble up the glucose they have stored as glycogen. As the activity continues, glucose from the blood pours into the muscles to supply their energy needs, lowering blood glucose levels. This march of glucose from the blood into the muscles doesn't end when the activity stops, however. The body needs to refill the muscles' glucose storage tanks in preparation for future movement. As a result, blood sugar levels can be reduced for up to 24 hours. While that can be great news for most people, it can spell trouble for those at risk of hypoglycemia.

The good news is that hypoglycemia can be avoided during exercise by following a few simple guidelines.

For starters, testing blood glucose more frequently can help you to better understand your body's response to exercise and prepare for it by adjusting medication or food intake. (You'll find advice on such adjustments later in this chapter.)

### heart disease

Before you increase your activity level, you need to consider the possible presence of heart disease. As you've already learned, coronary heart disease is very common in people with diabetes. To assess your risk, you and your doctor need to take into account your age, your blood pressure, your blood fats, whether you have protein in your urine, the length of time you have had diabetes, and your family history. So if you have not been physically active for a while, before you engage in anything more than light physical activity, consult your doctor and, if appropriate, have an exercise tolerance test. This test is done on a treadmill and reflects your heart's ability to work under stress. Your chances of having a positive result, indicating heart disease, increase with each risk factor you have. Even if you are at increased risk or have a positive test, you will still be able to be physically active; you will just need to work more closely with your diabetes care team to set safe guidelines for activity and, perhaps, to determine if medications to lower your risk of heart trouble are in order.

### diabetes complications

Before you increase your activity level, you need to account for any diabetic complications or related conditions that may be present. Some types of activity may not be wise for people with certain medical conditions.

Any activity that includes straining, such as weight lifting, can dramatically increase blood pressure during the actual activity, further aggravating any hypertension that is present. To lessen any potential problems, you need to have your blood pressure well controlled before you start increasing your activity level and especially before beginning an activity that involves straining.

Proliferative retinopathy may be aggravated by straining, which increases the pressure within some of the weakened blood vessels of the eyes. Activities that require straining or that involve jarring or rapid head motions may also cause an acute hemorrhage in those who already have weakened eye vessels. For this reason, it is important to have your eyes examined for signs of retinopathy before starting an exercise program and to have them rechecked annually.

If you have significant nerve disease in your feet, you may not be able to feel injuries to your feet, the most common of which are blisters and calluses. This does not mean you cannot exercise, but it means that you need to have your feet checked by your doctor first and you must observe good foot care at home, including inspecting your feet for sore spots and minor injuries daily. You'll also want to get expert advice on proper footwear for the activity and be sure that the footwear you choose is fitted properly to your feet.

## guidelines for activity

The following guidelines can help you increase your activity level safely. Be sure to work with your diabetes care team, too, so they can monitor you and provide specialized advice for your specific situation.

### screening

First, be screened by your doctor for any possible problems before you start any type of activity. This exam should include an exercise stress test for people with diabetes who fit certain criteria (see "Assess your risk before you start," at right), an eye examination for retinopathy, a urine test for elevated protein, and a medical evaluation of your feet.

### type of activity

Once you've received your team's okay for exercise, choose activities that fit your physical condition, lifestyle, and tastes. Many people with diabetes, especially those who have not been physically active for a while, find that low-impact activities such as walking and swimming are perfect.

Whatever you choose, make sure the activities are enjoyable for you and take into account your abilities and condition. The activities don't even have to be "exercises" in the traditional sense, as long as they get you moving. Dancing, taking your dog on long

### Assess your risk before you start

Before starting moderate- to high-intensity activity you should ask your physician if an exercise stress test is recommended, particularly if you have diabetes and meet any of these criteria:
- are older than 35
- have protein in your urine
- have high blood pressure
- have high blood cholesterol
- have a family history of heart disease
- smoke at all

Talk to your doctor about having a stress test if any of the above applies to you.

walks, riding your bike, gardening, and even walking the golf course all count. Vary them so you don't get bored and fall prey to easy excuses. Choose some that can be done with others and some that can be done alone; some that can be done indoors, some that can be done outdoors; some that can be done when your schedule is light, and some that can be fit in when you're strapped for time.

The American College of Sports Medicine recommends that people with type 2 diabetes perform at least 150 minutes a week of moderate to vigorous aerobic exercise spread out over at least three days of the week, with no more than two consecutive days between exercising. Experts also recommend that resistance exercise such as weight training be done at least twice a week—ideally three times—on days that are not consecutive.

### time, intensity, and duration

Begin each exercise session with a five- to ten-minute period of low-intensity warm-up activity (a very slow version of your exercise makes a good warm-up). The warm-up will prepare your heart for increased activity. After you warm up, start the aerobic portion of your activity. An aerobic activity is one that works large muscles—those in the legs and buttocks or arms and shoulders—continuously for an extended period of time. In so doing, it increases your body's demand for oxygen, forcing both your breathing and heart rate to speed up.

One way to determine how hard your body should work during physical activity is to use something called a target heart rate range.

To help establish your target range, you need to first determine your maximal heart rate. To calculate this number, simply subtract your age from 220. The high and low ends of your appropriate target heart rate range will be percentages of this number. For example, you might aim for the moderate intensity range, which is between 50 and 70 percent of your maximal heart rate. It is important, however, to

## WHAT'S YOUR TARGET RANGE?

| INTENSITY | % MAX HEART RATE* |
|---|---|
| very light | <35 |
| light | 35–54 |
| moderate | 55–70 |
| hard | 71–90 |
| very hard | >90 |
| maximal | 100 |

*maximal heart rate = 220 – age

## FIGURING YOUR TARGET RANGE

For a moderately intense (55–70% max) activity level:
[220 – (your age)]×.55 to [220 – (your age)]×.70

### EXAMPLE

Target heart rate range for 54-year-old doing moderately intense activity:
[220 – 54]×.55 to [220 – 54]×.70
91 to 116 beats per minute

work with your diabetes care team to determine the intensity range that is most appropriate for you. You will also want to ask for specific advice regarding how often and how long you should exercise. During the exercise, to determine if you are working in your target range, you will need to occasionally check your heart rate. To do this, count the number of heartbeats (by feeling the pulse on the inner side of your wrist) for six seconds and add a zero to the end of that number; that's the number of times your heart is beating per minute. And that's the number that should stay in your target range during the aerobic activity.

Another way to evaluate your intensity is with the "talk test." Essentially, you should be able to carry on a brief conversation (using short sentences) while you are exercising without becoming short of breath. However, if you can sing your favorite song, you may not be working hard enough.

It's always best to increase physical activity slowly and build up gradually. If it is uncomfortable to exercise near the higher end of your target range, talk to your diabetes care team. They will probably suggest that you shoot for a lower intensity but a longer duration. As time passes, you'll be able to maintain a higher and higher level of activity for longer and longer periods of time.

Regardless of the activity you choose, you should end each workout

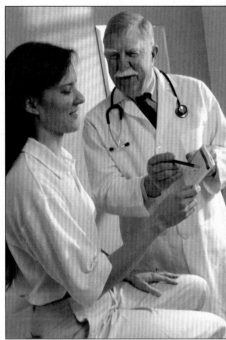

period with ten minutes of cooldown and gentle stretching. You want to slowly decrease the pace of your activity for several minutes rather than stop abruptly. You also want to take advantage of the fact that your muscles are warmed up to do some gentle stretching. The stretching will help you avoid tendon and muscle problems, which are common in people whose muscles and tendons have become tight after years of high blood glucose levels.

If you try to do some extra activity every other day, you will be amazed at the difference in your glucose control. Get moving every day, and the benefits will be even greater.

### avoiding glucose problems

To prevent problems with your glucose levels during exercise, there are a number of things you can do:

- Plan your activity to follow a meal so that it can help minimize the blood glucose spike that often follows eating.
- If you are at risk for hypoglycemia, check your blood glucose 30 minutes before and then just prior to activity. This way you can see which direction your glucose level is heading and anticipate a low in time to take preventive action. Still, plan for a possible hypoglycemic episode.

Carry glucose tablets with you; if symptoms of low blood glucose develop (see the chapter "Fighting Hypoglycemia" to learn how to recognize a low), stop the activity immediately and use the fast-acting glucose.

- If you manage your diabetes with insulin, know the peak time of your insulin and plan your activities accordingly. Avoiding the times when your insulin is peaking and at its strongest will help you prevent hypoglycemia.
- When injecting insulin, avoid the muscle areas that you will be using during the activity. For example, if you will be playing tennis, avoid using your racket arm and even, perhaps, your legs for your injection at the meal prior to your game. Most people find the abdomen or the buttocks work best before exercise.
- When planning to be extremely active, test your glucose level prior to getting started. If your blood glucose is near normal but you have the potential to develop hypoglycemia, you will need to eat some extra carbohydrate prior to the activity. (If you take insulin, you will either need to eat prior to the activity or lower your insulin dose.)
- If your blood glucose before the activity is more than 250 mg/dl,

check your urine for ketones. If they are present, activity will actually cause your blood glucose level to increase. An elevated glucose level and positive ketones indicate that your diabetes is uncontrolled and you need to contact your diabetes care team for advice immediately.

- Monitor your glucose during exercise to see what effect activity has on you. Check it every half hour during exercise and again when you are finished.
- Be sure to drink plenty of fluids. Sweating means you are losing fluids that need to be replaced. Water is usually a great choice.
- If, during any activity, you ever experience shortness of breath, chest pain, or leg cramps that go away with rest, contact your doctor immediately. These are all possible signs of blocked arteries and require an evaluation by your doctor.
- If you repeatedly experience episodes of hypoglycemia during and/or after increased levels of activity, you should contact your doctor and discuss the possibility of a change in your medications.

One final thought: Being active needs to be fun. Otherwise, you're much less likely to stick with an active lifestyle. So, choose your activities accordingly, then go out and play at least a little every day.

# using medications to treat diabetes

For many people who have type 2 diabetes, using food and activity to control blood glucose is not enough. For them, diabetes medications can be lifesavers—helping to lower their blood glucose levels and stave off diabetes complications.

## have I failed?

Imagine yourself sailing down a highway at 60 miles per hour. It is a flat, open road, and you require a steady amount of fuel to keep you at this speed. Then you hit a mountain range. Maintaining your speed as you begin to ascend requires more and more fuel—you must press farther down on the gas pedal to maintain a speed of 60 miles per hour. Diabetes is similar in a way. When first diagnosed, you may be able to maintain a steady speed, or steady glucose range, with a few modifications in your lifestyle. However, diabetes is a progressive, "uphill" condition that requires more and more "fuel" to keep your speed within your target range.

In general, the first steps taken to move your glucose levels back toward normal are to increase the level of activity in your life and to change your relationship with food. Sometimes these steps can't lower your glucose levels enough to reach a normal range or, over time, they may not continue to keep your level within your target range. You may then require medication to help you achieve or maintain your target glucose levels. If and when this happens, do not look at the use of medications as a failure on your part in any way. Keep in mind that diabetes is a chronic, progressive condition that requires progressive treatments to keep blood glucose under the same good control. Your goal, in the end, should not be to avoid medications but to avoid complications. Fortunately, recent years have seen the advent of several new and effective treatments that can help you reach that goal.

## how do diabetes medications work?

People with type 1 diabetes make very little, if any, insulin, so they are dependent on insulin

### Be intolerant!

Always remember that high glucose levels are extremely bad for you. Your body cannot tolerate them—nor should you. Don't count your prescriptions and feel that you've failed. It is not the number of medications you take, but rather the glucose levels you achieve, the complications you prevent, and the joyful life you lead that determine your treatment success.

injections to keep them alive. Since most medications used to treat diabetes are not the same as insulin and do not contain any insulin, they are of absolutely no use to people with type 1 diabetes. The pills used to treat diabetes can lower blood glucose levels, but only in people with type 2 diabetes whose bodies still make some insulin but either don't make enough or just don't use it well enough.

To understand how pills treat diabetes, you must first understand why your blood glucose levels are still high. For you and others with type 2 diabetes, your difficulties with glucose control stem from no fewer than three causes. First, your muscles are not taking up the glucose in your bloodstream the way they should. Second, the liver is taking up too little glucose and is over-secreting glucose, further increasing the glucose levels in your blood. And third, the insulin production by your pancreas cannot keep up with the high levels of glucose.

In this gradual system breakdown, the primary problem seems to be insulin resistance in your muscles and liver. Your muscles and liver are not responding properly to your insulin, and so the glucose is not being taken in; instead, the glucose builds up in your blood. It's as if each of your cells is in its own room, with the radio blasting. Insulin and glucose are both at the door, insulin knocking as hard as it can, but because the radio is up so loud, the cells cannot hear it.

The next problem lies in your liver. Your liver normally stops pumping out glucose when it "sees" insulin in your blood. When you eat, your glucose level rises, which prompts the release of insulin from your pancreas. The insulin's job is to get the muscle cells to take in the glucose. When your liver sees the insulin, it knows that glucose has entered the system, so it stops releasing its own glucose stores and begins absorbing insulin and packaging it in a storage form called "glycogen." The insulin levels in your body normally decrease when your glucose levels drop, such as when you fast overnight or when it has been several hours since you have eaten. Your liver does not see as much insulin, so it kicks into gear and begins to break down its glycogen stores and release glucose into the bloodstream to keep your blood sugar level in a normal range. When your liver cells become insulin resistant, however, they cannot see the insulin, and therefore they think, wrongly, that your glucose levels are low. So your liver pumps out more glucose despite the fact that there's already glucose in the bloodstream.

The last and crucial problem is the inability of the beta cells in your pancreas to make enough insulin to keep up with this resistance. As glucose and fatty acids build up in your bloodstream, your beta cells must pump out excessive amounts of insulin to keep up; eventually, this excessive demand exhausts the beta cells, and they begin to die off. When you reach a point where there are very few beta cells still living, your blood glucose level increases greatly, which further hampers the body's ability to take up glucose, causing the extremely elevated blood glucose levels that are seen in uncontrolled diabetes.

A second problem occurs when the beta cells become depleted. They do not produce sufficient amounts of the hormone amylin. Without enough amylin, food is digested faster than usual, resulting in a rapid blood glucose spike right after eating.

The pills available to treat diabetes work on these problem areas. They enhance your beta cells' ability to make and/or secrete more insulin, they decrease your liver's glucose production, they make your muscle cells more sensitive to insulin, and they put the brakes on the digestion of carbohydrates.

The diabetes medications available today fall into seven different catego-

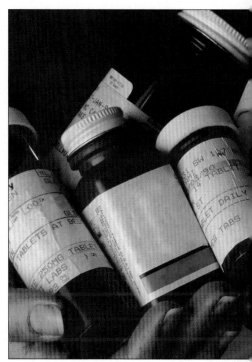

ries: sulfonylureas, meglitinides, biguanides, alpha-glucosidase inhibitors, thiazolidinediones (glitazones), DPP-4 inhibitors, and an injectable group of medications called incretin mimetics. The seven types have different actions and help you to control your diabetes in different ways. As you and your diabetes care team begin to consider one or more of these medications, make sure you stay completely informed. Know the names of all of your medications, how much you need to take, and when to take them. Be aware of any possible side effects and whether or not they can be taken with any other medications you currently take. The following discussions can help you become familiar with the medications available.

## sulfonylureas

The *sulfonylureas* (sul-fa-nul-ur-ee-ahs) are the original diabetes pills; they were the first pills ever available to treat diabetes. Prior to their introduction, insulin was the only treatment for elevated glucose levels. Around the time of World War II, it was noticed that antibacterial agents called sulfa drugs also seemed to lower blood glucose. But it wasn't until the 1950s that this discovery would lead to the introduction in the United States of sulfalike drugs, the sulfonylureas, for the treatment of diabetes.

Sulfonylureas work by stimulating your pancreas to increase insulin pro-duction. The first medication that was available in this category is called Orinase (known generically as tolbuta-mide); it was followed shortly by Diabi-nese (chlorpropamide) and Tolinase (tolazamide). These medications are

## NEWER SULFONYLUREAS IN A NUTSHELL

| BRAND NAME | GENERIC NAME | TYPICAL DAILY DOSE | MAXIMUM DAILY DOSE | DURATION OF ACTION |
|---|---|---|---|---|
| Micronase, Diabeta | glyburide | 1.25–20 mg Taken as a single or divided dose, once or twice a day | 20 mg | 24 hours |
| Glynase | micronized glyburide | 1.5–6 mg Taken as a single dose, once a day | 6 mg | 24 hours |
| Glucotrol | glipizide | 5–20 mg Taken as a single dose, once or twice a day | 20 mg | 12–24 hours |
| Glucotrol XL | extended-release glipizide | 5–20 mg Taken as a single dose, once a day | 20 mg | 24 hours |
| Amaryl | glimepiride | 1–8 mg Taken as a single or divided dose, once or twice a day | 8 mg | 24 hours |

## OLDER SULFONYLUREAS IN A NUTSHELL

| BRAND NAME | GENERIC NAME | TYPICAL DAILY DOSE | MAXIMUM DAILY DOSE | DURATION OF ACTION |
|---|---|---|---|---|
| Orinase | tolbutamide | 250–3,000 mg Taken as a divided dose, twice a day | 3,000 mg | 6–12 hours |
| Tolinase | tolazamide | 100–1,000 mg Taken as a single or divided dose, once or twice a day | 1,000 mg | 24 hours |
| Diabinese | chlorpropamide | 100–750 mg Taken as a single dose, once a day | 750 mg | 24–72 hours |

often referred to as "first generation sulfonylureas," since they were the first pills released in this category. Since the 1950s, newer and stronger sulfonylureas have been released. These include the "second generation" sulfonylureas Diabeta, Micronase, Glynase (all brand names for glyburide), Glucotrol, and Glucotrol XL (both brand names of glipizide), as well as the more recently introduced "third generation sulfonylurea" Amaryl (glimepiride). The sulfonylureas all operate by the same mechanism. They work on your beta cells, pushing them to make more insulin in order to lower your glucose level. Because of your insulin resistance, you require substantially more insulin than a non-insulin-resistant person to get the same amount of glucose into cells. In other words, it takes more insulin to keep your glucose levels normal just as it takes more gas to drive your car uphill compared to driving on a level road.

These pills help by lowering your blood glucose levels, but because they continually work on your pancreas, they cause insulin to be released even when it may not be needed. This is one of the major drawbacks, and major side effects, of all the sulfonylurea medications: They can cause hypoglycemia, or low blood glucose (see the chapter "Fighting Hypoglycemia" for more detailed information). And because extra insulin is being pro-

duced continuously, sulfonylureas tend to cause weight gain. Other side effects, although uncommon, include skin rashes, dark urine, stomach upset, and an increased sensitivity to the sun. But the most significant drawback to sulfonylureas is that they put stress on an already stressed-out system. Your overworked beta cells are forced to work harder than ever, which can result in a more rapid breakdown of these crucial cells.

Diabinese, a first generation sulfonylurea, has a longer duration of action in the body than the newer medications. With this very prolonged duration comes a greater risk of extended and severe hypoglycemia under certain conditions. Diabinese can also cause additional side effects including hyponatremia (low sodium in the blood) and a flushing of your skin when you ingest alcohol. Sulfonylureas are taken at the same time every day, generally about 30 minutes before a meal. If taken only once a day, they are usually taken with the first meal of the day. Because these medications are broken down by your liver and then eventually leave your body through your urine (via your kidneys), they should be used with caution if you have kidney or liver disease. In these diseases, the route by which the medication is broken down or eliminated may be blocked, and this can cause the medicine to accumulate in your body and cause very severe hypoglycemia.

Your sulfonylurea is working properly if your blood glucose values remain in a healthy range and you do not suffer from any episodes of hypoglycemia. Check your blood glucose often, both before and after meals, especially if this medication is newly prescribed or your dose has recently been changed. Pay particularly close attention to your glucose readings before your midday and evening meals. If your glucose levels are not within your target range most of the time, review your activity and eating patterns, ask yourself if you are missing medication doses, and see if there is any pattern to your high or low glucose levels. If your glucose readings remain too high or too low or you are not satisfied with your control, your doctor may need to change your dose or even switch your medication.

## meglitinides

*Meglitinides* (meh-gli-tin-eyeds) first became available in 1998, with the release of Prandin (repaglinide), and later Starlix (nateglinide). Meglitinides, which are similar to sulfonylureas, help to lower glucose levels by stimulating the beta cells of your pancreas to release insulin. However, they differ from the sulfonylureas in that they are much shorter-acting and begin working very quickly to increase your insulin level when it is needed most: while your food is being digested and glucose is entering your bloodstream. In addition to acting quickly, they also leave your bloodstream quickly, so your body doesn't keep releasing insulin beyond when it's needed, thus reducing your risk of hypoglycemia.

Sulfonylureas are generally taken just once a day and cause a steady release of insulin throughout the day, whether you eat or not. Meglitinides are different because they are taken just before meals. And because they work very quickly, they allow you to vary the timing and frequency of your meals each day. You take this medication one, two, three, or four times a day, depending on how many meals you eat. If you need or want to miss a meal, you simply skip that pill entirely.

Prandin comes in 0.5, 1, and 2 mg doses. The total daily dose should not exceed 16 mg. Starlix comes in 60 mg and 120 mg tablets. Because they prompt your pancreas to release insulin, meglitinides have the potential to cause hypoglycemia, especially if you take your pill but your meal is unexpectedly delayed or you eat significantly less than usual. However, the risk of hypoglycemia is less than it is with the sulfonylureas because meglitinides are much shorter-acting and therefore do not remain in your system for extended periods after the meal. Other side effects or symptoms that have been reported include cold and flulike symptoms, diarrhea, joint aches, and back pain. In addition, a rash and stomach upset can occur, but they are quite rare.

Another benefit of the meglitinides, when compared to sulfonylureas, is that they do not contain a sulfur group and thus are usually safe for people who have sulfa allergies.

## biguanides

*Biguanides* (bi-gwan-ides) are the most widely prescribed diabetes medications. Currently, the only biguanide available in the United States is Glucophage, also known by its generic name, metformin. In the 1960s, a precursor of metformin, DBI-TD (also known as phenformin), was introduced as a twice-a-day medication for the control of glucose levels. It was a very effective medication, but it was removed from the market because of a rare but fatal complication called lactic acidosis. Lactic acidosis is a condition in which lactic acids build up in the bloodstream; it is fatal in 50 percent of the people who develop it. This devastating side effect prompted researchers

to develop metformin, a safer version of DBI-TD. It was introduced in Europe about 40 years ago but was not available in the United States until 1995.

How metformin works is not yet completely understood. Its major action is to cause the liver to become more sensitive to insulin and secrete less glucose. Since metformin does not directly affect insulin levels, it is not very effective for controlling post-meal glucose levels. Its greatest benefit seems to be in decreasing the output of glucose by your liver during periods when you are fasting (such as between meals or at night).

Since the most extended period of fasting for many people occurs overnight, the liver tends to be very busy during that time; as a result, in those who are insulin resistant, the morning glucose levels can be the highest of the day. Metformin works well to prevent these early-morning highs by decreasing glucose production while you sleep. As an added benefit, it appears to cause less weight gain than most of the other diabetes medications and does not cause hypoglycemia. With all of these positives, it is not surprising that metformin is the most commonly prescribed diabetic medication in the United States and worldwide.

Metformin's side effects are generally minor. About 30 percent of the people who take metformin develop mild stomach upset or diarrhea; about 3 percent of those individuals find these side effects so intolerable that they cannot continue taking the medication. However, if you start out on a low dose of metformin and slowly increase it over time, and if you are disciplined about taking the medicine with or immediately after a meal, these gastrointestinal side effects can be minimized or eliminated. Sometimes, decreasing the total dose or only taking the medication with the evening meal can eliminate the side effects. If, after trying these adjustments, you are still plagued by diarrhea, loose stools, or frequent or uncontrollable bowel movements, talk to your doctor. Such side effects obviously can decrease your quality of life and you need not tolerate them, since there are other medications available to help you achieve glucose control. A new longer-acting version of metformin, Glucophage XR, is now available and has fewer gastrointestinal side effects. However, if you take Glucophage XR, be sure to have your triglyceride levels monitored, since this medication may cause them to increase.

Like its predecessor, metformin can cause lactic acidosis, but this is extremely rare. The signs and symptoms of lactic acidosis are unusual muscle pain, fast and shallow breathing, slow or unsteady heartbeat, vomiting, or a serious infection with dehydration and fever. To avoid this potentially dangerous effect, certain people should not use metformin:

- anyone who drinks heavily or is a binge drinker. Heavy alcohol intake is considered to be more than two to three drinks per day (a drink is 5 ounces of wine, 12 ounces of beer, or 1½ ounces of hard liquor).
- anyone who has liver disease, such as hepatitis. A test that measures a liver enzyme called alanine transaminase (ALT) should be done; elevated levels may indicate that the liver is irritated or diseased.
- anyone with kidney disease. The creatinine level in your blood is a measurement of your kidney function. For women, this level should be less than 1.4 mg/dl, and for men, less than 1.5 mg/dl.
- people more than 80 years of age, unless their kidney and liver functions are tested, frequently monitored, and found to be normal. After age 80, our kidney function naturally decreases. At this age, blood creatinine levels are no longer the best indicator of kidney function. Kidney function is best evaluated by a 24-hour measurement of your creatinine clearance, which requires you

to collect your urine for 24 hours so that your kidney function can be checked.

- anyone who has a condition that results in poor circulation, such as congestive heart failure, or a condition that results in a low level of oxygen, such as severe asthma or serious lung disease.

- Caution must also be taken if any type of medical test involving contrast dye is required. During tests that use contrast dye, the kidneys' excretion of lactic acid is slowed, which can allow the acid to build up in the blood. If you need to have such a test, you will need to stop taking metformin before the test and not start taking it again for two to three days afterward. You will also need to have your kidney function reevaluated before you restart the medication. However, do not stop taking metformin unless and until your doctor has directed you to do so.

Metformin comes in 500, 850, and 1,000 mg tablets. It is generally taken twice a day, once in the morning and once at night. Occasionally, to minimize side effects, it is taken just once a day, in the evenings. The initial dose is usually 500 mg with the evening meal. It is then increased 500 mg each week until the usual maximum dose of 2,000 mg per day is reached. This is generally taken as 1,000 mg, twice a day. Above 2,000 mg per day, there

appears to be little added benefit, and additional side effects are likely. If for any reason you must stop taking metformin for more than three days, you may find that you have to restart at the 500 mg dose to avoid side effects. However, most people who have to stop the medication for just three days to have a contrast-dye study done are able to restart the medication at their usual dose without experiencing significant side effects.

## alpha-glucosidase inhibitors

*Alpha-glucosidase* (glue-kos-a-dase) inhibitors are another type of medication available to treat diabetes. There are two medications available in the United States that fall into this class: Precose (acarbose) and Glyset (miglitol). Both medications work on your small intestines, where starches and large sugar molecules are broken down and absorbed.

One of the primary enzymes that allow glucose absorption into your blood is alpha-glucosidase. This enzyme is in the lining of your small intestines, and its effectiveness is partially blocked by these

medications. As a result, glucose is more slowly absorbed, and some glucose may not be absorbed at all but rather digested by bacteria found further down in your intestines. This delay in the absorption of glucose helps to prevent the sudden surges of glucose that can occur after eating. While these medications do not appear to cause weight loss, they cause a moderate lowering of blood glucose after meals.

When alpha-glucosidase inhibitors are used, not all of your food is absorbed, so it has ample time to react with the bacteria and yeast normally found in your bowels. These bacteria and yeast break down starches and sugars into gases. This results in the main side effects reported with these medicines—diarrhea and the tremendous production of gas. About 80 percent of all people who use either one of these medications experience these side effects, and many find they cannot tolerate these effects in the long term. Other side effects are more rare and include liver irritation, so these medications should not be used if you have liver disease. In addition, like metformin, the alpha-glucosidase inhibitors can build up in

your system if your kidneys are not functioning well. If your creatinine level exceeds 2.0 mg/dl, you should not take these medications.

Alpha-glucosidase inhibitors cannot cause hypoglycemia by themselves. However, caution is required if they are taken with a medication, such as a sulfonylurea, that can cause low blood glucose levels. Because the alpha-glucosidase inhibitors delay the absorption of certain sugars, hypoglycemia can only be treated with simple sugars such as those found in glucose tablets, honey, or fruit juices. The absorption of complex starches would be delayed, resulting in more prolonged episodes of hypoglycemia.

The usual dose of alpha-glucosidase inhibitors is 25 to 100 mg with each meal, taken no more than three times a day. Any dosage increases should be done very slowly, in order to lower the potential for side effects and help the body become accustomed to the changes these medications cause.

With their minimal effectiveness and frequent side effects, alpha-glucosidase inhibitors have not been extremely popular with people in the United States. However, these drugs are much more popular in some European countries.

## thiazolidinediones (TZDs)

*Thiazolidinediones* (thigh-ah-zo-la-deen-die-owns), commonly referred to as TZDs, are perhaps the most controversial group of medications available to treat diabetes. TZDs ushered in a new age in the treatment of type 2 diabetes when they were first introduced in 1997. For the first time ever, a medication was available to decrease the main problem of type 2 diabetes—insulin resistance.

The two TZDs that are currently available are Avandia (rosiglitazone) and Actos (pioglitazone). An early type of TZD called Rezulin (troglitazone) was withdrawn from the market more than 10 years ago due to a potential link with hepatitis.

TZDs mainly work on the genes inside your cells. They cause your fat cells to take up more fatty acids and glucose, leaving fewer fatty acids for your muscle cells. The muscle cells return to using glucose as their preferred fuel source and consequently increase their sensitivity to insulin. This is significant since the muscles normally take up the majority of the glucose from a meal.

A similar change occurs in your liver. As your insulin resistance decreases, your liver begins to make less glucose, because it can once again easily "see" the insulin in your bloodstream. Significant changes also happen in the beta cells of your pancreas. First, the decrease in glucose and fatty acids results in lower insulin levels in your blood. This drop, coupled with what appears to be a direct

protective effect that the TZDs have on the beta cells, may help beta cells to recover from the stress of diabetes and metabolic syndrome. So the TZDs may actually prevent the downhill slide that eventually leads to the inability of your pancreas to secrete insulin and the subsequent need for insulin injections. And the benefits don't end there.

TZDs help improve the blood lipids profile. When you take TZDs, your level of beneficial HDL cholesterol increases, your triglyceride level drops, your blood pressure decreases, and your clotting factors improve, all of which decrease your risk of circulatory problems. Unfortunately, controversy has surrounded the TZDs since 1999, when Rezulin (troglitazone), the first in this class of medications, made headline news. The news was not good. The early clinical trials of Rezulin had shown that it increases the likelihood of hepatitis. After Rezulin hit the market in 1997, case reports of liver failure and death began to trickle in to the U.S. Food & Drug Administration (FDA). Still, they appeared to be rare. At the time, Rezulin was the only TZD on the

## THE CURRENT TZD LINEUP

| BRAND NAME | GENERIC NAME | STRENGTHS | DOSE | MAXIMUM DOSE |
|---|---|---|---|---|
| Avandia | rosiglitazone | 2, 4, and 8 mg | once or twice a day | 8 mg |
| Actos | pioglitazone | 15, 30, and 45 mg | once a day | 45 mg |

market, and more than a million people were successfully managing their diabetes with it. Indeed, it was proving itself to be a very valuable medication. So the FDA agreed that Rezulin could continue to be prescribed but only with more closely monitored liver function testing.

As the liver side effects of Rezulin continued to make news throughout 1999 and early 2000, two new medications in this class hit the market. They were Actos (pioglitazone) and Avandia (rosiglitazone). These two new medications did not appear to cause the serious liver side effects of Rezulin. So the makers of Rezulin stopped making it and removed it from the market in March 2000.

The glucose-lowering effects of TZDs impressed users and healthcare providers alike. But as their use increased, certain problems became apparent. Rosiglitazone has been shown to cause fluid retention (a condition in which the body keeps excess fluid) that may lead to or worsen congestive heart failure. Some studies have shown that rosiglitazone may increase the risk of angina (chest pain), heart attack, and other problems that are caused by decreased blood flow to the heart. Other studies have not proven or ruled out that rosi-

glitazone increases this risk. The FDA has notified healthcare professionals and patients that the cardiovascular risks (including heart attack) of rosiglitazone have been added to the physician labeling and patient Medication Guide. This information was first announced by FDA in 2010 as part of new restrictions for prescribing and use of this drug. In addition to describing the cardiovascular risks, the drug labels have been revised to state that only rosiglitazone and medicines containing rosiglitazone should be used:

- In patients already being treated with these medicines
- In patients whose blood sugar cannot be controlled with other antidiabetic medicines and who, after consulting with their healthcare professional, do not wish to use medicines containing pioglitazone

(Rosiglitazone also is available in combination with metformin under the brand name Avandamet or glimepiride under the brand name Avandaryl.)

Pioglitazone has also been associated with cardiovascular risks. People with heart problems should not start taking Actos or medications that contain Actos (including ACTOplus met, ACTOplus met XR, or duetact). These medications can cause new heart problems or worsen existing heart failure.

An increased risk of pregnancy is also associated with the TZDs. All medications in this class can increase the risk (or, depending on your viewpoint, improve the chances) of pregnancy as a direct result of their ability to decrease insulin resistance.

Because Avandia and Actos are related to Rezulin, they carry with them the legacy of the Rezulin liver complications. The FDA has required that liver monitoring be done periodically during the first year of TZD use, even though there have been no reports of liver complications with these newer glitazones. It takes TZDs longer to become effective in your system than most diabetes medications, which can begin lowering glucose levels within hours of their ingestion. Because the TZDs work on a cellular level, through your genes, the decrease in insulin resistance and subsequent lower glucose levels are very slow to occur.

It can take up to four months for you to see the full effect of a TZD on your glucose levels, but usually you'll notice some improvement within the first one to two weeks. Because of this slow action, your doctor probably won't try increasing your TZD dose within the first four to six weeks of therapy in order to first see what effect it has had on your blood glucose levels.

## dpp-iv inhibitors

Among the newest diabetes medications are DPP-IV (4) inhibitors. They may be the perfect example of how one thing leads to another in diabetes treatment. Let's take a moment to examine how this class of drugs works.

When food passes through the stomach and enters the small intestine, specific cells of the intestine produce glucagonlike peptide-1 (GLP-1). Once in the circulation, GLP-1 does a number of things:

- Makes it easier for the pancreas to release its stored-up insulin, but only in the presence of elevated blood sugar (so it does not cause hypoglycemia)
- Decreases glucagon secretion from the pancreas (glucagon is a hormone that raises blood sugar)
- Promotes the growth and duplication of cells in the pancreas that produce insulin
- Slows the movement of food from the stomach into the intestines
- Decreases appetite

So GLP-1 is really good at helping to control blood sugar levels. Unfortunately, GLP-1 only lasts for a few minutes before it is broken down by an enzyme called DPP-IV. The job of a DPP-IV inhibitor is just that—to keep DPP-IV from breaking down GLP-1. This allows GLP-1 to circulate longer and work harder.

There are a number of companies working on this class of drugs, but the only ones currently available are sitagliptin (Januvia) and saxagliptin (Onglyza). Sitagliptin is available in

combination with metformin under the name Janumet. DPP-IV inhibitors can be used in combination with certain other medications but those with poor kidney function must use it very carefully. While it has been proven effective for improving blood sugar levels without causing hypoglycemia, it has not been shown to reduce weight. Side effects include occasional coldlike symptoms.

Given its minimal side effects and the multitude of ways it can improve blood sugar levels, DPP-IV inhibitors are becoming a major player in diabetes treatment. They are the only oral diabetes medications that actually promote the growth and function of insulin-producing cells in the pancreas. This may allow the pancreas to produce sufficient amounts of insulin to overcome significant insulin resistance. And by slowing the rate of digestion, it helps to minimize postmeal blood sugar spikes (as well as the pancreas' workload).

## injectable incretin mimetics

Until 2005, the only injectable treatment for diabetes was insulin. Now there are several other injectables available, with more on the way. Why the sudden upswing? As scientists learn more about how the body really regulates blood sugar levels, new and innovative treatments can be—and are—developed.

As mentioned earlier in our discussion of DPP-IV inhibitors, the importance of a protein called GLP-1 cannot be understated. Whenever we eat food that contains carbohydrates (sugar or starch), some of the sugar comes in contact with the inner lining of the small intestine. When this happens, special chemical messengers are secreted by cells of the intestine. One of these chemical messengers, called glucagon-like peptide-1, or GLP-1 for short, helps the pancreas to release a rapid burst of insulin, decreases other hormones that raise blood sugar levels, and slows digestion and decreases appetite. Unlike insulin taken by injection or the older classes of oral medications, GLP-1 does not promote low blood sugar or weight gain. Insulin secretion increases only when blood sugars are high and decreases as blood sugars approach normal.

Studies have shown that over time GLP-1 may preserve the health of the pancreas's insulin-producing cells. Since progressive loss of these cells is an underlying cause of type 2 diabetes, GLP-1 has the potential to halt or reverse this process. We know that DPP-IV inhibitors increase the amount of GLP-1 available in circulation. Well, what if you could take GLP-1 directly? Now you can.

## WHERE DO THEY WORK?

| TYPE OF MEDICATION | GLITAZONE | BIGUANIDE | ALPHA-GLUCOSIDASE INHIBITOR | MEGLITINIDE | SULFO-NYLUREA | DDP-IV INHIBITORS | INJECTABLE INCRETINS |
|---|---|---|---|---|---|---|---|
| **brand names** | Actos Avandia | Glucophage | Precose Glyset | Prandin Starlix | Micronase Diabeta Glynase Glucotrol Amaryl | Januvia, Onglyza | Byetta, Victoza, Symlin |
| **site of action and metabolic effect** | **muscle** Makes muscles more sensitive to insulin | **liver** Causes liver to produce less glucose | **small intestine** Delays absorption of glucose in small intestine | **pancreas** Stimulates the beta cells to make more insulin | **pancreas** Stimulates the beta cells to make more insulin | **pancreas** Eases secretion of stored-up insulin | **stomach, central nervous system, pancreas** Slows gastric emptying, blocks hunger, inhibits glucagon (except for Symlin) and stimulates beta-cell proliferation |

Exenatide (Byetta) is very similar to GLP-1, except that it lasts much longer in the body. Currently, exenatide is a twice-daily injectable medication. Plans are underway to develop a form of Byetta that only needs to be taken once a week. Liraglutide (Victoza) works similarly to exenatide but only requires one injection daily.

Exenatide and liraglutide can be used alone or in combination with metformin or sulfonylureas. For those who are not taking any medications for their diabetes but are having a difficult time keeping blood glucose levels near normal, they may be all that is needed. For those already taking oral medications, adding exenatide or liraglutide may allow for a reduction or eventual elimination of the oral medications. Exenatide and liraglutide can also prevent or delay the need for insulin injections.

Because they require a functioning pancreas to work correctly, exenatide and liraglutide are intended only for people with type 2 diabetes. Varying degrees of nausea are common during the first few weeks of use, but this usually subsides over time. Those with gastrointestinal problems or kidney disease are usually not good candidates. The pens used to administer the injections (which are prefilled and contain 60 fixed doses) utilize very small disposable needles.

For those with type 1 or type 2 diabetes who take rapid-acting insulin at mealtimes, another type of injectable medication is available: pramlintide (Symlin).

When the beta cells of the pancreas secrete insulin, they also secrete a second hormone called amylin. People with type 1 diabetes secrete no amylin at all, and people with type 2 diabetes usually secrete very little amylin. Classified as an "incretin" hormone, pramlintide influences other hormone-secreting glands. It acts directly on the central nervous system to do the following:

- Slow the emptying of the stomach's contents into the small intestine for absorption.
- Blunt the secretion of glucagon by the pancreas (ironically, the pancreas of people with diabetes secretes blood glucose-raising glucagon just after meals).
- Enhance satiety and decrease appetite.

By slowing digestion, limiting food intake, and keeping the body from raising blood glucose levels on its own, pramlintide helps to prevent the sharp blood sugar rise that occurs after meals in most people with diabetes. Pramlintide can also be a valuable weight-loss tool: Pramlintide users lose an average of 6.6 pounds over the first six months of use, mainly by consuming smaller portions at meals and snacking less often. Given that many people with diabetes have difficulty controlling their appetite (likely due to lack of the amylin hormone), pramlintide has obvious lifestyle benefits.

On the downside, pramlintide's effects only last for about three hours, so it needs to be injected at just about every meal in order to work throughout the day. It is administered in the same manner as insulin: injected into the subcutaneous fat. It cannot be mixed with insulin because it is slightly acidic (which causes it to sting a bit when injected).

Pramlintide is intended for people who take mealtime insulin, with or without oral medications.

The most common side effect associated with pramlintide is nausea. Once a therapeutic dose is achieved, mild nausea (sometimes called "sour stomach") may occur 30 to 60 minutes after injection. This nausea tends to last for about 30 minutes, and usually dissipates entirely after a few weeks, as the body becomes reaccustomed to having the amylin hormone present.

Another potential complication when using pramlintide is the challenge in treating hypoglycemia. During its peak action time (30 to 60 minutes after injection), pramlintide blocks the secretion of glucagon and slows digestion considerably. Attempts to treat hypoglycemia during this time may be unsuccessful. As a result, special efforts must be made to prevent hypoglycemia when taking pramlintide. For those who take insulin at mealtimes, it may be necessary to reduce or delay the doses when using pramlintide.

Pramlintide is not for those who take a casual approach to diabetes management. It takes considerable effort to use pramlintide successfully. But once that happens, the benefits can be significant. It may be the most potent tool for controlling after-meal blood sugar levels, and it is very effective at curbing hunger and preventing grazing and overeating.

## combination therapy

All of these new diabetes medications have certainly changed the face of diabetes treatment. Each one helps fix a particular treatment problem; but increasingly they are being used in various combinations to make diabetes treatment more individualized—and more successful.

### meeting more needs

In type 2 diabetes, there are usually multiple problems that need to be addressed, and one pill just can't do it all. Problems include insulin resistance by the body's cells, oversecretion of glucose by the liver, insufficient insulin production by the pancreas, and altered rates of food digestion. Sometimes a combination of medications is much more effective at lowering glucose levels than is a single medicine.

### the one-by-one approach

There are now dozens of different combinations of medications that can be used to treat diabetes.

The most commonly used method of prescribing medications to improve glucose control is called the "Step System." In this traditional approach, medications are slowly and systematically added, with the goal of achieving glucose control. Because metformin offers considerable benefit with few side effects, and because there is no risk of hypoglycemia when using metformin alone, it is usually considered the best first-line treatment.

The next step is to add a sulfonylurea or meglitinide for its additional effect on the pancreas. If glucose levels still continue to increase despite the use of these medications, the addition of a DPP-IV inhibitor, TZD, or injectable incretin mimetic may be necessary. Acarbose

## Combination Medications

Currently, the following classes of medications are available in combined pill form:

- Biguanide and Sulfonylurea
- Biguanide and TZD
- Biguanide and DPP IV Inhibitor
- TZD and Sulfonylurea

(Precose) is occasionally used either prior to or after the addition of a sulfonylurea, but its use, at least in the United States, is less extensive because of its side effects. The final addition to the treatment plan has historically been insulin. The Step System usually fails because it just never seems to catch up to the ever-rising glucose levels. It is a slow approach, and sometimes the doses are not increased quickly enough, which means that glucose levels remain elevated for months before a dose increase or additional medication is tried.

### the total overhaul

The reality for most people, when they discover they have diabetes or when they finally decide that they need to take better care of themselves, is that their glucose levels are generally quite high. One medication will rarely make the grade. Glucose levels are likely to be so high that they are causing direct damage to the beta cells, and insulin resistance is off the charts. Because everything is so out of control, the "blast and taper fast" system may be a more appropriate method of attack. This approach involves the immediate use of several different medications, with or without insulin, to alleviate insulin resistance and force glucose levels down toward normal. Blood glucose levels are checked frequently (four times per day), and as soon as the glucose levels begin to fall below 120 mg/dl (6.7 mmol/l), the insulin

and sulfonylurea or meglitinide doses are decreased rapidly; they may even be stopped as blood glucose falls into the goal range. Other medications may be decreased or discontinued as well, as long as the blood glucose remains below 120 mg/dl (6.7 mmol/l).

The goal with the "blast and taper fast" system is to eliminate potential glucose toxicity caused by very high glucose levels and then see how well the pancreas performs when glucose is closer to normal. Once glucose levels begin to respond and before hypoglycemia becomes an issue, medications are quickly tapered off, starting with any that can cause hypoglycemia. In this way, even people whose diabetes is way out of control can begin to improve their condition and lower their risk of complications immediately.

### fixed combinations

To make diabetes management easier, some drug manufacturers are now making fixed combinations of medications, in which specific doses of two or more drugs are included in a single pill. These combination medications are generally cheaper than buying the individual medications separately and allow you to take a smaller number of pills. On the downside, fixed combinations do not allow adjustments to be made to the dosages of the individual medicines. (For a list of combination medicines available, see box at left.)

# using insulin

Many people view insulin as the "beginning of the end" or some form of punishment for doing a poor job. Nothing could be further from the truth. Due to advances in technology, taking insulin injections has become extremely safe and simple, and it's virtually pain-free. And insulin remains the most natural and effective medication for treating high blood sugar.

## sticking to control

Mention the word insulin and just about everyone has a sad story. "My aunt started insulin, and soon afterward she ended up going blind." "I know this guy, he takes insulin and he's always sick." "My friend had to start insulin, and she's gained 40 pounds over the last year!" In addition to personal tales like this, health care professionals have been known to threaten their patients with insulin as a motivational tool. The person is told, "If you don't get your act together, take your pills, strictly follow your diet, and start exercising regularly, I'll have to put you on insulin," or "If you fail this, the only thing we have left to try is insulin."

To understand insulin's value, you need to remember the chronic, progres-sive nature of diabetes. You need to recognize that the enemy is not insulin but rather uncontrolled glucose levels. And you need to keep your eye on the ultimate goal: a life free of diabetes complications.

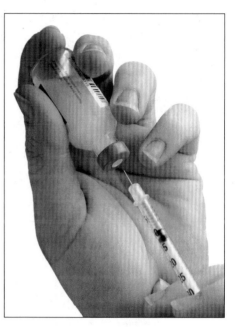

As we've said, diabetes is a chronic disease that progressively takes more aggressive treatment to keep glucose levels in a healthy range. You might start out with dietary changes and increased activity as prescribed treatments; then you need a pill; then two pills; then a handful of pills; and finally, a handful of pills and insulin—all to keep your glucose levels within your goal range. Because of the progressive nature of diabetes, if you live long enough, you will need insulin. Some need it sooner than others. You might have to live to be 137 before you would need it, but given what is known about diabetes today and the treatments currently available, you would need insulin eventually.

People often say they'd do anything to get their diabetes under control—anything, that is, but inject insulin. Insulin is viewed by many people with diabetes as signaling the ultimate failure: They've lost control of their diabetes, and there is no hope. They now have the "bad" or "serious" type of diabetes. The reality is that there are only two types of diabetes, the kind that is under control and the kind that isn't. And if you're smart, you want to be in the "controlled" group. What you have to do to keep your glucose level under control in no way indicates failure or success, good or bad, serious or not. All diabetes is serious, regardless of what type you have. Commit yourself to doing whatever it takes to keep yourself healthy.

Elevated glucose levels result in poor quality of life and serious complications, and if you need to inject insulin to prevent these problems, do it!

## the first diabetes treatment

On January 23, 1922, at the University of Toronto, Dr. Frederick Banting and his student C. H. Best made one of the greatest discoveries of the 20th century. They successfully used insulin to treat a person with diabetes, a disease that, up to that time, was an automatic death sentence for anyone diagnosed with it. Prior to their discovery, there was no treatment for diabetes. Those with type 1 died very quickly, while those with type 2 died more slowly, suffering horrible complications prior to death. The University of Toronto immediately gave pharmaceutical companies license to produce insulin free of royalties. In early 1923, about a year after the first test injection, insulin became widely available when Eli Lilly and Company marketed Iletin, the first commercially available insulin, which was extracted from the pancreas of stockyard animals.

Animal insulin worked well overall, saving millions of lives, but it was not an exact match with human insulin and sometimes caused side effects such as skin rashes and other allergic reactions. For the next 60 years, insulin would become one of the most studied medications in the world. Up until the 1980s, people with diabetes relied on insulin from animals, primarily cattle and pigs.

In 1978, a fledgling biotechnology company named Genentech produced the first synthetically manufactured insulin that could be made in large amounts. Using bacteria or yeast as miniature "factories," the gene for human insulin was inserted into bacterial DNA. The result was human insulin, called recombinant DNA insulin, which did not cause the problems that animal insulin sometimes did. It became widely available in the early 1980s and has been the standard ever since.

## one type does not fit all

If you need insulin, the decision to take it is a good one. One thing that we know about insulin is that it always works. It *will* lower your glucose levels when taken correctly.

As described previously, insulin is a small protein molecule made by the beta cells in the pancreas. Its major actions are to get your muscle, fat, and liver cells to take in glucose and to tell your liver to make less glucose. If you have type 1 diabetes, you are insulin dependent and rely on insulin injections to live. Your pancreas does not make enough insulin, if any at all, to maintain the functions of your body. If you have type 2 diabetes, you may be insulin requiring; you may require insulin to supplement what your pancreas makes in order to achieve desirable blood glucose levels, but you probably still make enough to at least keep yourself alive.

There are different kinds of insulin, all with different characteristics. When determining the best insulin for you,

there are three important characteristics to understand and consider. The first is the onset of the insulin. This is the length of time it takes the insulin to reach your bloodstream and begin to lower your glucose level. Next is the peak time of the insulin. This is the time when your insulin is at its maximum strength in terms of lowering your glucose level. The last characteristic is the duration. This is the length of time that insulin remains in your body, continuing to work and lower your glucose levels.

With an understanding of these characteristics, you and your diabetes-care team have five different types of insulin to consider. Very often these insulins will be used in some sort of combination in order to meet your required onset, peak-time, and duration-of-action needs. And while the characteristics of insulin types have been studied and documented at length, you need to understand that your response to each insulin may vary from what is predicted. For this reason, taking complete, detailed notes of your glucose-testing results, the timing of your tests, and your insulin injections becomes vitally important to understanding how insulin works in your body.

## the types, your choices

Since carbohydrates raise blood sugar levels quickly, everyone with type 1 diabetes and many people with type 2

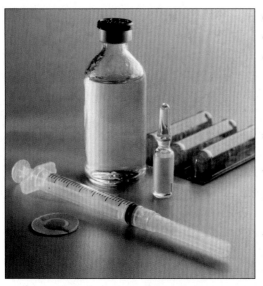

diabetes require a quick-acting insulin at mealtimes.

When insulin first became available in 1923, there was only one type, Regular insulin. While it was animal-based back then, it is still available today, in a recombinant DNA form. Regular insulin, also called R insulin, is a short-acting insulin that usually begins working within 30 to 60 minutes, peaks two to four hours after injection, and is usually out of your system in six to eight hours.

These days, Regular insulin is rarely used. It does a poor job of covering the blood sugar rise that occurs after meals. With most carbohydrates raising the blood sugar 30 to 90 minutes after eating, Regular insulin is just too slow. Even when Regular insulin is taken 15 to 30 minutes before eating, blood sugars tend to spike very high after the meal, and then drop suddenly 3 to 6 hours later after the food is done working. Clearly, there is a need for faster, shorter-acting insulin.

Introducing the rapid-acting insulin analogs. They are called "analogs" because they are slightly altered forms of Regular insulin. By altering their molecular structure ever so slightly,

these insulins absorb and work much faster than Regular. Currently, three rapid-acting analog insulins are available: aspart (Novolog, or NovoRapid), glulisine (Apidra), and lispro (Humalog). These types of insulin begin to work 10 to 15 minutes after injection, peak in about 60 to 90 minutes, and are finished working in three to five hours. These rapid-acting insulins can be injected shortly before a meal rather than 30 minutes before a meal, which is recommended for Regular insulin. Because they work so fast, they do a better job keeping blood glucose levels down right after eating. Also, because they are cleared from the body so quickly, there is less risk of hypoglycemia several hours later. Furthermore, because of its fast action, rapid insulin does a much better job of bringing high blood sugar levels down to normal.

## insulin to cover the body's metabolism

Food isn't the only influence on blood sugar levels. They are also influenced by the liver's ongoing production of glucose. Insulin is needed not only to limit how much glucose the liver secretes, but also to take that glucose and pack it into the body's cells for nourishment. This is how our brain, nerves, heart, lungs, and other "always-active" organs have energy.

In the early days of insulin therapy, the needles that were used to inject insulin were thick and needed to be sharpened by hand with a honing stone or razor strap before each use. The syringes were made of glass and needed to be boiled and cleaned every day. The pain and inconvenience of injecting insulin created the drive to develop an insulin that was longer-acting so that fewer injections would be needed. In the 1950s, European researchers developed two new insulin preparations that required only two injections a day instead of four to six injections.

The first of these new insulin preparations was NPH insulin, which added a fish protein, protamine, to Regular insulin to slow its absorption and action. NPH is an intermediate-acting insulin that generally starts working in two hours, peaks in four to eight hours, and is gone from the system in 16 to 24 hours.

The other new preparation yielded two insulin types, Lente and Ultralente insulin. These insulins were made by crystallizing Regular insulin to different degrees. Crystallized insulin takes

## ACTIVITY OF THE VARIOUS INSULIN TYPES AVAILABLE TODAY

| TYPE OF INSULIN | ONSET | PEAK | DURATION | LOW BLOOD GLUCOSE MOST LIKELY TO OCCUR |
|---|---|---|---|---|
| **rapid-acting** lispro, aspart, glulisine | 10–15 minutes | 60–90 minutes | 3–5 hours | 2–3 hours |
| **regular** | 30–60 minutes | 2–4 hours | 6–8 hours | 3–5 hours |
| **intermediate-acting** | | | | |
| NPH | 2–4 hours | 4–8 hours | 16–24 hours | 6–12 hours |
| Lantus | 2 hours | None | 13–24 hours | 2–24 hours |
| Levemir | 2 hours | (mild) 6–10 hours | 18–22 hours | 2–22 hours |
| **premixed** | | | | |
| 70/30 (NPH/R) | 30–60 minutes | 2 & 6 hours | 16–24 hours | 4 & 8 hours |
| 50/50 NPH/Humalog mix | 30–60 minutes | 2 & 8 hours | 16–24 hours | 2 & 8 hours |
| 75/25 NPH/Humalog mix | 10–15 minutes | 1 & 8 hours | 16–24 hours | 3 & 8 hours |
| 70/30 NPH/Novolog mix | 10–15 minutes | 1 & 8 hours | 16–24 hours | 3 & 8 hours |

*Onset, peak, and duration times are all approximate. Each person is different and will have a unique response to insulin.*

longer to be absorbed, thus prolonging its action in the body. Lente insulin, an intermediate-acting insulin like NPH, generally starts working in three to four hours, peaks in 6 to 12 hours, and lasts for 20 to 24 hours.

By comparison, Ultralente is crystallized to a greater extent and is considered a long-acting insulin. It generally starts working in four to six hours, has its peak action at 10 to 20 hours, and is usually gone from the body 24 to 36 hours after the injection. However, studies have shown that Ultralente and Lente insulin are absorbed at very different rates in different people. For some people, Ultralente works like an intermediate-acting insulin, while for other people it is very long-acting. For these reasons, as well as the development of new "basal" insulin, Lente and Ultralente are no longer being manufactured.

The newest insulin, introduced soon after the turn of the century, is called "basal" insulin. Two types of basal insulin are currently available. Lantus, also known asglargine, is a true "peakless" insulin. This insulin is taken once or twice a day, works consistently for 20 to 24 hours, and then tapers off. Lantus is rapidly replacing NPH, but because it has a flat, peakless action, Lantus does nothing to lower the glucose rise that results from eating. In addition, because it has a lower pH than other insulins (making it more acidic), it may sting slightly when injected, and it cannot be mixed with other insulins in the same syringe.

The other basal insulin is called Levemir (generic name detemir). Levemir is usually taken twice daily to produce a relatively steady level of insulin in the bloodstream. It has a slight peak six to ten hours after injection, and begins tapering off after 16 to 20 hours. Unlike Lantus, the action profile (onset, peak, duration) is not affected by the size of the dose taken.

Onset, peak, and duration times are all approximate. Each person is different and will have a unique response to insulin.

The final type of insulin is premixed insulin. Premixed insulins consist of different insulins that are combined in fixed percentages. These insulins are convenient for some people who combine two different insulins together, such as NPH and Humalog. The most typical mixture is 75 percent NPH and 25 percent Humalog, called 75/25 insulin. Other mixtures that are available are 50/50 insulin, which is 50 percent NPH and 50 percent Humalog; 70/30 Novolog mix, a combination of 70 percent NPH and 30 percent Novolog; and 70/30 NPH/Regular-mix, a combination of 70 percent NPH and 30 percent Regular.

Because premixed insulin preparations represent a combination of two different insulins, the onset, peak, and duration of these mixed insulins are a combination of the onset, peak, and duration of each individual insulin they contain. This requires considerably more rigidity in your life, allowing for little variance in meal timing or amount of food eaten. Premixed insulin is best used by those unwilling or unmotivated to take multiple injections each day, those unable or unwilling to test blood glucose levels frequently, those who have trouble drawing up insulin out of two different bottles, and those without the ability to adjust insulin dosing based on blood glucose readings. You are generally unable to achieve normal glucose control using premixed insulin, and the major goals of this type of rigid insulin therapy are to prevent both very low and very high blood glucose levels.

## a measure of strength

Pure insulin is a very small, white crystal. When it is made into a solution, it is dissolved or suspended in a liquid. These liquid solutions have different strengths, and the strengths are measured in units of active insulin. The most common insulin available in the United States is U-100 insulin. A U-100 insulin has 100 units of active insulin in each milliliter (mL) of liquid. You can think of it as 100 pieces of insulin in each milliliter of liquid. Using your math skills, this would mean that there are

1,000 units of insulin (10 mL times 100 units/mL) in one 10-mL vial of insulin. Other concentrations of insulin, such as U-40, U-50 are available, but they are rarely used in the United States today. In Europe and Latin America, U-40 can still be found in use, an important bit of information to know if you are a frequent international traveler. Another more concentrated form of Regular insulin, U-500, is being used more and more often with those who are extremely insulin resistant (requiring more than 200 units of insulin daily). U-500 is five times more concentrated than U-100, so 10 units of U-500 acts like 50 units or U-100. However, the action profile of U-500 Regular insulin is almost like NPH insulin: It has a slower onset, later peak, and longer duration of action than U-100 Regular insulin.

## pick your best shot

Insulin is a protein and therefore cannot be taken orally because the body's digestive juices would destroy it; it must be given by injection. The timing and frequency of insulin injections depend on a number of factors, including the type of insulin, amount and type of food eaten, and the person's level of physical activity. By testing your blood glucose levels frequently and working together with your diabetes care team to analyze your glucose patterns, you and your team will identify the right insulin "fit" for you.

Once your patterns are identified, you then need to choose the insulin delivery system that is right for you. Not too long ago, your only option was a glass syringe with its "sharpen after each use" detachable needle. As metal technology advanced, it was replaced by the disposable needle-and-syringe combination, which had a very sharp, very strong, yet significantly thinner (and thus less painful) needle. Today, syringe needles are so small that in most instances the injection is almost painless. You often need to look to make sure the needle is through the skin when giving yourself a shot. And when asked, most people who use insulin say that it is a much bigger deal, and more painful, to test your glucose than to administer an injection.

While syringes have greatly improved over the last 75 years, they still require the insulin to be drawn from a vial. This can be inconvenient for anyone attempting to lead a normal, active life, and studies have shown that miscalculated insulin doses are not uncommon. Concerns such as these led to the development of insulin pens, which were first used in Europe and then introduced in the United States in the early 1990s. An insulin pen looks very similar to a fountain pen, except that insulin goes where you would normally find an ink cartridge, and a needle replaces the point of the pen. You "dial up" your desired insulin dose, then you press down on the top to deliver the insulin. Simplifying the injection process has increased compliance with frequent insulin injections (especially those during the middle of the day, when people are likely to be away from home) and increased the accuracy of the delivered doses. Insulin pens come in two forms: prefilled disposable pens that contain 300 units of insulin, and reusable pens that use replaceable 300-unit insulin cartridges. The types of insulin that are found in insulin pens and pen cartridges include Regular, Humalog, Novolog, Apidra, NPH, Lantus, Levemir, Premixed 70/30, 50/50, and 75/25.

Despite these advances and the improved compliance they've brought, there are still several bumps in the road to tighter glucose control. The first is the difficulty in accurately matching the peak-time variability of the intermediate- and long-acting insulins with the rise in glucose levels you have first thing in the morning. This is called the dawn phenomenon and is caused by the liver's tendency to increase its glucose output during the early morning hours. In order to accurately match your insulin needs, it would be best not to take any long-acting insulin at all but rather to get up at 3:00 A.M. every night to inject Regular insulin to correct for this condition. Since that doesn't make for a very good long-term treatment plan, the longer-lasting insulins have been the best alternative.

The second problem occurs when the rate of insulin absorption does not match the glucose rise after meals. This variation can result from the sites you select for injection or the repeated use of a favorite site. For Regular, NPH insulin, and premixed insulins, the absorption rate depends on where you inject. Insulin injections in the stomach act faster than injections in your arm, injections in your arm act faster than those in your leg, and injections in the buttocks are slowest acting of all. The blood flow to the injection site also governs absorption, so cold skin makes for slower absorption than does warm skin. Blood flow is also changed when injections are continually given at the same site, because excessive insulin in one area promotes the development of scar tissue and either fat overgrowth or breakdown—a condition called lipodystrophy. Tissue that has lipodystrophy absorbs insulin poorly. By changing and rotating injection sites (pick a spot about 1 inch from the last injection site), you can usually prevent this problem.

Finally, your daytime, base insulin needs are sometimes difficult to match.

## GIVING YOURSELF A SHOT OF INSULIN

| WHAT YOU NEED TO DO | WHY YOU NEED TO DO IT |
|---|---|
| Look at the vial or cartridge of insulin before you use it. | Clumps that do not dissolve, a color change, or cloudiness (of a clear insulin) means the insulin may be damaged and thus no good. |
| Check the expiration date of the insulin. | Old insulin has lost some of its effectiveness and will not work well or as expected. |
| If using a normally cloudy insulin, such as NPH or 70/30, gently roll the vial between the palms of your hands. If you are using an insulin pen, invert the pen 15 times to mix the insulin. | Cloudy insulin is a mixture of insulins and/or additives that prolong or change its action. If you don't mix it, you will receive an incorrect percentage of the insulin in this dose as well as in future doses from the same vial. |
| Wash your hands and clean your injection site. | This prevents infection. |
| Use a new syringe or new pen needle each time. | This prevents infection. In addition, new needles are sharp. Dull needles hurt. |
| If using a vial, first draw up air equal to your dose, then inject this air into the vial. | This fills the vial with pressure to help with the withdrawal of the insulin dose. |
| Turn the vial upside down, and withdraw more than the number of units you need, then push up to the amount you need. | This prevents bubbles in the syringe. |
| If using an insulin pen, once you attach a new needle to the pen, prime the pen with a 2-unit shot into the air. | This assures that the pen is delivering insulin and fills the needle with insulin in preparation for injecting the proper dose. |
| Pinch the skin, push the needle straight in, and push the plunger down. Count to 5 before removing the needle. Stop pinching and remove the needle. | This allows for complete delivery of the insulin and prevents insulin leaking back out of the injection site. Congratulations, and well done. |

Your base insulin need, also called your basal, is what your body requires to function when you are in a fasting state between meals. The same variation that is associated with the dawn phenomenon occurs in some people in a milder form during the day as well.

To address these problems and to meet the needs of people desiring the best glucose control possible, the insuline pump was introduced in the late 1970s. It provided continuous delivery of Regular insulin directly under the skin. Unfortunately, the first pumps were not very reliable. By the 1990s, the kinks had been addressed and the pumps improved so dramatically that they are currently considered the best method for delivering insulin in almost all people who require insulin. The number of people using pumps in the United States rose from 20,000 in 1995 to more than 200,000 today. This number has been increasing by more than 20,000 each year and continues to climb.

The modern pumps are quite similar to the IV (intravenous) machines used in hospitals to deliver medication, only much smaller, more sophisticated, and more comfortable since they infuse insulin into the fat below the skin

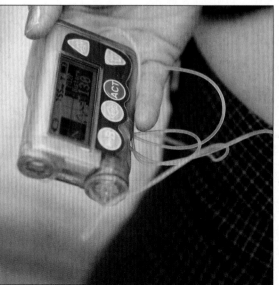

instead of a vein. They are usually the size of a pager and weigh about four ounces. Each pump has a thin plastic tube, with one end connected to the insulin reservoir inside the pump and the other end to a thin plastic catheter. This catheter is generally placed under the skin of your abdomen, hips, thighs, buttocks or sides using an insertion needle, which is removed once the catheter is in place. The catheter site is changed every two to three days. That means that instead of requiring 8 to 12 insulin injections over the course of two to three days, you need only one needlestick, to place the catheter, during the same time period when you use a pump. Your insulin pump is then programmed to deliver basal insulin at specific rates throughout the day and night (your basal rate) to compensate for the dawn phenomenon and meet your daytime base needs. This leaves you free to eat any time, and you are no longer tied to the timing of insulin injections, which significantly reduces the risk of hypoglycemia. Each time you eat, you simply direct the pump to deliver a bolus (or an added amount) of insulin to match the amount of food that you want to eat.

But there are downsides to the pump. One of the major drawbacks is the risk of infection at the insertion site. This is usually remedied by making sure that the site is changed often enough and that a good, clean insertion technique is used. Another and quite serious problem is the very high glucose levels and life-threatening ketoacidosis that can occur if insulin delivery is disrupted for longer than a few hours. This can happen if the pump malfunctions, the tubing becomes kinked or blocked, or the pump runs out of insulin. With all the bells and whistles available on today's pumps, however, a vigilant user is likely to notice such a pump problem long before insulin delivery is disrupted for any serious length of time.

The last two hurdles tend to be cost (a pump costs about $6,000) and the issue of constantly being "hooked up" to something. While the cost of a pump is daunting, the cost of keeping an individual with diabetes well is far less than treating someone with complications. Many insurance companies are becoming more aware of this and are beginning to find that the cost of the pump is small compared to the long-term costs of medical care for someone in poor health and poor control. For this reason, with prior authorization, many insurance companies, including Medicare, do cover insulin pumps.

Finally, the concern about being attached to a machine usually fades quickly. Pumps are so small that they are easily slipped into a pocket, clipped onto a belt, or hidden under clothes. Not convinced? Look up pictures of Nicole Johnson, Miss America 1999, wearing her evening gown during the competition. Insulin dependent, she had her pump on during all but the swimsuit portion of the contest.

## know when to test for ketones

People whose bodies no longer produce insulin and are insulin dependent are at risk of developing a serious condition called ketoacidosis. Ketoacidosis can result from high levels of ketones (acids) in the blood coupled with dehydration. If you use insulin, you need to understand what ketoacidosis is, why it happens, how to detect it, and what you should do when it occurs.

Ketones are formed when the body doesn't have enough insulin available to allow it to use glucose for energy. Without the required insulin, your body simply can't get glucose into its cells. So instead, the body tries to break down stored fat to make fuel available to the cells. The fat in fat cells is broken down into fatty acids, which pass through the liver and form acidic by-products called ketones. The ketones begin to build up in the blood; eventually, they spill over into the urine, as well. At high levels, ketones in the blood are toxic and can cause diabetic ketoacidosis (DKA), which is a medical emergency.

Ketones can be detected through a simple urine test you can do at home (you can buy the test strips at any pharmacy without a prescription). There are also blood glucose meters that can measure ketone levels in the blood using special test strips. It is important, however, for you to discuss with your team ahead of time when you should test for ketones and what to do if you detect an elevated level. It is generally recommended that urine be tested for ketones

- when the blood sugar is higher than 240 mg/dl (13 mmol/l),
- during any acute illness (such as pneumonia or severe flu),
- when nausea and/or vomiting are occurring,
- during pregnancy (discuss with your team how often).

If your ketone reading is above normal, especially if it is accompanied by an elevated blood glucose level, call your doctor at once. And again, be sure you know ahead of time if there are any other situations in which your doctor would like you to test your urine more frequently for ketones.

## new directions, new delivery systems

To eliminate the need for insulin injections, various delivery methods have been tried and used, but with limited, if any, success. Mechanical devices, called jet injectors, use compressed air to blow the insulin under the skin. They have proven to be expensive, are bulky, and can still be painful, even more so than syringes. Administering insulin through the nose was tried, but without success, because of the irritation that it caused to the mucous membranes of the nose. And the use of rectal insulin suppositories before meals has proven to be socially unacceptable for widespread use.

Inhaled-insulin delivery systems are currently being tested by several manufacturers. With these systems, packages of insulin become airborne in an enclosed cavity and are then inhaled through the mouth. The inhaled insulin is rapidly absorbed, so a long-acting "basal" insulin would still need to be taken by injection. The current systems are also bulky and require training and special attention to technique in order to work properly. Still, studies are underway with hopes of FDA approval sometime in the near future.

Other promising avenues of investigation are the use of ultrasound pulses to deliver insulin through skin patches; implanted, extended-release insulin pellets; and an oral form of insulin.

While oral insulin is really a misnomer, researchers have discovered a plantlike substance that can be taken orally and that appears to have effects similar to insulin. Research is underway.

While implantable insulin pumps have been available for years, they are advancing in use quite slowly. A very high insulin concentration (U-400 and higher) is delivered via remote control in both basal (ongoing) and bolus (for after meals) forms. The implanted pump is about the size of a hockey puck and needs to be refilled about every three months and, until recently, was plagued by incidents of blockage in the delivery catheter. Reformulations of the insulin being delivered through these pumps seem to have improved the blockage situation. By combining this implantable pump with an implantable glucose sensor, the diabetes loop would be closed, creating a "mechanical" cure for diabetes. Such a system may become a reality sometime in the near future.

Several years ago, Canadian scientists made an exciting breakthrough in islet cell transplant research. They demonstrated a possible cure for type 1 diabetes, with people remaining insulin independent, with normal glucose levels by transplanting islet cells from a nondiabetic donor pancreas and suppressing the immune system in a novel yet gentle way. This research led to worldwide trials, using what is now called the Edmonton Protocol. Other research has focused on ways to help the body to regenerate its own insulin-producing cells by stimulating the pancreas with a special protein. This, coupled with discoveries by California researchers who have been able to grow beta cells, resulting in an unlimited source of transplant material, may someday foretell an end to insulin-dependent diabetes.

Even though insulin is not a cure for diabetes, the 1922 medical discovery saved, and continues to save, millions of lives around the world. And while this Nobel Prize–winning accomplishment is among one of the greatest medical achievements ever, the Flame of Hope still burns outside of Sir Frederick G. Banting Square at the Banting Museum in London, Ontario. Only when a cure, rather than a treatment, for diabetes is found will the flame be extinguished.

# fighting hypoglycemia

Diabetes management focuses on lowering high blood glucose, but there's an opposite effect called a hypoglycemic reaction that can be equally dangerous. Especially for people who have had diabetes for a long time or who take medication or insulin, being able to recognize and treat hypoglycemia is a basic skill that must be mastered.

## strange happenings

It's 5:00 P.M.: You test your blood glucose and take your diabetes medication. You start to eat your dinner but, midway through, the phone rings, taking you away from the meal. By the time you return to the table, the food is cold and you decide not to finish what's left on your plate. All is fine until a few hours later, when you start to feel dizzy, begin sweating, and notice that your heart is beating very fast and hard. You test your blood glucose—

the meter reads 52 mg/dl (3 mmol/l)! You grab some orange juice, a few cookies, and a handful of grapes. After a while, you start feeling a bit better, and by the time you finish a glass of milk and a turkey sandwich, you're on solid ground and everything is back to normal. You check your glucose again before heading to bed and are shocked to find a reading of 269 mg/dl. What the heck is going on?

In two words, you experienced a hypoglycemic reaction. The high blood glucose level that followed, called a food rebound, resulted from the life-saving steps you took to increase your blood glucose.

## what is hypoglycemia?

As its name suggests, hypoglycemia means low blood sugar (hypo means low and glycemia means sugar in the blood). It's sometimes referred to as "an insulin reaction," "a low," "insulin shock," or just plain "shock." No matter the term used, hypoglycemia is one of the most common, and most dangerous, side effects of any medication for lowering blood glucose. For the person with diabetes, the goal of treatment is to lower blood glucose levels to as close to normal as possible. If the treatment plan to obtain this goal includes insulin and/or one of the insulin-stimulating medications (a sulfonylurea or meglitinide), then hypoglycemia is definitely a risk. Hypoglycemia can occur if you take too much insulin or too large a dose of medication, miss or delay a meal, eat too little food for the amount of insulin or pills taken, increase your normal level of activity, drink alcohol, or any combination of these factors.

Any time your blood glucose falls below 70 mg/dl (4 mmol/l) you're depriving some of your body's important systems of having the energy they need. Remember, your brain and nervous system depend solely on glucose for energy. In an attempt to raise the glucose level, your brain sends out emergency signals. As a result, your

alpha cells, located in your pancreas, release glucagon. The glucagon signals your liver and muscles to release stored glycogen and change it back to glucose to try to raise your blood glucose level to a normal range. Meanwhile, the release of the hormone epinephrine increases your hunger, causes a resistance to insulin's action, and further stimulates the breakdown of the liver's glycogen into glucose. Other hormones, cortisol and growth hormone, are also released to counteract insulin and raise your blood glucose levels.

Outwardly, you may begin to feel dizzy, hungry, shaky, or very fatigued and weak. You may notice that you are

## SYMPTOMS OF HYPOGLYCEMIA

| EARLY SYMPTOMS<br>CAUSED BY THE RELEASE OF EPINEPHRINE AND<br>DECREASING BLOOD GLUCOSE LEVELS | LATER SYMPTOMS<br>CAUSED BY THE DECREASING AVAILABILITY<br>OF GLUCOSE TO YOUR BRAIN |
|---|---|
| Dizziness | Headache |
| Pale or flushed face | Blurred vision |
| Irritability | Slurred speech |
| Hunger | Confusion |
| Sweating | Euphoria |
| Rapid heartbeat | Hostility |
| Fatigue or weakness | Lack of coordination |
| Nervousness or anxiousness | Drowsiness |
| Shakiness | Convulsions/seizure |
| | Loss of consciousness |

## How to treat a low blood glucose level

1. Check your blood glucose, if you are able.

2. If you are in doubt and unable to check your blood glucose, ALWAYS assume that your glucose level is low.

3. Eat 15 grams (or the amount recommended by your caregiver) of a fast-acting carbohydrate. That's equal to any of the following:
   3–4 glucose tabs
   4 ounces of fruit juice
   5 sugar cubes
   1 small box of raisins
   1 tablespoon of honey
   6 hard candies

4. Wait 15 minutes, then check your blood glucose level again.

5. If symptoms are still present or blood sugar is less than 70 (4mmol/l), repeat step 3.

6. **If the person is unable to swallow or becomes unconscious, a glucagon injection must be given immediately!** This should be done even if you are unsure that the person's blood sugar is low.

7. Call your doctor if you experience frequent or severe hypoglycemic reactions.

sweaty, your heart is beating fast, your face is pale or flushed, or your mouth and lips are tingling or numb. These early signs of low blood glucose are primarily caused by the release of epinephrine.

If the glucose continues to drop, less and less is available to your brain. You may develop a headache, blurred vision, slurred speech, and confusion. You may become quite uncoordinated, and your state of mind may be either euphoric or quite hostile and belligerent. If the low glucose level continues, you may lose consciousness, have a seizure, and possibly lapse into a coma. Hypoglycemia can even result in death.

## how do I treat it?

The best time to treat hypoglycemia is as soon as you recognize the first symptoms. Do not wait! Food is the best remedy for hypoglycemia, but not just any food. You want something that will get into your system fast and raise your glucose levels quickly.

While a chocolate bar may seem like a wonderful choice, it actually takes quite a bit of time for it to raise your blood glucose levels. The sucrose from the granulated sugar in the candy bar starts the process, but the fat in the chocolate actually delays the rise in your blood glucose.

Instead, you want something that will get into your system quickly and work immediately to raise your blood glucose levels. Simple carbohydrates and liquid carbohydrates are your best choices for this. Glucose tablets, sugar cubes, fruit juice, and sugary candies are your best bets. They are absorbed quickly into your bloodstream and begin raising blood glucose levels within five to ten minutes of ingestion.

Untreated hypoglycemia or a delay in treating a low blood glucose level can result in a severe hypoglycemic reaction in which you are unable to swallow liquids or food and may even become unconscious. Anyone who takes insulin to manage their diabetes is most at risk for this type of reaction. Others at risk for severe hypoglycemia are those who have had diabetes for many years and have developed something called hypoglycemia unawareness, in which they have difficulty recognizing the symptoms of low blood sugar until it is too late and they are unable to help themselves.

For anyone who takes insulin and anyone with hypoglycemia unawareness, an additional safety net, a glucagon emergency kit, should be kept on hand for emergencies. The glucagon in the kit can be given by injection to the person having the severe hypoglycemic reaction. This injected glucagon is a synthetic version of the hormone found naturally in the alpha cells of the pancreas, the hormone that signals the liver and muscles to release stored glycogen. Anyone who is at risk for severe hypoglycemia should have a glucagon emergency kit and needs to train those around them how to use it. The kit is available, with a doctor's prescription, at pharmacies. Be sure to have the pharmacist or your diabetes care team demonstrate the use of the kit to you so that you can show others how to use it.

## prepare yourself and others

If you take insulin or a medication that stimulates insulin, you can reduce your risk of hypoglycemia. It's all a matter of education and preparation. Check your blood glucose levels frequently. Anticipate situations that may trigger hypoglycemia and take steps to adjust; plan ahead for increased activity or changes in routine. Learn how to recognize and treat symptoms of low blood glucose, and stash sugar everywhere. Wear identification that states you have diabetes. Teach friends and family how to recognize symptoms of low blood glucose and how to help if you display symptoms of a low. And if you take insulin, make sure those around you know how to treat you in case you become disoriented or unconscious. They should also know where you keep your glucagon emergency kit.

# expand your options, improve your choices

**There's no question** that your food choices and eating habits can have a major impact on your diabetes control. And because you have diabetes, you may assume you must follow a very strict diet. The problem is, diets tend to be seen as temporary. They can also be boring, inconvenient, and even frustrating. And, if they cut out foods you truly enjoy, they can lead to problem eating habits such as bingeing. If instead you expand your food options and learn to make healthier food choices that match your tastes and your body's needs for carbohydrate, fat, and other nutrients, you build a skill that will last a lifetime. And that skill can help you control not only your glucose levels, but your blood pressure, cholesterol level, and weight, as well.

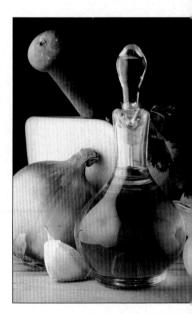

# learning to choose

Many of us know what it's like to be on a diet, whether it's for our weight, blood pressure, cholesterol, or diabetes. We're quick with the phrase, "I can't, I'm on a diet." That's what dieting is about after all—not being able to eat all the foods we enjoy. Most often, the foods we are allowed are bland or boring. We'd give up anything to have something sweet or rich or flavorful. Eventually, we give up the diet instead. We go back to old habits, or develop new ones, like bingeing, that leave us back where we started—or worse off. It's unfortunate, too, since how and what we eat and how we live can go a long way toward helping us improve our blood pressure, cholesterol levels, and glucose control, as well as shed some unwanted pounds— all of those metabolic syndrome problems that people with diabetes struggle with.

There is a better way. It's a path that in many ways is the opposite of dieting. It's called learning to choose. It's a path you can stay on for life. It's a skill that can bring the joy and pleasure back into eating as it tackles diabetes, metabolic syndrome, and heart disease. Unlike dieting, which is all about restrictions, learning to choose healthier foods and eating habits is about expanding your dietary horizons. Here's some advice on learning to choose:

**know how foods affect your body.** As discussed in "Eating for Better Control," you need to check your glucose after meals to find out how different levels of carbohydrates affect your blood glucose. And in the pages that follow, you'll learn how various types of fat affect blood cholesterol and how salt affects blood pressure. Use this information and food labels to compare foods and make healthier choices.

**never call a food good or bad.** No single food, in and of itself, is good or bad. A chocolate bar, an ice cream sundae, a piece of prime rib, a slice of bread—not one of these is bad, despite what you may have heard. Nor does eating one of these mean you've failed somehow. Even though you have diabetes, each food can fit into your healthy eating plan, as long as you adjust for it. Likewise, having one of these foods will not make or break your efforts at lowering your cholesterol or losing weight. It won't erase progress you've already made. And if enjoying it once in a while, in a reasonable portion, keeps you satisfied and out of the denial-binge trap, then it helps you in the end.

**expand your food options.** Go ahead, dive into those grocery aisles and start experimenting! Use the recipes in this book for tasty, healthful new dishes. The more foods you try, the more likely you are to find a wide variety of tasty, desirable foods that match your body's nutrient needs and move you closer to your health goals. Again, it doesn't mean you can't have your old favorites once in a while. But when you want something chewy or creamy or crunchy, you'll also have some options that are lower in calories, fat, or sodium.

**say no to quick—or temporary—fixes.** When you go on a diet, you generally pick a date to begin (and binge on all your favorites the night before). And when you start, there's often an assumption that you will reach a certain goal—or give up—and go off the diet. Learning to choose isn't like that. It's more like learning how to ride a bike. It may take a while to get the hang of it, but once you learn how, you don't really ever forget. Each time you eat becomes an opportunity to

choose something lower in salt or fat, something higher in fiber, a carbohydrate that's richer in vitamins, or a lower-calorie food or snack. You make the changes as you are able. Eventually, making healthier choices becomes the norm, so there's no reason to fret about an occasional sloppy burger or scoop of double-fudge ice cream. What's more, along the way, you discover you've actually dropped a few pounds, improved your control, and lowered your blood pressure and cholesterol.

By learning to choose rather than trying yet another diet, the ball is in your court. It is up to you how often you make a healthier food choice, how quickly you move toward your goals, and exactly what a healthy, enjoyable diet consists of for you. It can seem daunting at first. With freedom comes responsibility. There's nobody telling you what you can and can't eat every day. But once you begin to expand your food choices and discover how truly flavorful even healthier foods can be, you'll realize why learning to choose is such a great choice.

# opting for less salt

## *Relieving the pressure*

In addition to limiting sodium, there are other dietary factors that play a role in controlling high blood pressure. In general, high blood pressure can be lowered with a diet that is:
- low in saturated fat, cholesterol, total fat, red meat, and simple carbohydrates
- rich in fruits, vegetables, low-fat dairy foods, whole-grain products, fish, poultry, and nuts

Blood pressure is also helped by a diet that is rich in magnesium (widely available; nuts, seeds, dried beans, and bananas are rich sources), potassium (fruits and vegetables), and calcium (dairy products), as well as protein and fiber.

Sodium, a component of salt, is an essential mineral for the human body. It controls fluid balance, and too little of it can cause serious problems. For some people, however, too much sodium contributes to high blood pressure, which increases the risk of heart attack, stroke, and kidney problems. High blood pressure, as we've said, is especially common in, and dangerous for, people with type 2 diabetes. So it just makes sense, as you're learning to choose more foods—and healthier foods—to keep an eye out for sodium content and tilt your food choices toward lower-sodium options.

So how much sodium do you need, and how much is too much? The minimum sodium requirement, under normal conditions, is approximately 400 milligrams (mg) a day. That may sound like a lot, but it only equals about one-fifth of a teaspoon of table salt. The maximum recommended salt intake, according to the US Department of Agriculture, is less than 2,300 milligrams (mg) for most Americans, and just 1,500 mg for people over age 50 and for those of any age who are African American or have hyperten-

sion, diabetes, or chronic kidney disease. The 1,500 mg recommendation applies to about half of the U.S. population, including children, and the majority of adults.

Keep in mind, too, that these minimums and maximums include not only salt you sprinkle on your food, but also the salt used in cooking, preparing, and/or processing the food. And you'd be surprised at the amount of sodium there is in most processed foods (see "Sodium Surprises" on the next page).

Processed foods account for most of the salt and sodium consumed, so it's important to read food labels to see just how much sodium foods contain. A good rule of thumb when it comes to sodium is that if the food comes in a bag, in a box, in a can, out a window (of a fast-food joint), or on a restaurant platter, it probably has more sodium than you expect or want (unless you've specifically chosen a lower-salt version). Here are some additional tips to help you lower your sodium intake:
- Choose reduced-sodium or no-salt-added products.
- Buy fresh. There's no salt added to fresh produce.

- Use fresh poultry, fish, and lean meats more often than canned, smoked, or processed types.
- If you're a fan of soy sauce or teri-yaki sauce, try a low-sodium version.
- Experiment with spices. Try fresh herbs in cooking, in salsa and dips, and in salads. Make your own blend of favorite herbs and spices. You might even consider growing a miniature herb garden on your kitchen windowsill so you'll have fresh herbs at hand year-round.
- Go for brown rice, whole-grain pasta, and whole-grain hot cereals cooked without salt.
- If you like tuna, buy water-packed and rinse the meat to remove some of the salt.
- Take the salt shaker off the table. Always taste your food before add-ing any salt.
- Choose only small portions of foods that are pickled, cured, in broth, or bathed in soy sauce, since these will have higher sodium contents.
- When dining out, ask that your food be prepared without added salt, monosodium glutamate (MSG), or high-sodium ingredients. If they won't accommodate your request, choose another restaurant next time.
- Try limiting salty condiments such as ketchup, mustard, pickles, and may-onnaise. Experiment: Try at least one bite of your food without condiments.

## SODIUM SURPRISES

| MINIMAL SODIUM | LOW SODIUM | MODERATE SODIUM | HIGH SODIUM |
|---|---|---|---|
| apple, 1 = 2 mg | applesauce, 1 cup = 6 mg | apple pie, ⅛ pie = 200 mg | apple turnover, 1 fast-food = 400 mg |
| low-sodium bread, 1 slice = 8 mg | white bread, 1 slice = 114 mg | pound cake, 1 slice = 170 mg | English muffin, 1 whole = 200 mg |
| olive oil, 1 tbsp = 0 mg | unsalted butter, 1 tbsp = 2 mg | butter, salted, 1 tbsp = 116 mg | margarine, 1 tbsp = 140 mg |
| fresh corn, 1 ear = 1 mg | frozen corn, 1 cup = 7 mg | corn flakes, 1 cup = 256 mg | canned corn, 1 cup = 384 mg |
| cucumber, 7 slices = 2 mg | sweet pickle, 1 = 128 mg | cucumber w/ salad dressing = 234 mg | dill pickle, 1 = 928 mg |
| lemon, 1 = 1 mg | ketchup, 1 tbsp = 156 mg | soy sauce, 1 tbsp = 1,029 mg | salt, 1 tbsp = 1,938 mg |
| potato, 1 = 5 mg | potato chips, 10 chips = 200 mg | mashed potatoes, instant, 1 cup = 485 mg | potato salad, ½ cup = 625 mg |
| tuna, fresh, 3 oz = 50 mg | tuna, canned, 3 oz = 384 mg | tuna pot pie, 1 frozen = 715 mg | fish sandwich, 1 fast-food = 882 mg |
| peanuts, unsalted, 1 cup = 8 mg | peanut butter, 1 tbsp = 81 mg | peanut brittle, 1 oz = 145 mg | dry roasted peanuts, salted, 1 cup = 986 mg |

If you still miss them, add on just enough to get a hint of their taste, but not so much that you hide the flavor of the food itself. If you don't like the taste of the food without the condiments, choose a different food next time—one whose unadorned flavor you do enjoy.

# falling for less fat

## More for less!

Eating less fat can do more than help lower your blood cholesterol and keep your heart and blood vessels healthy. Eating less fat can also help you control your weight, since fat packs more than twice the calories of protein or carbohydrate. And, as previously discussed, because fat can indirectly elevate blood glucose levels by blocking the action of insulin, eating less fat can help improve your blood glucose control.

The connection may not seem obvious, but if you have diabetes, you need to be concerned about your heart. People with diabetes are three times more likely to develop heart disease. One factor contributing to that increased risk is the high blood cholesterol common among people with type 2 diabetes (it's one of the metabolic syndrome conditions). So as you learn to choose healthier foods, it's important to keep your blood cholesterol level and your risk of heart disease in mind—and in check. To do so, research suggests you choose a diet in which less than 30 percent of calories comes from fat, and of that fat, very little comes from saturated and trans fats.

That's not to say fat is bad, of course. Fat provides energy, and we need some fat to absorb the fat-soluble vitamins A, D, E, and K. And no one can deny that fat adds flavor and juiciness to food. It's just that we tend to eat more of it than our bodies can handle in a healthy manner. And because we are inundated with processed foods, we tend to choose foods higher in the fats that can raise our cholesterol and damage our arteries.

To improve our fat choices, then, we need to understand our fat options. There are three main types of fats: saturated, monounsaturated, and polyunsaturated. The more saturated a fat is, the more detrimental it can be when eaten in excess. Too much saturated fat leads to more of those nasty little LDL molecules, the "bad" cholesterol that lingers in the bloodstream and makes damaging cholesterol deposits in our arteries. Monounsaturated fats have the opposite effect, lowering the number of LDL molecules. As for polyunsaturated fats, their effect depends on their type. One type, called omega 6 fatty acids, when eaten in large amounts, can cause water retention, raise blood pressure, increase blood clotting, and decrease "good" HDL cholesterol. The other type, omega 3 fatty acids, tends to lower blood cholesterol and heart disease risk by making blood less likely to clot. As for trans fats, they're created when unsaturated fats are "resaturated," making them more solid and increasing their shelf life but also making them act more like saturated fats in the body; they tend to raise total blood cholesterol.

While this may sound a bit complicated, it boils down to choosing more foods that have less total fat and substituting healthier fats for some of the saturated ones you usually eat. Here's some advice to guide you:

- Use this book and the labels on foods to help you opt more often for foods that have less total fat and less saturated fat.
- Spend more of your choices on a variety of fruits and vegetables, whole-grain products, beans, and nuts. Fruits and vegetables are naturally low in fat (if not slathered with fatty sauces) and provide loads of nutrients. Whole-grain foods and beans are low in fat but are nutrient dense and pack a load of fiber, which fills you up on fewer calories. And nuts, while not low in fat, are filled with mostly monounsaturated fats.
- Choose fish (its fat is mostly monounsaturated) more often than poultry (its fat is more saturated), and choose poultry (lower in saturated fat and usually lower in total fat) more often than beef (higher in saturated fats).
- Trim visible fat (it's saturated) from meat and fat and skin from poultry before eating. Instead of frying, which requires added fat, try baking, broiling, roasting, or grilling.
- Include fat-free and low-fat milk products.
- Choose fats and oils that are trans-fat free and have two grams or less

saturated fat per tablespoon, such as liquid and tub margarine, canola oil, and olive oil. (Try dipping fresh, crusty bread into olive oil instead of slathering it with butter.)

### WHERE ARE THEY?

| | |
|---|---|
| **Saturated fats** | Red meat, poultry, cheese, butter, and full-fat dairy products; some plant products, such as palm, coconut, and palm kernel oils |
| **Monounsaturated fats** | Olive, canola, and peanut oils; olives; avocados; most nuts, including almonds, cashews, pecans, and pistachios; and peanuts and natural peanut butter |
| **Polyunsaturated fats** | **Omega 6s:** Corn, sunflower, soybean, and cottonseed oils; MANY processed foods<br>**Omega 3s:** Many fish, including wild salmon, mackerel, sardines, herring, anchovies, rainbow trout, bluefish, caviar, white albacore tuna; canola oil; flaxseed and flaxseed oil; walnuts and walnut oil; and dark green, leafy vegetables |
| **Trans fats** | Many breads, crackers, cookies, doughnuts, frozen pie crusts, deep-fried foods, foods with chocolate coatings, fast foods, packaged and convenience foods, snack items such as chips, cake mixes, pastries, whipped toppings, nondairy creamers, shortening, and some margarines |

# weighing the benefits

By now you probably realize (or your doctor has told you) that being overweight—especially carrying too much fat in your abdominal area—hampers diabetes control. So you may be wondering where you'll find the weight-loss diet in this book. Well, you won't. It's not that we think weight loss is unimportant—far from it. It's just that a restrictive diet is not the best way to achieve the benefits of weight loss. For people with diabetes, the best path to weight loss is the same one that leads to getting well and staying well. It's the one you take each time you choose a healthier food or more physical activity. That's right! Rather than deprive yourself to achieve some ideal body size, you simply focus on making one simple choice at a time that will help you control your glucose, blood pressure, and cholesterol. Along the way, you leave an excess pound here, a little excess risk there, and you end up feeling better and more in control.

## losing weight does help

There's no denying weight loss is beneficial for people with type 2 diabetes who are overweight. But you don't need to lose 50 or 100 pounds to reap the benefits. Even a weight loss of just 5 to 10 percent of your total body weight can bring impressive improvements in your health. For a person who weighs 200 pounds, that's a weight loss of as little as ten pounds!

Studies show that when a person who has recently been diagnosed with diabetes loses weight, blood glucose levels drop, blood pressure improves, and cholesterol levels return to a healthier range. Medications may be decreased or even stopped altogether.

For a person with long-standing diabetes (of more than 8 to 12 years), weight loss causes the same improvements in glucose, blood pressure, and cholesterol, which can improve well-being and help delay complications. However, losing weight is no longer likely to mean less medication or a delay in the need for insulin. That's because diabetes is a progressive condition, and despite weight loss, over time the beta cells of the pancreas gradually fail. This is not a failure of the person or of the lifestyle changes; it's the sad nature of a progressive condition.

## so why not diet?

The reasons are many. An important one is that you're not trying to lose pounds to look better at a reunion or fit into swimwear. It's your health on the line. And when being healthier is your goal, it makes no sense to use unhealthy habits, like restricting foods or food groups, skipping meals, or depriving yourself of needed energy or nutrients, to reach it.

Besides, it's possible to be slimmer and still have the poor eating habits and inactive lifestyle that cause problems with glucose control, high blood pressure, and high blood cholesterol.

And diets simply don't work in the long run. Within two years of going off a diet, 70 percent of dieters will regain at least half their lost weight, and the five-year success rate of any diet is a measly 3 percent.

## what does work?

Basically, the same changes you need to make to improve your glucose control, including an overall diet that gets less than 30 percent of its calories from fat, but here are a few more tips:

**fill up on fiber.** Foods that are high in fiber can help you feel fuller longer on fewer calories and without increasing your blood sugar.

**think small.** Choose smaller, more reasonable portions of everything, served on smaller plates (never eat directly from a bag or box or while standing at the kitchen counter), and eat more slowly so you'll "hear it" when your stomach tells you that you're full.

**check your thirst.** Many people confuse feelings of thirst for hunger. So enjoy a large glass of ice water, hot tea, low-sodium broth, or another calorie-free beverage before reaching for food. You may discover that you were really just thirsty.

**make trades.** When you opt for a food or meal that's fat rich and/or calorie dense, choose other foods and meals that day that are low in fat and light in calories.

**add even more activity.** The more you move, the more you'll lose. We've pointed out that physical activity is an essential element in controlling diabetes. But every extra bit of planned exercise and even unplanned activity (running errands, taking stairs instead of elevators, parking farther from stores, etc.) helps burn calories.

# enjoy
# diabetic recipes

**Once you dig into** these delicious recipes, you'll be amazed that dishes so good for you could be so scrumptious. Each recipe comes with the nutritional information you need to determine how the food will affect your blood sugar as well as how it will fit your calorie, fat, and sodium goals. The nutritionals can also help you mix and match foods within a meal and throughout your day so your overall diet brings you better health and tighter control. Keep in mind that the nutritional analysis for each recipe is based on a single serving, does not include garnishes or optional ingredients, and, when a range is given for an ingredient, reflects the lesser amount. Meats were trimmed of all visible fat, and cooked rice and noodles were prepared without added salt and fat.

# breakfast & brunch

## farmstand frittata

### nutrients per serving:

1 frittata wedge
(¼ of total recipe)
Calories: 163
Carbohydrate: 19 g
Dietary Fiber: 2 g
Total Fat: 2 g
Calories From Fat: 12%
Saturated Fat: 1 g
Cholesterol: 8 mg
Sodium: 686 mg
Protein: 17 g

**Exchanges:** 1½ Starch,
1 Vegetable, 2 Lean Meat

**Nonstick cooking spray**
**½ cup chopped onion**
**1 medium red bell pepper, seeded and cut into thin strips**
**1 cup broccoli florets, blanched and drained**
**1 cup cooked, quartered unpeeled red potatoes**
**1 cup cholesterol-free egg substitute**
**6 egg whites**
**1 tablespoon chopped fresh parsley**
**½ teaspoon salt**
**¼ teaspoon black pepper**
**½ cup (2 ounces) shredded reduced-fat Cheddar cheese**

1. Spray large nonstick ovenproof skillet with cooking spray; heat over medium heat until hot. Add onion and bell pepper; cook and stir 3 minutes or until crisp-tender.

2. Add broccoli and potatoes; cook and stir 1 to 2 minutes or until heated through.

3. Whisk together egg substitute, egg whites, parsley, salt and black pepper in medium bowl.

4. Spread vegetables into even layer in skillet. Pour egg white mixture over vegetables; cover and cook over medium heat 10 to 12 minutes or until egg mixture is set.

5. Meanwhile, preheat broiler. Sprinkle frittata with cheese. Broil 4 inches from heat 1 minute or until cheese is melted. Cut into 4 wedges to serve.     *Makes 4 servings*

**farmstand frittata**

# brunch-time zucchini-date bread

**nutrients per serving:**

1 slice
(1/16 of loaf) with about
1 tablespoon spread
Calories: 124
Carbohydrate: 24 g
Dietary Fiber: 2 g
Total Fat: 1 g
Calories From Fat: 7%
Saturated Fat: <1 g
Cholesterol: 27 mg
Sodium: 260 mg
Protein: 5 g

**Exchanges:** 1½ Starch

**Bread**
- 1 cup chopped pitted dates
- 1 cup water
- 1 cup whole wheat flour
- 1 cup all-purpose flour
- 2 tablespoons granulated sugar
- 1 teaspoon baking powder
- ½ teaspoon baking soda
- ½ teaspoon salt
- ½ teaspoon ground cinnamon
- ¼ teaspoon ground cloves
- 2 eggs
- 1 cup shredded zucchini, pressed dry with paper towels

**Cream Cheese Spread**
- 1 package (8 ounces) fat-free cream cheese
- ¼ cup powdered sugar
- 1 tablespoon vanilla
- ⅛ teaspoon ground cinnamon
- Dash ground cloves

1. Preheat oven to 350°F. Spray 8×4×2-inch loaf pan with nonstick cooking spray.

2. For bread, combine dates and water in small saucepan. Bring to a boil over medium-high heat. Remove from heat; let stand 15 minutes.

3. Combine flours, granulated sugar, baking powder, baking soda, salt, cinnamon and ¼ teaspoon ground cloves in large bowl. Beat eggs in medium bowl; stir in date mixture and zucchini. Stir egg mixture into flour mixture just until dry ingredients are moistened. Pour batter evenly into prepared pan. Bake 30 to 35 minutes or until toothpick inserted into center comes out clean. Cool 5 minutes. Remove from pan. Cool completely on wire rack.

4. Meanwhile, prepare cream cheese spread. Combine cream cheese, powdered sugar, vanilla, cinnamon and dash ground cloves in small bowl. Beat until smooth. Cover and refrigerate until ready to use.

5. Cut bread into 16 slices. Serve with cream cheese spread. *Makes 16 servings*

**brunch-time zucchini-date bread**

# blueberry-sour cream corn muffins

**nutrients per serving:**

1 muffin with about 1 tablespoon spread
Calories: 150
Carbohydrate: 23 g
Dietary Fiber: 1 g
Total Fat: 4 g
Calories From Fat: 24%
Saturated Fat: 3 g
Cholesterol: 29 mg
Sodium: 252 mg
Protein: 5 g
**Exchanges:** 1 Starch, ½ Fruit, 1 Fat

**1 cup all-purpose flour**
**¾ cup cornmeal**
**2 teaspoons baking powder**
**½ teaspoon baking soda**
**¼ teaspoon salt**
**1 egg, beaten**
**1 cup reduced-fat sour cream**
**⅓ cup frozen unsweetened apple juice concentrate, thawed**
**1½ cups fresh or frozen (not thawed) blueberries**
**⅔ cup reduced-fat whipped cream cheese**
**2 tablespoons no-sugar-added blueberry fruit spread**

1. Preheat oven to 400°F. Spray 12 medium-size muffin cups with nonstick cooking spray, or line with paper liners; set aside.

2. Combine flour, cornmeal, baking powder, baking soda and salt in medium bowl. Add combined egg, sour cream and apple juice concentrate; mix just until dry ingredients are moistened. Gently stir in blueberries.

3. Spoon batter into prepared muffin cups, filling each cup ¾ full. Bake 18 to 20 minutes or until golden brown. Let stand in pan on wire rack 5 minutes. Remove from pan; cool slightly. Combine cream cheese and fruit spread in small serving bowl; serve with warm muffins.

*Makes 1 dozen muffins*

**blueberry-sour cream corn muffins**

# eggs primavera

**4 small round loaves (4 inches each) whole wheat bread**
   **Nonstick cooking spray**
**1½ cups chopped onions**
 **¾ cup chopped yellow summer squash**
 **¾ cup chopped zucchini**
 **½ cup chopped red bell pepper**
 **2 ounces snow peas, trimmed and cut diagonally into thirds**
 **¼ cup finely chopped fresh parsley**
**1½ teaspoons finely chopped fresh thyme *or* ¾ teaspoon dried thyme leaves**
 **1 teaspoon finely chopped fresh rosemary *or* ½ teaspoon dried rosemary leaves, crushed**
 **2 whole eggs**
 **4 egg whites**
 **¼ teaspoon black pepper**
 **½ cup (2 ounces) shredded reduced-fat Swiss cheese**

1. Preheat oven to 350°F. Slice top off each loaf of bread. Carefully hollow out each loaf, leaving sides and bottom ½ inch thick. Reserve centers for another use. Place loaves and tops, cut sides up, on baking sheet. Spray all surfaces of bread with cooking spray; bake 15 minutes or until well toasted.

2. Spray large nonstick skillet with cooking spray and heat over medium heat until hot. Add onions; cook and stir 3 minutes or until soft. Add yellow squash, zucchini and bell pepper; cook and stir 3 minutes or until crisp-tender. Add snow peas and herbs; cook and stir 1 minute.

3. Whisk eggs, egg whites and black pepper in small bowl until blended. Add to vegetable mixture; gently stir until eggs begin to set. Sprinkle cheese over top; gently stir until cheese melts and eggs are set but not dry.

4. Fill each bread bowl with ¼ of egg mixture, about 1 cup. Place tops back on bread bowls before serving. Garnish, if desired.                    *Makes 4 servings*

**eggs primavera**

# strawberry oat mini muffins

**nutrients per serving:**

3 mini muffins
Calories: 135
Carbohydrate: 23 g
Dietary Fiber: 2 g
Total Fat: 3 g
Calories From Fat: 21%
Saturated Fat: <1 g
Cholesterol: 1 mg
Sodium: 310 mg
Protein: 4 g

**Exchanges:** 1½ Starch, ½ Fat

  1 cup all-purpose flour
  ¾ cup uncooked oat bran cereal
2½ teaspoons baking powder
  ½ teaspoon baking soda
  ⅛ teaspoon salt
  ¾ cup buttermilk
  ⅓ cup frozen apple juice concentrate, thawed
  ⅓ cup unsweetened applesauce
  ½ teaspoon vanilla
  ¾ cup diced strawberries
  ¼ cup chopped pecans

1. Preheat oven to 400°F. Spray 24 miniature muffin cups with nonstick cooking spray.

2. Combine flour, oat bran, baking powder, baking soda and salt in medium bowl. Whisk together buttermilk, apple juice concentrate, applesauce and vanilla in small bowl.

3. Stir buttermilk mixture into flour mixture just until dry ingredients are almost moistened. Fold strawberries and pecans into batter. *Do not overmix.*

4. Spoon batter into muffin cups. Bake 17 to 18 minutes or until lightly browned and toothpick inserted into centers comes out clean. Let cool in pan 5 minutes; remove to wire racks. Serve warm or cool completely.

*Makes 2 dozen mini muffins*

**strawberry oat mini muffins**

nutrients per serving:

1 cup strata
Calories: 155
Carbohydrate: 20 g
Dietary Fiber: 3 g
Total Fat: 2 g
Calories From Fat: 12%
Saturated Fat: 1 g
Cholesterol: 8 mg
Sodium: 642 mg
Protein: 15 g

**Exchanges:** 1½ Starch, 2 Lean Meat

# brunch strata

**2 cups cholesterol-free egg substitute *or* 8 eggs**
**1 can (10¾ ounces) reduced-fat condensed cream of celery soup, undiluted**
**1 cup fat-free (skim) milk**
**1 can (4 ounces) sliced mushrooms, drained (optional)**
**¼ cup sliced green onions**
**1 teaspoon dry mustard**
**½ teaspoon salt (optional)**
**¼ teaspoon black pepper**
**6 slices reduced-fat white bread, cut into 1-inch cubes**
**4 links reduced-fat precooked breakfast sausage, thinly sliced**

1. Preheat oven to 350°F. Spray 2-quart baking dish with nonstick cooking spray; set aside.

2. Combine egg substitute, soup, milk, mushrooms, if desired, green onions, mustard, salt, if desired, and pepper in medium bowl; mix well.

3. Combine bread cubes, sausage and soup mixture in prepared baking dish; toss to coat. Bake 35 to 40 minutes or until set. Garnish as desired.

*Makes 6 servings*

## tip

Look for the words "light," "lite," "reduced-fat" or "fat-free" when you're shopping for the ingredients in this recipe.

**brunch strata**

# scrambled egg burritos

**Nonstick cooking spray**
**1 medium red bell pepper, chopped**
**5 green onions, sliced**
**½ teaspoon red pepper flakes**
**1 cup cholesterol-free egg substitute *or* 8 egg whites**
**1 tablespoon chopped fresh cilantro or parsley**
**4 (8-inch) flour tortillas**
**½ cup (2 ounces) shredded low-sodium reduced-fat Monterey Jack cheese**
**⅓ cup salsa**

1. Spray medium nonstick skillet with cooking spray. Heat over medium heat until hot. Add bell pepper, green onions and red pepper flakes; cook and stir 3 minutes or until vegetables are crisp-tender.

2. Add egg substitute to vegetables. Reduce heat to low. Cook and stir 3 minutes or until set. Sprinkle with cilantro.

3. Stack tortillas and wrap in paper towels. Microwave at HIGH 1 minute or until tortillas are hot.

4. Place ¼ egg mixture on each tortilla. Sprinkle with 2 tablespoons cheese. Fold sides over to enclose filling. Serve with salsa.                      *Makes 4 servings*

# tip

Store the cilantro or parsley for this recipe in a tall glass in the refrigerator. Fill the glass with enough cold water to cover about 1 inch of the stems, then top the leaves with a plastic bag. Use a rubber band to attach the bag to the top of the glass.

**scrambled egg burrito**

## nutrients per serving:

1 frittata wedge
(¼ of total recipe)

Calories: 129
Carbohydrate: 14 g
Dietary Fiber: 2 g
Total Fat: 3 g
Calories From Fat: 22%
Saturated Fat: 1 g
Cholesterol: 108 mg
Sodium: 371 mg
Protein: 12 g

**Exchanges:** ½ Starch,
1 Vegetable, 1 Lean Meat

# spicy mexican frittata

**1 fresh jalapeño pepper***
**1 clove garlic**
**1 medium tomato, peeled, halved, quartered and seeded**
**½ teaspoon ground coriander**
**½ teaspoon chili powder**
**Nonstick cooking spray**
**½ cup chopped onion**
**1 cup frozen corn**
**6 egg whites**
**2 eggs**
**¼ cup fat-free (skim) milk**
**¼ teaspoon salt**
**¼ teaspoon black pepper**
**¼ cup (1 ounce) shredded part-skim farmer or mozzarella cheese**

*Jalapeño peppers can sting and irritate the skin. Wear rubber gloves when handling peppers and do not touch eyes. Wash hands after handling peppers.*

1. Place jalapeño pepper and garlic in food processor or blender. Cover; process until finely chopped. Add tomato, coriander and chili powder. Cover; process until tomato is almost smooth.

2. Spray large skillet with cooking spray; heat over medium heat until hot. Cook and stir onion until tender. Stir in tomato mixture and corn; cook 3 to 4 minutes or until liquid is almost evaporated, stirring occasionally.

3. Combine egg whites, eggs, milk, salt and black pepper in medium bowl. Add egg mixture all at once to skillet. Cook, without stirring, 2 minutes or until eggs begin to set. Run large spoon around edge of skillet, lifting eggs for even cooking. Remove skillet from heat when eggs are almost set but surface is still moist.

4. Sprinkle with cheese. Cover; let stand 3 to 4 minutes or until surface is set and cheese is melted. Cut into 4 wedges.                    *Makes 4 servings*

**spicy mexican frittata**

# snacks & appetizers

## veggie quesadilla appetizers

**10 (8-inch) flour tortillas**
**1 cup finely chopped broccoli**
**1 cup thinly sliced small mushrooms**
**¾ cup shredded carrots**
**¼ cup chopped green onions**
**1¼ cups (5 ounces) reduced-fat sharp Cheddar cheese**
**2 cups Zesty Pico de Gallo (recipe follows)**

1. Brush both sides of tortillas lightly with water. Heat small nonstick skillet over medium heat until hot. Heat tortillas, one at a time, 30 seconds on each side. Divide vegetables among 5 tortillas; sprinkle evenly with cheese. Top with remaining 5 tortillas.

2. Cook quesadillas, one at a time, in large nonstick skillet or on griddle over medium heat 2 minutes on each side or until surface is crisp and cheese is melted.

3. Cut each quesadilla into 4 wedges. Serve with Zesty Pico de Gallo.

*Makes 20 servings*

## zesty pico de gallo

**2 cups chopped seeded tomatoes**
**1 cup chopped green onions**
**1 can (8 ounces) tomato sauce**
**½ cup minced fresh cilantro**
**1 to 2 tablespoons minced jalapeño peppers***
**1 tablespoon fresh lime juice**

*\*Jalapeño peppers can sting and irritate the skin. Wear rubber gloves when handling peppers and do not touch eyes. Wash hands after handling peppers.*

Combine all ingredients in medium bowl. Cover and refrigerate at least 1 hour.

*Makes about 4 cups*

**veggie quesadilla appetizer**

nutrients per serving:

1 mini pizza
Calories: 64
Carbohydrate: 9 g
Dietary Fiber: <1 g
Total Fat: 2 g
Calories From Fat: 23%
Saturated Fat: 1 g
Cholesterol: 4 mg
Sodium: 211 mg
Protein: 3 g

**Exchanges:** ½ Starch, ½ Fat

# lox and cheese mini pizzas

**New York-Style Pizza Crust (page 148)**
**4 ounces reduced-fat cream cheese**
**2 tablespoons finely chopped red onion**
**1 tablespoon fresh lemon juice**
**2 teaspoons grated fresh lemon peel**
**1½ teaspoons olive oil**
**4 ounces thinly sliced lox or smoked salmon**
**Black pepper**
**1 tablespoon small capers, 2 teaspoons snipped fresh chives *or* 20 tiny sprigs fresh dill, for garnish (optional)**

1. Prepare New York-Style Pizza Crust as directed through step 2. Preheat oven to 500°F. Lightly grease 2 large baking sheets; set aside.

2. Combine cream cheese, onion, lemon juice and lemon peel in small bowl; set aside.

3. Roll dough into 10-inch log on lightly floured surface. Cut log into 20 (½-inch-thick) slices. Pat slices into 2¼- to 2½-inch discs. Place slightly apart on prepared baking sheets. Pierce discs several times with fork; brush evenly with oil. Bake, 1 sheet at a time, 6 minutes or until light golden. Transfer to wire rack to cool slightly.

4. Spoon about 1 teaspoon cream cheese mixture onto center of each warm crust. Spread over surface, leaving ¼-inch border. Cut lox into 2-inch pieces. Place over cream cheese. Sprinkle with pepper. Garnish, if desired.          *Makes 20 mini pizzas*

**Note:** To prepare the mini pizza crusts in advance, let the baked crusts cool completely on wire racks after being removed from the oven. Store the crusts in an airtight container at room temperature for up to one day.

*continued on page 148*

**lox and cheese mini pizza**

*lox and cheese mini pizzas, continued*

## new york-style pizza crust

**⅔ cup warm water (110°F to 115°F)**
**1 teaspoon sugar**
**½ (¼-ounce) package rapid-rise or active dry yeast**
**1¾ cups all-purpose or bread flour plus additional for kneading**
**½ teaspoon salt**
**1 tablespoon cornmeal (optional)**

1. Combine water and sugar in small bowl; stir to dissolve sugar. Sprinkle yeast over top; stir to combine. Let stand 5 to 10 minutes or until foamy.

2. Combine flour and salt in medium bowl. Stir in yeast mixture. Mix until mixture forms soft dough. Remove dough to lightly floured surface. Knead 5 minutes or until dough is smooth and elastic, adding additional flour, 1 tablespoon at a time, as needed. Place dough in medium bowl coated with nonstick cooking spray. Turn dough in bowl so top is coated with cooking spray; cover with towel or plastic wrap. Let rise in warm place 30 minutes or until doubled in bulk. Punch dough down; place on lightly floured surface and knead about 2 minutes or until smooth.

3. Pat dough into flat disc about 7 inches in diameter. Let rest 2 to 3 minutes. Pat and gently stretch dough from edges until dough seems to not stretch anymore. Let rest 2 to 3 minutes. Continue patting and stretching until dough is 12 to 14 inches in diameter.

4. Spray 12- to 14-inch pizza pan with nonstick cooking spray; sprinkle with cornmeal, if desired. Press dough into pan.

5. Preheat oven to 500°F. Follow directions for individual recipes, baking pizza on bottom rack of oven.

*Makes 20 (2½-inch) mini pizza crusts, 1 medium-thin 12-inch crust, 1 very thin 14-inch crust, 2 (8- to 9-inch) crusts or 4 (6- to 7- inch) crusts*

# cheesy potato skin appetizers

**⅔ cup Zesty Pico de Gallo (page 144) or purchased salsa**
**5 potatoes (4 to 5 ounces each)**
   **Butter-flavored nonstick cooking spray**
**4 ounces fat-free cream cheese**
**2 tablespoons reduced-fat sour cream**
**⅓ cup (about 1.3 ounces) shredded reduced-fat sharp Cheddar cheese**
**2 tablespoons sliced ripe olives (optional)**
**¼ cup minced fresh cilantro**

1. Prepare Zesty Pico de Gallo; set aside.

2. Preheat oven to 425°F. Scrub potatoes; pierce several times with fork. Bake 45 minutes or until soft. Cool.

3. Split each potato lengthwise into halves. Scoop out potato with spoon, leaving ¼-inch-thick shell. (Reserve potato for another use, if desired.) Place potato skins on baking sheet; spray lightly with cooking spray.

4. Preheat broiler. Broil potato skins 6 inches from heat 5 minutes or until lightly browned and crisp.

5. Preheat oven to 350°F. Combine cream cheese and sour cream in small bowl; stir until well blended. Divide evenly among potato skins; spread to cover. Top with Zesty Pico do Gallo, cheese and olives, if desired. Bake 15 minutes or until heated through. Sprinkle with cilantro. *Makes 10 servings*

## nutrients per serving:

1 potato skin appetizer with about 1 tablespoon pico de gallo

Calories: 86
Carbohydrate: 15 g
Dietary Fiber: 3 g
Total Fat: 1 g
Calories From Fat: 10%
Saturated Fat: 1 g
Cholesterol: 4 mg
Sodium: 149 mg
Protein: 4 g

**Exchanges:** 1 Starch, ½ Lean Meat

# portobello mushrooms sesame

**4 large portobello mushrooms**
**2 tablespoons sweet rice wine**
**2 tablespoons reduced-sodium soy sauce**
**2 cloves garlic, minced**
**1 teaspoon dark sesame oil**

1. Remove and discard stems from mushrooms; set caps aside. Combine remaining ingredients in small bowl.

2. Brush both sides of mushroom caps with soy sauce mixture. Grill mushrooms, top sides up, on covered grill over medium coals 3 to 4 minutes. Brush tops with soy sauce mixture and turn over; grill 2 minutes more or until mushrooms are lightly browned. Turn again and grill, basting frequently, 4 to 5 minutes or until tender when pressed with back of metal spatula. Remove mushrooms; cut diagonally into ½-inch-thick slices.

*Makes 4 servings*

**nutrients per serving:**

1 grilled mushroom cap
Calories: 67
Carbohydrate: 9 g
Dietary Fiber: <1 g
Total Fat: 2 g
Calories From Fat: 21%
Saturated Fat: <1 g
Cholesterol: 0 mg
Sodium: 268 mg
Protein: 4 g

**Exchanges:** 2 Vegetable, ½ Fat

# mediterranean pita pizzas

**1 cup canned cannellini beans, rinsed and drained**
**2 teaspoons lemon juice**
**2 medium cloves garlic, minced**
**2 (8-inch) pita bread rounds**
**1 teaspoon olive oil**
**½ cup thinly sliced radicchio or escarole lettuce (optional)**
**½ cup chopped seeded tomato**
**½ cup finely chopped red onion**
**¼ cup (1 ounce) crumbled feta cheese**
**2 tablespoons thinly sliced pitted black olives**

1. Preheat oven to 450°F. Place beans in small bowl; mash lightly with fork. Stir in lemon juice and garlic.

2. Arrange pita rounds on baking sheet; brush tops with oil. Bake 6 minutes.

3. Spread bean mixture onto pita rounds to within ½ inch of edges. Arrange remaining ingredients on pitas. Bake 5 minutes or until topping is thoroughly heated and crust is crisp. Cut each pizza into 4 wedges. Serve hot. *Makes 8 servings*

**nutrients per serving:**

1 pizza wedge
Calories: 98
Carbohydrate: 14 g
Dietary Fiber: 2 g
Total Fat: 3 g
Calories From Fat: 29%
Saturated Fat: 1 g
Cholesterol: 7 mg
Sodium: 282 mg
Protein: 4 g

**Exchanges:** 1 Starch, ½ Fat

**portobello mushrooms sesame**

# señor nacho dip

**4 ounces fat-free cream cheese**
**½ cup (2 ounces) shredded reduced-fat Cheddar cheese**
**¼ cup mild or medium chunky salsa**
**2 teaspoons reduced-fat (2%) milk**
**4 ounces baked tortilla chips or assorted fresh vegetable dippers**

1. Combine cream cheese and Cheddar cheese in small saucepan; cook and stir over low heat until melted. Stir in salsa and milk; heat thoroughly, stirring occasionally.

2. Transfer dip to small serving bowl. Serve with tortilla chips. Garnish with hot peppers and cilantro, if desired. *Makes 4 servings*

**Olé Dip:** Substitute reduced-fat Monterey Jack cheese or reduced-fat taco cheese for Cheddar cheese.

**Spicy Mustard Dip:** Omit tortilla chips. Substitute 2 teaspoons spicy brown mustard or honey mustard for salsa. Serve with fresh vegetable dippers or pretzels.

nutrients per serving:
about 3½ tablespoons dip with 10 tortilla chips
Calories: 181
Carbohydrate: 25 g
Dietary Fiber: 2 g
Total Fat: 4 g
Calories From Fat: 18%
Saturated Fat: 1 g
Cholesterol: 11 mg
Sodium: 629 mg
Protein: 11 g
**Exchanges:** 1½ Starch, 1 Lean Meat

# california rolls

**1 cup reduced-fat ricotta cheese**
**2 (11-inch) flour tortillas**
**1 medium tomato, thinly sliced**
**2 cups stemmed, washed and torn fresh spinach leaves**
**1 cup chopped onion**
**½ teaspoon dried oregano leaves**
**½ teaspoon dried basil leaves**
**1 cup alfalfa sprouts**
**4 ounces sliced turkey breast**

Spread cheese evenly over tortillas to within ¼ inch of edges. Layer tomato, spinach, onion, oregano, basil, alfalfa sprouts and turkey over ⅔ of each tortilla. Roll up tortillas. Wrap in plastic wrap; refrigerate 1 hour. Cut each rolled tortilla crosswise into 10 slices before serving. *Makes 4 servings*

nutrients per serving:
5 rolls
Calories: 209
Carbohydrate: 28 g
Dietary Fiber: 2 g
Total Fat: 4 g
Calories From Fat: 17%
Saturated Fat: <1 g
Cholesterol: 28 mg
Sodium: 233 mg
Protein: 16 g
**Exchanges:** 1½ Starch, 1 Vegetable, 1½ Lean Meat

**señor nacho dip**

## nutrients per serving:

1 baguette slice

Calories: 98

Carbohydrate: 14 g

Dietary Fiber: 1 g

Total Fat: 3 g

Calories From Fat: 25%

Saturated Fat: 1 g

Cholesterol: 7 mg

Sodium: 239 mg

Protein: 4 g

**Exchanges:** 1 Starch, ½ Fat

# stuffed party baguette

**2 medium red bell peppers**
**1 French bread loaf (about 14 inches long)**
**¼ cup plus 2 tablespoons prepared fat-free Italian dressing, divided**
**1 small red onion, very thinly sliced**
**8 large fresh basil leaves**
**3 ounces Swiss cheese, very thinly sliced**

1. Preheat oven to 425°F. Cover large baking sheet with foil; set aside.

2. To roast bell peppers, cut peppers in half; remove stems, seeds and membranes. Place peppers, cut sides down, on prepared baking sheet. Bake 20 to 25 minutes or until skins are browned, turning occasionally.

3. Transfer peppers from baking sheet to paper bag; close bag tightly. Let stand 10 minutes or until peppers are cool enough to handle and skins are loosened. Using sharp knife, peel off skins; discard skins. Cut peppers into strips.

4. Trim ends from bread; discard. Cut loaf lengthwise in half. Remove soft insides of loaf; reserve removed bread for another use, if desired.

5. Brush ¼ cup Italian dressing evenly onto cut sides of bread. Arrange pepper strips in even layer in bottom half of loaf; top with even layer of onion. Brush onion with remaining 2 tablespoons Italian dressing; top with layer of basil and cheese. Replace bread top. Wrap loaf tightly in heavy-duty plastic wrap; refrigerate at least 2 hours or overnight.

6. When ready to serve, remove plastic wrap. Cut loaf crosswise into 1-inch slices. Secure with toothpicks and garnish, if desired.             *Makes 12 servings*

**stuffed party baguette**

# spicy orange chicken kabob appetizers

        2 boneless skinless chicken breasts (4 ounces each)
        1 small red or green bell pepper
       24 small fresh button mushrooms
        ½ cup orange juice
        2 tablespoons reduced-sodium soy sauce
        1 tablespoon vegetable oil
       1½ teaspoons onion powder
        ½ teaspoon Chinese five-spice powder

1. Cut chicken and pepper each into 24 (¾-inch) square pieces. Place chicken, pepper and mushrooms in large resealable plastic food storage bag. Combine orange juice, soy sauce, oil, onion powder and five-spice powder in small bowl. Pour over chicken mixture. Close bag securely; turn to coat. Marinate in refrigerator 4 to 24 hours, turning frequently.

2. Soak 24 small wooden skewers or toothpicks in water 20 minutes. Meanwhile, preheat broiler. Coat broiler pan with nonstick cooking spray.

3. Drain chicken, pepper and mushrooms, reserving marinade. Thread 1 piece chicken, 1 piece pepper and 1 mushroom onto each skewer. Place on prepared pan. Brush with marinade; discard remaining marinade. Broil 4 inches from heat 5 to 6 minutes or until chicken is no longer pink in center. Serve immediately.     *Makes 12 servings*

**nutrients per serving:**

2 kabobs
Calories: 30
Carbohydrate: 2 g
Dietary Fiber: <1 g
Total Fat: <1 g
Calories From Fat: 26%
Saturated Fat: <1 g
Cholesterol: 10 mg
Sodium: 38 mg
Protein: 4 g
**Exchanges:** ½ Lean Meat

# snackin' cinnamon popcorn

        3 to 4 teaspoons brown sugar substitute
       1½ teaspoons salt
       1½ teaspoons cinnamon
        8 cups hot air-popped popcorn
          Butter-flavored nonstick cooking spray

1. Combine brown sugar substitute, salt and cinnamon in small bowl; mix well.

2. Spread hot popped popcorn onto jelly-roll pan. Coat popcorn with cooking spray; immediately sprinkle cinnamon mixture over top. Serve immediately or store in container at room temperature up to 2 days.     *Makes 4 servings*

**nutrients per serving:**

2 cups popcorn
Calories: 63
Carbohydrate: 13 g
Dietary Fiber: 3 g
Total Fat: 1 g
Calories From Fat: 9%
Saturated Fat: <1 g
Cholesterol: 0 mg
Sodium: 873 mg
Protein: 2 g
**Exchanges:** 1 Starch

**spicy orange chicken kabob appetizers**

# oven-fried tex-mex onion rings

½ cup plain dry bread crumbs
⅓ cup yellow cornmeal
1½ teaspoons chili powder
⅛ to ¼ teaspoon ground red pepper
⅛ teaspoon salt
1 tablespoon plus 1½ teaspoons margarine, melted
1 teaspoon water
2 medium onions (about 10 ounces), sliced ⅜ inch thick
2 egg whites

1. Preheat oven to 450°F. Spray large nonstick baking sheet with nonstick cooking spray; set aside.

2. Combine bread crumbs, cornmeal, chili powder, ground red pepper and salt in medium shallow dish; mix well. Stir in margarine and water.

3. Separate onion slices into rings. Place egg whites in large bowl; beat lightly. Add onions; toss lightly to coat evenly. Transfer to bread crumb mixture; toss to coat evenly. Place in single layer on prepared baking sheet. Bake 12 to 15 minutes or until onions are tender and coating is crisp.

*Makes 6 servings*

**nutrients per serving:**

about 8 onion rings
Calories: 111
Carbohydrate: 16 g
Dietary Fiber: 2 g
Total Fat: 4 g
Calories From Fat: 30%
Saturated Fat: 1 g
Cholesterol: 0 mg
Sodium: 188 mg
Protein: 4 g
**Exchanges:** 1 Starch, ½ Fat

# rock 'n' rollers

4 (6- to 7-inch) flour tortillas
4 ounces Neufchâtel cheese, softened
⅓ cup peach preserves
1 cup (4 ounces) shredded fat-free Cheddar cheese
½ cup packed stemmed and washed fresh spinach leaves
3 ounces thinly sliced regular or smoked turkey breast

1. Spread each tortilla evenly with 1 ounce Neufchâtel cheese; cover with thin layer of preserves. Sprinkle with ¼ cup Cheddar cheese.

2. Arrange spinach leaves and turkey over Cheddar cheese. Roll up tortillas; trim ends. Cover and refrigerate until ready to serve.

3. Cut "rollers" crosswise in half or diagonally into 1-inch pieces.

*Makes 4 servings*

**nutrients per serving:**

2 rock 'n' roller halves
Calories: 315
Carbohydrate: 41 g
Dietary Fiber: 2 g
Total Fat: 9 g
Calories From Fat: 26%
Saturated Fat: 5 g
Cholesterol: 31 mg
Sodium: 865 mg
Protein: 17 g
**Exchanges:** 2½ Starch, 1 Lean Meat, 1½ Fat

**oven-fried tex-mex onion rings**

nutrients per serving:

1 smoked salmon appetizer
Calories: 80
Carbohydrate: 10 g
Dietary Fiber: 1 g
Total Fat: 2 g
Calories From Fat: 21%
Saturated Fat: 1 g
Cholesterol: 6 mg
Sodium: 241 mg
Protein: 6 g

**Exchanges:** ½ Starch, ½ Lean Meat

# smoked salmon appetizers

¼ cup reduced-fat or fat-free cream cheese, softened
1 tablespoon chopped fresh dill *or* 1 teaspoon dried dill weed
⅛ teaspoon ground red pepper
4 ounces thinly sliced smoked salmon or lox
24 melba toast rounds or other low-fat crackers
Fresh dill sprigs, for garnish (optional)

1. Combine cream cheese, dill and red pepper in small bowl; stir to blend. Spread evenly over each slice of salmon. Roll up salmon slices jelly-roll fashion. Place on plate; cover with plastic wrap. Chill at least 1 hour or up to 4 hours before serving.

2. Using sharp knife, cut salmon rolls crosswise into ¾-inch pieces. Place pieces, cut side down, on melba rounds. Garnish each salmon roll with dill sprig, if desired. Serve cold or at room temperature.            *Makes about 2 dozen appetizers*

nutrients per serving:

6 nachos
Calories: 176
Carbohydrate: 23 g
Dietary Fiber: 2 g
Total Fat: 5 g
Calories From Fat: 26%
Saturated Fat: 2 g
Cholesterol: 16 mg
Sodium: 683 mg
Protein: 10 g

**Exchanges:** 1½ Starch, 1 Lean Meat

# super nachos

12 large baked low-fat tortilla chips (about 1½ ounces)
½ cup (2 ounces) shredded reduced-fat Cheddar cheese
¼ cup fat-free refried beans
2 tablespoons chunky salsa

**Microwave Directions**

1. Arrange chips in single layer on large microwavable plate. Sprinkle cheese evenly over chips. Spoon 1 teaspoon beans over each chip; top with ½ teaspoon salsa.

2. Microwave at MEDIUM (50% power) 1½ minutes; rotate dish. Microwave 1 to 1½ minutes more or until cheese is melted.            *Makes 2 servings*

**Conventional Directions:** Substitute foil-covered baking sheet for microwavable plate. Assemble nachos as directed on prepared baking sheet. Bake at 350°F 10 to 12 minutes or until cheese is melted.

**smoked salmon appetizers**

# spicy vegetable quesadillas

nutrients per serving:

1 quesadilla
(3 wedges)
Calories: 153
Carbohydrate: 23 g
Dietary Fiber: 1 g
Total Fat: 4 g
Calories From Fat: 22%
Saturated Fat: 1 g
Cholesterol: 8 mg
Sodium: 201 mg
Protein: 7 g

**Exchanges:** 1½ Starch,
½ Vegetable, ½ Lean Meat

**Nonstick cooking spray**
**1 small zucchini, chopped**
**½ cup *each* chopped onion and chopped green bell pepper**
**2 cloves garlic, minced**
**½ teaspoon *each* chili powder and ground cumin**
**8 (6-inch) flour tortillas**
**1 cup (4 ounces) shredded reduced-fat Cheddar cheese**
**¼ cup chopped fresh cilantro**

1. Spray large nonstick skillet with cooking spray. Heat over medium heat until hot. Add zucchini, onion, bell pepper, garlic, chili powder and cumin; cook and stir 3 to 4 minutes or until vegetables are crisp-tender. Remove vegetables; set aside. Wipe skillet clean.

2. Spoon vegetable mixture evenly over half of each tortilla. Sprinkle each evenly with cheese and cilantro. Fold each tortilla in half.

3. Spray same skillet with cooking spray. Add tortillas; heat 1 to 2 minutes per side over medium heat or until lightly browned. Cut into thirds before serving.

*Makes 8 servings*

# avocado salsa

nutrients per serving:

2 tablespoons salsa
Calories: 13
Carbohydrate: 1 g
Dietary Fiber: <1 g
Total Fat: 1 g
Calories From Fat: 60%
Saturated Fat: <1 g
Cholesterol: 0 mg
Sodium: 38 mg
Protein: <1 g

**Exchanges:** Free

**1 medium avocado, peeled and diced**
**1 cup chopped seeded peeled cucumber**
**1 cup chopped onion**
**1 Anaheim chili, seeded and chopped***
**½ cup chopped fresh tomato**
**2 tablespoons chopped fresh cilantro**
**½ teaspoon salt**
**¼ teaspoon hot pepper sauce**

*\*Chili peppers can sting and irritate the skin. Wear rubber gloves when handling peppers and do not touch eyes. Wash hands after handling chili peppers.*

Combine avocado, cucumber, onion, chili, tomato, cilantro, salt and hot pepper sauce in medium bowl; mix well. Refrigerate, covered, at least 1 hour to allow flavors to blend. Serve as dip or condiment.

*Makes about 32 servings (4 cups)*

**spicy vegetable quesadillas**

# light lunches

nutrients per serving:

⅙ of total recipe (with 2 tablespoons dressing)

Calories: 182
Carbohydrate: 19 g
Dietary Fiber: 4 g
Total Fat: 2 g
Calories From Fat: 10%
Saturated Fat: 1 g
Cholesterol: 38 mg
Sodium: 140 mg
Protein: 22 g

**Exchanges:** ½ Fruit, 2 Vegetable, 2 Lean Meat

## mandarin turkey salad with buttermilk-herb dressing

**Buttermilk-Herb Dressing (recipe follows)**
**1 can (about 14 ounces) fat-free reduced-sodium chicken broth**
**1¼ pounds turkey tenderloins, cut in half lengthwise**
**½ teaspoon dried basil leaves**
**½ pound (about 8 cups) mesclun salad greens, washed and dried**
**2 pounds (about 10 cups) raw cut-up vegetables such as broccoli florets, red or yellow bell peppers, carrots and red onion**
**1 can (11 ounces) mandarin orange segments, drained**

1. Prepare Buttermilk-Herb Dressing; set aside.

2. Place broth in medium saucepan; bring to a boil over high heat. Add turkey and basil. Return to a boil; reduce heat. Simmer, covered, 12 to 14 minutes or until turkey is no longer pink.

3. Remove turkey from broth. When cool enough to handle, shred turkey into strips.

4. Arrange salad greens on individual plates. Divide turkey evenly over salad greens. Arrange vegetables and orange segments around turkey. Drizzle each serving with 2 tablespoons Buttermilk-Herb Dressing. *Makes 6 servings*

## buttermilk-herb dressing

**½ cup plus 1 tablespoon nonfat buttermilk**
**3 tablespoons raspberry-flavored vinegar**
**1 tablespoon chopped fresh basil leaves**
**1½ teaspoons snipped fresh chives**
**¼ teaspoon minced garlic**

Place all ingredients in small bowl; stir to combine. Store, covered, in refrigerator up to 2 days. *Makes about ¾ cup*

**mandarin turkey salad with buttermilk-herb dressing**

# tangy italian chicken sandwiches

nutrients per serving:
2 filled pita halves
Calories: 330
Carbohydrate: 39 g
Dietary Fiber: 6 g
Total Fat: 7 g
Calories From Fat: 20%
Saturated Fat: 3 g
Cholesterol: 53 mg
Sodium: 610 mg
Protein: 28 g
**Exchanges:** 2½ Starch, 2 Lean Meat, ½ Fat

    **2 cups (8 ounces) chopped cooked boneless skinless chicken or turkey breast**
    **⅓ cup drained bottled hot or mild pickled vegetables (jardinière)**
    **2 ounces reduced-fat provolone cheese slices, diced**
    **¼ cup chopped fresh parsley**
    **3 tablespoons prepared reduced-fat Italian salad dressing**
    **¼ teaspoon dried oregano leaves**
    **4 pita bread rounds (2 ounces each)**
    **8 leaves romaine or red leaf lettuce**

1. Combine chicken, pickled vegetables, cheese, parsley, dressing and oregano in medium bowl; mix well.

2. Cut pitas in half crosswise; gently open. Line each half with lettuce leaf. Divide chicken mixture evenly among pita pockets. *Makes 4 servings*

# garden tuna salad

nutrients per serving:
1 pita half with about ½ cup tuna salad, 1 lettuce leaf and 1 tomato slice
Calories: 213
Carbohydrate: 22 g
Dietary Fiber: 4 g
Total Fat: 6 g
Calories From Fat: 23%
Saturated Fat: 2 g
Cholesterol: 24 mg
Sodium: 605 mg
Protein: 19 g
**Exchanges:** 1½ Starch, 2 Lean Meat

    **1 can (6 ounces) tuna packed in water, drained**
    **1 medium carrot, chopped**
    **1 rib celery, chopped**
    **½ cup reduced-fat Monterey Jack cheese cubes (¼ inch each)**
    **¼ cup frozen green peas, thawed and drained**
    **¼ teaspoon dried parsley flakes**
    **⅓ cup prepared reduced-fat Italian salad dressing**
    **2 pita bread rounds (2 ounces each)**
    **4 lettuce leaves**
    **4 tomato slices**

1. Place tuna in large bowl; break into chunks. Add carrot, celery, cheese, peas and parsley; toss to blend. Pour dressing over tuna mixture; toss lightly to coat.

2. Cut each pita in half crosswise; gently open. Place lettuce leaf and tomato slice in each pita half. Divide tuna salad evenly among pita pockets. *Makes 4 servings*

**tangy italian chicken sandwiches**

# turkey vegetable chili mac

**nutrients per serving:**

1 bowl chili mac (⅙ of total recipe)

Calories: 236

Carbohydrate: 34 g

Dietary Fiber: 6 g

Total Fat: 6 g

Calories From Fat: 21%

Saturated Fat: 1 g

Cholesterol: 25 mg

Sodium: 445 mg

Protein: 17 g

**Exchanges:** 1½ Starch, 2 Vegetable, 1 Lean Meat, ½ Fat

**Nonstick cooking spray**
**¾ pound 93% lean ground turkey**
**½ cup chopped onion**
**2 cloves garlic, minced**
**1 can (about 15 ounces) black beans, rinsed and drained**
**1 can (14½ ounces) Mexican-style stewed tomatoes, undrained**
**1 can (14½ ounces) no-salt-added diced tomatoes, undrained**
**1 cup frozen corn**
**1 teaspoon Mexican seasoning**
**½ cup uncooked elbow macaroni**
**⅓ cup reduced-fat sour cream**

1. Spray large nonstick saucepan or Dutch oven with cooking spray; heat over medium heat until hot. Add turkey, onion and garlic; cook and stir 5 minutes or until turkey is no longer pink.

2. Stir beans, tomatoes with juice, corn and Mexican seasoning into saucepan; bring to a boil over high heat. Cover; reduce heat to low. Simmer 15 minutes, stirring occasionally.

3. Meanwhile, cook pasta according to package directions, omitting salt. Rinse and drain pasta; stir into saucepan. Simmer, uncovered, 2 to 3 minutes or until heated through.

4. Top each serving with dollop of sour cream. Garnish as desired.

*Makes 6 servings*

**turkey vegetable chili mac**

# raspberry mango salad

**nutrients per serving:**

¼ of total recipe
Calories: 98
Carbohydrate: 12 g
Dietary Fiber: 2 g
Total Fat: 8 g
Calories From Fat: 74%
Saturated Fat: 3 g
Cholesterol: 8 mg
Sodium: 227 mg
Protein: 3 g
**Exchanges:** ½ Vegetable, 2 Fat

**2 cups arugula**
**1 cup torn Bibb or Boston lettuce**
**1 cup diced mango**
**¾ cup fresh raspberries**
**½ cup watercress, stems removed**
**¼ cup (1½ ounces) crumbled blue cheese**
**1 tablespoon olive oil**
**1 tablespoon water**
**1 tablespoon raspberry vinegar**
**⅛ teaspoon salt**
**⅛ teaspoon black pepper**

1. Combine arugula, lettuce, mango, raspberries, watercress and cheese in medium bowl.

2. Place remaining ingredients in small jar; shake to combine. Pour over salad; toss to coat. Serve immediately.

*Makes 4 servings*

# vegetable-chicken noodle soup

**nutrients per serving:**

about 1 cup soup
Calories: 98
Carbohydrate: 12 g
Dietary Fiber: 1 g
Total Fat: 2 g
Calories From Fat: 14%
Saturated Fat: <1 g
Cholesterol: 18 mg
Sodium: 73 mg
Protein: 10 g
**Exchanges:** ½ Starch, ½ Vegetable, 1 Lean Meat

**¼ cup chopped celery**
**¼ cup thinly sliced leek (white part only)**
**¼ cup chopped carrot**
**¼ cup chopped turnip**
**3 cups fat-free reduced-sodium chicken broth, divided**
**1 teaspoon minced fresh parsley**
**½ teaspoon fresh thyme *or* pinch dried thyme leaves**
**½ teaspoon fresh rosemary *or* pinch dried rosemary leaves, crushed**
**½ teaspoon balsamic vinegar**
**⅛ teaspoon black pepper**
**½ ounce uncooked yolk-free wide noodles**
**¼ cup diced cooked boneless skinless chicken breast**

1. Place celery, leek, carrot, turnip and ⅓ cup broth in medium saucepan. Cover; cook over medium heat 12 to 15 minutes or until vegetables are tender, stirring occasionally.

2. Stir in remaining broth, parsley, thyme, rosemary, vinegar and pepper; bring to a boil. Add noodles; cook until noodles are tender. Stir in chicken. Reduce heat to medium; simmer until heated through.

*Makes 2 servings*

**raspberry mango salad**

# tuscan chicken with white beans

nutrients per serving:

1½ cups soup
Calories: 215
Carbohydrate: 24 g
Dietary Fiber: 7 g
Total Fat: 6 g
Calories From Fat: 25%
Saturated Fat: 2 g
Cholesterol: 34 mg
Sodium: 321 mg
Protein: 17 g

**Exchanges:** 1 Starch,
1½ Vegetable,
2 Lean Meat

**1 large fresh fennel bulb (about ¾ pound)**
**1 teaspoon olive oil**
**8 ounces boneless skinless chicken thighs, cut into ¾-inch pieces**
**1 teaspoon dried rosemary leaves, crushed**
**½ teaspoon black pepper**
**1 can (14½ ounces) no-salt-added stewed tomatoes, undrained**
**1 can (about 14 ounces) fat-free reduced-sodium chicken broth**
**1 can (about 15 ounces) cannellini beans, rinsed and drained**
**Hot pepper sauce (optional)**

1. Cut off and reserve ¼ cup chopped feathery fennel tops. Chop bulb into ½-inch pieces. Heat oil in large saucepan over medium heat. Add chopped fennel bulb; cook 5 minutes, stirring occasionally.

2. Sprinkle chicken with rosemary and pepper; add to saucepan. Cook and stir 2 minutes. Add tomatoes with juice and chicken broth; bring to a boil. Cover and simmer 10 minutes. Stir in beans; simmer, uncovered, 15 minutes or until chicken is cooked through and sauce thickens. Season to taste with hot sauce, if desired. Ladle into 4 shallow bowls; top with reserved fennel tops. *Makes 4 servings*

# chunky chicken stew

nutrients per serving:

1 bowl stew
(½ of total recipe)
Calories: 287
Carbohydrate: 31 g
Dietary Fiber: 8 g
Total Fat: 6 g
Calories From Fat: 18%
Saturated Fat: 1 g
Cholesterol: 66 mg
Sodium: 337 mg
Protein: 30 g

**Exchanges:** 6 Vegetable,
3 Lean Meat

**1 teaspoon olive oil**
**1 small onion, chopped**
**1 cup thinly sliced carrots**
**1 cup fat-free reduced-sodium chicken broth**
**1 can (14½ ounces) no-salt-added diced tomatoes, undrained**
**1 cup diced cooked chicken breast**
**3 cups sliced kale or baby spinach leaves**

1. Heat oil in large saucepan over medium-high heat. Add onion; cook and stir about 5 minutes or until golden brown. Stir in carrots, then broth; bring to a boil.

2. Reduce heat; simmer, uncovered, 5 minutes. Add tomatoes with juice; simmer 5 minutes or until carrots are tender. Add chicken; heat through. Add kale, stirring until kale is wilted. Simmer 1 minute. Ladle into 2 soup bowls. *Makes 2 servings*

**tuscan chicken with white beans**

nutrients per serving:

1 filled pepper (without cheese topping)
Calories: 216
Carbohydrate: 27 g
Dietary Fiber: 2 g
Total Fat: 4 g
Calories From Fat: 16%
Saturated Fat: 1 g
Cholesterol: 26 mg
Sodium: 574 mg
Protein: 19 g

**Exchanges:** 1 Starch, 2 Vegetable, 2 Lean Meat

# pasta and tuna filled peppers

¾ **cup uncooked ditalini pasta**
4 **large green bell peppers**
1 **cup chopped seeded fresh tomatoes**
1 **can (6 ounces) white tuna packed in water, drained and flaked**
½ **cup chopped celery**
½ **cup (2 ounces) shredded reduced-fat Cheddar cheese**
¼ **cup fat-free mayonnaise or salad dressing**
1 **teaspoon salt-free garlic and herb seasoning**
2 **tablespoons shredded reduced-fat Cheddar cheese (optional)**

**Microwave Directions**

1. Cook pasta according to package directions, omitting salt. Rinse and drain. Set aside.

2. Cut thin slice from top of each pepper. Remove seeds and membranes from insides of peppers. Rinse peppers; place, cut side down, on paper towels to drain.*

3. Combine cooked pasta, tomatoes, tuna, celery, ½ cup cheese, mayonnaise and seasoning in large bowl until well blended; spoon evenly into pepper shells.

4. Place peppers on large microwavable plate; cover with waxed paper. Microwave at HIGH 7 to 8 minutes, turning halfway through cooking time. Top evenly with remaining 2 tablespoons cheese before serving, if desired. Garnish as desired.

*Makes 4 servings*

*For more tender peppers, cook in boiling water 2 minutes. Rinse with cold water; drain upside down on paper towels before filling.*

**pasta and tuna filled pepper**

nutrients per serving:

1 sandwich
Calories: 282
Carbohydrate: 37 g
Dietary Fiber: 7 g
Total Fat: 7 g
Calories From Fat: 19%
Saturated Fat: 1 g
Cholesterol: 47 mg
Sodium: 282 mg
Protein: 27 g

**Exchanges:** 2 Starch,
1½ Vegetable,
2 Lean Meat

# turkey sandwiches with roasted bell peppers

**2 large red bell peppers**
**8 slices whole-grain or millet bread**
**¼ cup reduced-fat mayonnaise**
**4 romaine lettuce leaves** *or* **8 spinach leaves**
**8 thin slices red onion**
**8 ounces thinly sliced skinless roasted turkey breast**
**8 large basil leaves (optional)**

1. Preheat broiler. Cut bell peppers into quarters; discard stems, membranes and seeds. Place peppers, skin side up, on foil-lined baking sheet. Broil 3 inches from heat 10 minutes or until skin is blackened. Wrap peppers in foil from baking sheet; let stand 10 minutes. Peel off and discard skin.

2. Spread 4 bread slices with mayonnaise. Top with lettuce, onion, turkey, peppers and basil, if desired. Top with remaining 4 bread slices.          *Makes 4 servings*

## tip

Cool and Creamy Pea Salad with Cucumbers and Red Onion (page 208) makes a great side dish for this healthy, tasty sandwich.

**turkey sandwich with roasted bell peppers**

# grilled mozzarella & roasted red pepper sandwich

**nutrients per serving:**

1 sandwich
(2 sandwich halves)
Calories: 303
Carbohydrate: 35 g
Dietary Fiber: 2 g
Total Fat: 9 g
Calories From Fat: 29%
Saturated Fat: 5 g
Cholesterol: 25 mg
Sodium: 727 mg
Protein: 16 g

**Exchanges:** 2 Starch, 1 Vegetable, 1 Lean Meat, 1½ Fat

> **1 tablespoon reduced-fat olive oil vinaigrette or prepared reduced-fat Italian salad dressing**
> **2 slices (2 ounces) Italian-style sandwich bread**
> **Basil leaves (optional)**
> **⅓ cup roasted red peppers, rinsed, drained and patted dry**
> **2 slices (1 ounce each) part-skim mozzarella or reduced-fat Swiss cheese**
> **Nonstick olive oil cooking spray**

1. Brush dressing onto one side of one slice of bread; top with basil, if desired, peppers, cheese and second bread slice. Lightly spray both sides of sandwich with cooking spray.

2. Heat skillet over medium heat until hot. Place sandwich in skillet; grill 4 to 5 minutes on each side or until brown and cheese is melted. Cut in half before serving, if desired.

*Makes 1 sandwich*

# sunburst chicken salad

**nutrients per serving:**

½ of total recipe
Calories: 195
Carbohydrate: 18 g
Dietary Fiber: 2 g
Total Fat: 6 g
Calories From Fat: 29%
Saturated Fat: 1 g
Cholesterol: 39 mg
Sodium: 431 mg
Protein: 18 g

**Exchanges:** 1 Fruit, 2 Lean Meat, ½ Fat

> **1 tablespoon fat-free mayonnaise**
> **1 tablespoon fat-free sour cream**
> **2 teaspoons frozen orange juice concentrate, thawed**
> **¼ teaspoon grated fresh orange peel**
> **1 boneless skinless chicken breast, cooked and chopped**
> **1 large kiwi, thinly sliced**
> **⅓ cup canned mandarin oranges, drained**
> **¼ cup finely chopped celery**
> **4 lettuce leaves, washed**
> **2 tablespoons coarsely chopped cashews**

Combine mayonnaise, sour cream, orange juice concentrate and orange peel in small bowl. Add chicken, kiwi, oranges and celery; toss to coat. Cover; refrigerate 2 hours. Serve on lettuce leaves. Top with cashews.

*Makes 2 servings*

**grilled mozzarella & roasted red pepper sandwich**

# crab spinach salad with tarragon dressing

nutrients per serving:

¼ of total recipe
Calories: 170
Carbohydrate: 14 g
Dietary Fiber: 4 g
Total Fat: 4 g
Calories From Fat: 18%
Saturated Fat: <1 g
Cholesterol: 91 mg
Sodium: 481 mg
Protein: 22 g

**Exchanges:** 2 Vegetable, 2½ Lean Meat

**12 ounces coarsely flaked cooked crabmeat**
 **1 cup chopped tomatoes**
 **1 cup sliced cucumber**
 **⅓ cup sliced red onion**
 **¼ cup fat-free salad dressing or mayonnaise**
 **¼ cup reduced-fat sour cream**
 **¼ cup chopped fresh parsley**
 **2 tablespoons fat-free (skim) milk**
 **2 teaspoons chopped fresh tarragon** *or* **½ teaspoon dried
     tarragon leaves**
 **1 clove garlic, minced**
 **¼ teaspoon hot pepper sauce**
 **8 cups torn washed stemmed spinach**

1. Combine crabmeat, tomatoes, cucumber and onion in medium bowl. Combine salad dressing, sour cream, parsley, milk, tarragon, garlic and hot pepper sauce in small bowl.

2. Line four salad plates with spinach. Place crabmeat mixture on spinach; drizzle with dressing. *Makes 4 servings*

# grilled portobello open-faced sandwich

nutrients per serving:

1 sandwich
Calories: 155
Carbohydrate: 17 g
Dietary Fiber: 1 g
Total Fat: 8 g
Calories From Fat: 44%
Saturated Fat: 1 g
Cholesterol: 2 mg
Sodium: 300 mg
Protein: 4 g

**Exchanges:** 1 Starch, 1 Vegetable, 1½ Fat

**1 portobello mushroom cap, rinsed and stem removed**
**2 teaspoons balsamic vinegar**
**1 tablespoon prepared pesto sauce**
**1 slice bread, toasted**
**1 teaspoon grated Parmesan cheese**

1. Preheat broiler. Sprinkle mushroom cap with balsamic vinegar. Place on rack under broiler about 4 inches from heat. Cook 3 to 4 minutes on each side or until tender.

2. Spread pesto onto toast. Top with mushroom cap and sprinkle with Parmesan cheese. Serve immediately. *Makes 1 serving*

**crab spinach salad with tarragon dressing**

# pizza turnovers

**5 ounces reduced-fat mild Italian bulk turkey sausage**
**½ cup prepared pizza sauce**
**1 package (10 ounces) refrigerated pizza dough**
**⅓ cup shredded reduced-fat Italian cheese blend**

1. Preheat oven to 425°F. Cook and stir sausage in nonstick saucepan over medium-high heat until browned. Drain fat. Add pizza sauce. Cook and stir until hot.

2. Spray baking sheet with nonstick olive oil cooking spray. Unroll pizza dough onto baking sheet. Pat into 12×8-inch rectangle. Cut into 6 (4×4-inch) squares. Divide sausage mixture evenly among squares. Sprinkle with cheese. Lift 1 corner of each square; fold over filling to opposite corner. Press edges with tines of fork to seal.

3. Bake 11 to 13 minutes or until golden brown. Serve immediately or follow directions for freezing and reheating.                    *Makes 6 servings*

**Note:** To freeze turnovers, remove to wire rack to cool 30 minutes. Individually wrap in plastic wrap, or place in freezer container or plastic freezer bag and freeze. To reheat, preheat oven to 400°F. Unwrap turnovers. Place in ungreased baking pan. Cover loosely with foil. Bake 18 to 22 minutes or until hot. Or, place one turnover on a paper-towel-lined microwavable plate. Heat on DEFROST (30% power) 3 to 3½ minutes or until hot, turning once.

**nutrients per serving:**

1 turnover
Calories: 188
Carbohydrate: 24 g
Dietary Fiber: 3 g
Total Fat: 6 g
Calories From Fat: 28%
Saturated Fat: 2 g
Cholesterol: 17 mg
Sodium: 502 mg
Protein: 10 g

**Exchanges:** 1½ Starch, ½ Vegetable, ½ Lean Meat, ½ Fat

# salmon pasta salad

**1 cup cooked medium pasta shells**
**1 can (6 ounces) canned red salmon, rinsed and drained**
**½ cup finely chopped celery**
**2 tablespoons finely chopped red bell pepper**
**2 tablespoons chopped fresh parsley**
**2 tablespoons fat-free mayonnaise**
**1 green onion, finely chopped**
**1 tablespoon lemon juice**
**2 teaspoons capers**
**⅛ teaspoon paprika**

Combine all ingredients in medium bowl. Cover; refrigerate before serving.
                    *Makes 2 servings*

**nutrients per serving:**

½ of total recipe
Calories: 262
Carbohydrate: 26 g
Dietary Fiber: 2 g
Total Fat: 9 g
Calories From Fat: 32%
Saturated Fat: 2 g
Cholesterol: 21 mg
Sodium: 627 mg
Protein: 18 g

**Exchanges:** 1½ Starch, 1 Vegetable, 2 Lean Meat, ½ Fat

**pizza turnovers**

# broiled turkey burgers

**nutrients per serving:**

1 sandwich
(without toppings)
Calories: 243
Carbohydrate: 20 g
Dietary Fiber: 0 g
Total Fat: 3 g
Calories From Fat: 12%
Saturated Fat: 1 g
Cholesterol: 74 mg
Sodium: 384 mg
Protein: 31 g

**Exchanges:** 1½ Starch,
3½ Lean Meat

    **1 pound 93% lean ground turkey**
    **¼ cup finely chopped green onions**
    **¼ cup finely chopped fresh parsley**
    **2 tablespoons dry red wine**
    **1 teaspoon dried Italian seasoning**
    **¼ teaspoon salt**
    **¼ teaspoon black pepper**
    **4 whole wheat hamburger buns**
      **Toppings: lettuce, grilled pineapple slices and bell pepper strips (optional)**

1. Preheat broiler.

2. Combine turkey, green onions, parsley, wine, Italian seasoning, salt and black pepper in large bowl; mix well. Shape turkey mixture into 4 (¾-inch-thick) burgers.

3. Spray rack of broiler pan with nonstick cooking spray; place burgers on rack. Broil burgers 4 inches from heat 5 to 6 minutes per side or until no longer pink in center. Serve on whole wheat buns with lettuce, grilled pineapple slices and bell pepper strips, if desired.

*Makes 4 servings*

# black and white chili

**nutrients per serving:**

1 cup chili
Calories: 260
Carbohydrate: 34 g
Dietary Fiber: 8 g
Total Fat: 2 g
Calories From Fat: 6%
Saturated Fat: <1 g
Cholesterol: 44 mg
Sodium: 403 mg
Protein: 27 g

**Exchanges:** 2 Starch,
½ Vegetable, 2 Lean Meat

    **Nonstick cooking spray**
    **1 pound chicken tenders, cut into ¾-inch pieces**
    **1 cup coarsely chopped onion**
    **1 can (15½ ounces) Great Northern beans, rinsed and drained**
    **1 can (15 ounces) black beans, rinsed and drained**
    **1 can (14½ ounces) Mexican-style stewed tomatoes, undrained**
    **2 tablespoons Texas-style chili powder seasoning mix**

1. Spray large saucepan with cooking spray; heat over medium heat until hot. Add chicken and onion; cook and stir over medium to medium-high heat 5 to 8 minutes or until chicken is browned.

2. Stir beans, tomatoes with juice and seasoning mix into saucepan; bring to a boil. Reduce heat to low; simmer, uncovered, 10 minutes.

*Makes 6 servings*

**broiled turkey burger**

# main dishes

## browned pork chops with gravy

**nutrients per serving:**

1 pork chop with ½ cup noodles and ¼ of gravy
Calories: 315
Carbohydrate: 30 g
Dietary Fiber: 2 g
Total Fat: 10 g
Calories From Fat: 29%
Saturated Fat: 3 g
Cholesterol: 67 mg
Sodium: 296 mg
Protein: 25 g

**Exchanges:** 1½ Starch, 1 Vegetable, 3 Lean Meat

  **4 boneless pork loin chops (about ¾ pound)**
½ **teaspoon dried sage leaves**
½ **teaspoon dried marjoram leaves**
¼ **teaspoon black pepper**
⅛ **teaspoon salt**
  **Nonstick olive oil cooking spray**
¼ **cup coarsely chopped onion**
  **1 clove garlic, minced**
  **1 cup sliced mushrooms**
¾ **cup beef broth**
⅓ **cup fat-free sour cream**
  **1 tablespoon all-purpose flour**
  **1 teaspoon Dijon mustard**
  **2 cups hot cooked noodles**
  **Snipped parsley (optional)**

**1.** Trim fat from chops. Combine sage, marjoram, pepper and salt in small bowl; rub on both sides of chops. Spray large nonstick skillet with cooking spray; heat over medium heat. Place chops in skillet. Cook 5 minutes, turning once, or until chops are just barely pink. Remove chops from skillet; keep warm.

**2.** Add onion and garlic to skillet; cook and stir 2 minutes. Add mushrooms and broth. Bring to a boil. Reduce heat; simmer, covered, 3 to 4 minutes or until mushrooms are tender.

**3.** Whisk together sour cream, flour and mustard in medium bowl. Whisk in about 3 tablespoons broth mixture from skillet. Stir sour cream mixture into skillet. Cook, stirring constantly, until mixture comes to a boil. Serve over pork chops and noodles. Sprinkle with parsley, if desired. *Makes 4 servings*

**browned pork chop with gravy**

# lemon-dijon chicken with potatoes

**2 medium lemons**
**½ cup chopped fresh parsley**
**2 tablespoons Dijon mustard**
**4 cloves garlic, minced**
**2 teaspoons extra-virgin olive oil**
**1 teaspoon dried rosemary leaves, crushed**
**¾ teaspoon black pepper**
**½ teaspoon salt**
**1 whole chicken (about 3½ pounds)**
**1½ pounds small red potatoes, cut into halves**

1. Preheat oven to 350°F.

2. Squeeze 3 tablespoons juice from lemons; reserve squeezed lemon halves. Combine parsley, lemon juice, mustard, garlic, oil, rosemary, pepper and salt in small bowl; blend well. Reserve 2 tablespoons mixture.

3. Place chicken on rack in baking pan. Gently slide fingers between skin and meat of chicken breasts and drumsticks to separate skin from meat, being careful not to tear skin. Spoon parsley mixture between skin and meat. (Secure breast skin with toothpicks, if necessary.) Discard any remaining parsley mixture (not reserved 2 tablespoons). Place lemon halves in cavity of chicken. Bake 30 minutes.

4. Meanwhile, toss potatoes with reserved parsley mixture until coated. Arrange potatoes around chicken; bake 1 hour or until juices in chicken run clear and thermometer inserted into thickest part of thigh registers 180°F. Remove chicken from oven; let stand 10 minutes. Remove skin; discard. Slice chicken. Sprinkle any accumulated parsley mixture from pan over chicken and potatoes. *Makes 6 servings*

**lemon-dijon chicken with potatoes**

# teriyaki salmon with asian slaw

**nutrients per serving:**

1 salmon fillet with about 2 cups slaw

Calories: 354
Carbohydrate: 32 g
Dietary Fiber: 5 g
Total Fat: 11 g
Calories From Fat: 28%
Saturated Fat: 2 g
Cholesterol: 75 mg
Sodium: 730 mg
Protein: 32 g

**Exchanges:** 1 Starch, 4 Vegetable, 3½ Lean Meat

**4 tablespoons light teriyaki sauce, divided**
**2 (5- to 6-ounce) boneless salmon fillets with skin (1 inch thick)**
**2½ cups packaged coleslaw mix**
**1 cup fresh or frozen snow peas, cut lengthwise into thin strips**
**½ cup thinly sliced radishes**
**2 tablespoons orange marmalade**
**1 teaspoon dark sesame oil**

1. Preheat broiler or prepare grill for direct cooking. Spoon 2 tablespoons teriyaki sauce over fleshy sides of salmon. Let stand while preparing vegetable mixture.

2. Combine coleslaw mix, snow peas and radishes in large bowl. Combine remaining 2 tablespoons teriyaki sauce, marmalade and sesame oil in small bowl. Add to coleslaw mixture; toss well.

3. Broil salmon 4 to 5 inches from heat source or grill, flesh side down, over medium coals, without turning, 6 to 10 minutes or until center is opaque.

4. Transfer coleslaw mixture to serving plates; top with salmon.     *Makes 2 servings*

# fajita-seasoned grilled chicken

**nutrients per serving:**

1 chicken breast

Calories: 176
Carbohydrate: 8 g
Dietary Fiber: 2 g
Total Fat: 8 g
Calories From Fat: 39%
Saturated Fat: 1 g
Cholesterol: 43 mg
Sodium: 186 mg
Protein: 19 g

**Exchanges:** 1½ Vegetable, 2½ Lean Meat, ½ Fat

**2 boneless skinless chicken breasts (about 4 ounces each)**
**1 bunch green onions, ends trimmed**
**1 tablespoon olive oil**
**2 teaspoons fajita seasoning mix**

1. Preheat grill for direct cooking.

2. Brush chicken and green onions with oil. Sprinkle both sides of chicken breasts with seasoning mix. Grill chicken and onions 6 to 8 minutes or until chicken is no longer pink in center. Serve chicken with onions.     *Makes 2 servings*

**teriyaki salmon with asian slaw**

nutrients per serving:

1 lamb chop with ¼ cup chutney

Calories: 260
Carbohydrate: 24 g
Dietary Fiber: 2 g
Total Fat: 8 g
Calories From Fat: 28%
Saturated Fat: 3 g
Cholesterol: 71 mg
Sodium: 293 mg
Protein: 22 g

**Exchanges:** 1½ Fruit, 3 Lean Meat

# lamb chops with cranberry-pear chutney

**Chutney**
   ½ cup water
   ¼ cup dried cranberries
   ¼ cup dried apricots, cut into quarters
   ¼ cup no-sugar-added raspberry spread
   1 tablespoon red wine vinegar
   ¼ teaspoon ground cinnamon
   ⅛ teaspoon salt
   1 medium pear, peeled and cut into ½-inch pieces
   ½ teaspoon vanilla

**Lamb**
   4 bone-in lamb loin chops (about 5 ounces each)
   2 cloves garlic, minced
   ¼ teaspoon dried rosemary leaves, crushed
   ¼ teaspoon salt
   Black pepper

1. Preheat broiler. For chutney, combine water, cranberries, apricots, raspberry spread, vinegar, cinnamon and ⅛ teaspoon salt in medium saucepan; bring to a boil over high heat. Reduce heat to medium-low; simmer, uncovered, 12 minutes or until mixture is thickened. Remove from heat; stir in pear and vanilla.

2. For lamb, rub both sides of chops with garlic. Sprinkle with rosemary, ¼ teaspoon salt and pepper. Coat broiler pan and rack with nonstick cooking spray. Place lamb on rack; broil at least 5 inches from heat source 7 minutes; turn and broil 7 minutes more or until of desired doneness. Serve lamb chops with chutney. *Makes 4 servings*

**lamb chop with cranberry-pear chutney**

# fresh vegetable lasagna

**8 ounces uncooked lasagna noodles**
**1 package (10 ounces) frozen chopped spinach, thawed and well drained**
**1 cup shredded carrots**
**½ cup sliced green onions**
**½ cup sliced red bell pepper**
**¼ cup chopped fresh parsley**
**½ teaspoon black pepper**
**1½ cups low-fat (1%) cottage cheese**
**1 cup buttermilk**
**½ cup plain nonfat yogurt**
**2 egg whites**
**1 cup sliced mushrooms**
**1 can (14 ounces) artichoke hearts, drained and chopped**
**2 cups (8 ounces) shredded part-skim mozzarella cheese, divided**
**¼ cup freshly grated Parmesan cheese**

1. Cook pasta according to package directions, omitting salt; drain. Rinse under cold water; drain well. Set aside.

2. Preheat oven to 375°F. Pat spinach with paper towels to remove excess moisture. Combine spinach, carrots, green onions, bell pepper, parsley and black pepper in large bowl; set aside.

3. Combine cottage cheese, buttermilk, yogurt and egg whites in food processor or blender. Cover; process until smooth.

4. Spray 13×9-inch baking pan with nonstick cooking spray. Arrange third of lasagna noodles in bottom of pan. Spread with half of cottage cheese mixture, half of vegetable mixture, half of mushrooms, half of artichokes and ¾ cup mozzarella. Repeat layers, ending with noodles. Sprinkle with remaining ½ cup mozzarella and Parmesan.

5. Cover; bake 30 minutes. Remove cover; continue baking 20 minutes or until bubbly and heated through. Remove from oven; let stand 10 minutes. Cut into 8 pieces to serve.

*Makes 8 servings*

**fresh vegetable lasagna**

# oven-fried chicken

**nutrients per serving:**

1 chicken breast plus 1 drumstick

Calories: 208
Carbohydrate: 14 g
Dietary Fiber: 1 g
Total Fat: 4 g
Calories From Fat: 18%
Saturated Fat: 1 g
Cholesterol: 75 mg
Sodium: 348 mg
Protein: 27 g

**Exchanges:** 1 Starch, 3 Lean Meat

**2 boneless skinless chicken breasts (about 4 ounces each)**
**4 small skinless chicken drumsticks (about 2½ ounces each)**
**3 tablespoons all-purpose flour**
**½ teaspoon poultry seasoning**
**¼ teaspoon garlic salt**
**¼ teaspoon black pepper**
**1½ cups cornflakes, crushed**
**1 tablespoon dried parsley flakes**
**1 egg white**
**1 tablespoon water**
**Nonstick cooking spray**

**1.** Preheat oven to 375°F. Rinse chicken; pat dry with paper towels. Trim fat from chicken; discard.

**2.** Combine flour, poultry seasoning, garlic salt and pepper in large resealable plastic food storage bag. Combine cornflake crumbs and parsley in small shallow bowl. Whisk together egg white and water in small bowl.

**3.** Add chicken to flour mixture, one or two pieces at a time. Seal bag; shake until chicken is well coated. Remove chicken from bag, shaking off excess flour. Dip into egg white mixture, coating all sides. Roll in crumb mixture. Place in shallow baking pan. Repeat with remaining chicken, flour mixture, egg white and crumb mixture.

**4.** Lightly spray chicken pieces with cooking spray. Bake breasts 18 to 20 minutes or until no longer pink in center. Bake drumsticks about 25 minutes or until juices run clear.

*Makes 4 servings*

**oven-fried chicken**

# seared pork roast with currant cherry salsa

nutrients per serving:

3 ounces cooked pork with 1 tablespoon drippings and 3 tablespoons salsa
Calories: 217
Carbohydrate: 10 g
Dietary Fiber: 1 g
Total Fat: 9 g
Calories From Fat: 38%
Saturated Fat: 3 g
Cholesterol: 72 mg
Sodium: 300 mg
Protein: 23 g

**Exchanges:** 1 Fruit, 3 Lean Meat

1½ **teaspoons chili powder**
¼ **teaspoon salt**
½ **teaspoon garlic powder**
½ **teaspoon paprika**
¼ **teaspoon ground allspice**
 1 **boneless pork loin roast (2 pounds)**
  **Nonstick cooking spray**
½ **cup water**
 1 **bag (1 pound) frozen pitted dark cherries, thawed, drained and halved**
¼ **cup currants or dark raisins**
 1 **teaspoon balsamic vinegar**
 1 **teaspoon grated orange peel**
⅛ **to** ¼ **teaspoon red pepper flakes**

**Slow Cooker Directions**

1. Combine chili powder, salt, garlic powder, paprika and allspice in small bowl. Coat roast evenly with spice mixture, pressing spices into roast.

2. Spray large skillet with cooking spray; heat over medium-high heat. Brown roast on all sides. Place in 4-quart slow cooker.

3. Pour water into skillet, stirring to scrape up browned bits. Pour into slow cooker around roast. Cover; cook on LOW 6 to 8 hours or until pork reaches 160°F. (For tender pork, do not cook on HIGH.)

4. Remove roast from slow cooker. Tent with foil; keep warm. Strain juices from slow cooker; discard solids. Pour juice into small saucepan; keep warm over low heat.

5. *Turn slow cooker to HIGH.* Add cherries, currants, vinegar, orange peel and red pepper flakes. Cover; cook 30 minutes. Slice pork and spoon warm juices over meat. Serve with salsa. *Makes 8 servings*

**Note:** To thicken the salsa, mix 1 teaspoon cornstarch with 1 tablespoon water. Stir into the cherry mixture. Cook, uncovered, on HIGH until thickened.

**seared pork roast with currant cherry salsa**

# sassy chicken & peppers

**2 teaspoons Mexican seasoning***
**2 boneless skinless chicken breasts (about 4 ounces each)**
**2 teaspoons vegetable oil**
**1 small red onion, sliced**
**½ medium red bell pepper, cut into thin strips**
**½ medium yellow or green bell pepper, cut into long, thin strips**
**¼ cup chunky salsa or chipotle salsa**
**1 tablespoon lime juice**
**Lime wedges, for garnish (optional)**

*If Mexican seasoning is not available, substitute 1 teaspoon chili powder, ½ teaspoon ground cumin, ½ teaspoon salt and ⅛ teaspoon ground red pepper.*

1. Sprinkle seasoning over both sides of chicken.

2. Heat oil in large nonstick skillet over medium heat. Add onion; cook 3 minutes, stirring occasionally.

3. Add bell pepper strips; cook 3 minutes, stirring occasionally.

4. Push vegetables to edge of skillet. Add chicken to skillet. Cook 5 minutes; turn. Stir salsa and lime juice into vegetables. Continue to cook 4 minutes or until chicken is no longer pink in center and vegetables are tender.

5. Transfer chicken to serving plates; top with vegetable mixture. Garnish with lime wedges, if desired.                    *Makes 2 servings*

**sassy chicken & peppers**

# cannelloni with tomato-eggplant sauce

nutrients per serving:

2 filled manicotti shells with about ½ cup sauce and ¼ cup mozzarella cheese (2 tablespoons per shell)

Calories: 338
Carbohydrate: 40 g
Dietary Fiber: 3 g
Total Fat: 7 g
Calories From Fat: 19%
Saturated Fat: 4 g
Cholesterol: 26 mg
Sodium: 632 mg
Protein: 30 g

**Exchanges:** 1½ Starch, 3 Vegetable, 3 Lean Meat

  **1 package (10 ounces) fresh spinach, stemmed**
  **1 cup fat-free ricotta cheese**
  **4 egg whites, beaten**
  **¼ cup grated Parmesan cheese**
  **2 tablespoons finely chopped fresh parsley**
  **½ teaspoon salt (optional)**
  **8 manicotti shells (about 4 ounces uncooked), cooked (without added salt) and cooled**
  **Tomato-Eggplant Sauce (recipe follows)**
  **1 cup (4 ounces) shredded reduced-fat mozzarella cheese**

1. Preheat oven to 350°F. Wash spinach; do not pat dry. Place spinach in large saucepan; cook, covered, over medium-high heat 3 to 5 minutes or until spinach is wilted. Cool slightly; drain. Chop finely.

2. Combine ricotta cheese, spinach, egg whites, Parmesan cheese, parsley and salt, if desired, in large bowl; mix well. Spoon mixture into cooked manicotti shells; arrange in 13×9-inch baking pan. Spoon Tomato-Eggplant Sauce over manicotti; sprinkle with mozzarella cheese. Bake, uncovered, 25 to 30 minutes or until hot and bubbly.
*Makes 4 servings*

# tomato-eggplant sauce

  **Nonstick olive oil cooking spray**
  **1 small eggplant, coarsely chopped**
  **½ cup chopped onion**
  **2 cloves garlic, minced**
  **½ teaspoon dried tarragon leaves**
  **¼ teaspoon dried thyme leaves**
  **1 can (16 ounces) no-salt-added whole tomatoes, undrained, coarsely chopped**

1. Spray large skillet with cooking spray; heat over medium heat until hot. Add eggplant, onion, garlic, tarragon and thyme; cook and stir about 5 minutes or until vegetables are tender.

2. Stir in tomatoes with juice; bring to a boil. Reduce heat; simmer, uncovered, 3 to 4 minutes.
*Makes about 2½ cups*

**cannelloni with tomato-eggplant sauce**

# beef tenderloin with roasted vegetables

**1 beef tenderloin roast (about 3 pounds), trimmed of fat**
**½ cup chardonnay or other dry white wine**
**½ cup reduced-sodium soy sauce**
**2 cloves garlic, sliced**
**1 tablespoon fresh rosemary**
**1 tablespoon Dijon mustard**
**1 teaspoon dry mustard**
**1 pound small red or white potatoes, cut into 1-inch pieces**
**1 pound brussels sprouts**
**1 package (12 ounces) baby carrots**
**Fresh rosemary, for garnish (optional)**

1. Place roast in large resealable plastic food storage bag. Combine wine, soy sauce, garlic, rosemary, Dijon mustard and dry mustard in small bowl. Pour over roast. Seal bag; turn to coat. Marinate in refrigerator 4 to 12 hours, turning several times.

2. Preheat oven to 425°F. Spray 13×9-inch baking pan with nonstick cooking spray. Place potatoes, brussels sprouts and carrots in pan. Remove roast from marinade. Pour marinade over vegetables; toss to coat well. Cover vegetables with foil; bake 30 minutes. Stir.

3. Place tenderloin on vegetables. Roast, uncovered, 35 to 45 minutes or until internal temperature of roast reaches 135°F for medium-rare to 150°F for medium when tested with meat thermometer inserted into thickest part of roast.

4. Transfer roast to cutting board; cover with foil. Let stand 10 to 15 minutes before carving. (Internal temperature will continue to rise 5°F to 10°F during stand time.)

5. Stir vegetables; test for doneness. Continue to bake if not tender. Slice tenderloin; arrange on serving platter with roasted vegetables. Garnish with fresh rosemary, if desired. *Makes 10 servings*

**beef tenderloin with roasted vegetables**

# chicken with spinach and celery hash

**nutrients per serving:**

¼ of total recipe

Calories: 294
Carbohydrate: 22 g
Dietary Fiber: 8 g
Total Fat: 9 g
Calories From Fat: 27%
Saturated Fat: 1 g
Cholesterol: 65 mg
Sodium: 217 mg
Protein: 31 g

**Exchanges:** 1 Starch, 1 Vegetable, 3 Lean Meat, ½ Fat

**1 package (16 ounces) refrigerated pre-cooked fat-free hash browns**
**1 package (8 ounces) ready-to-use celery sticks, thinly sliced**
**3 teaspoons olive oil, divided**
**12 chicken tenders (about 1 pound)**
**½ teaspoon dried thyme leaves**
**¼ teaspoon ground white pepper**
**2 packages (5 ounces each) ready-to-use baby spinach**
**¼ cup water**

1. Combine hash browns and celery in medium bowl.

2. Heat 1½ teaspoons oil in large nonstick skillet over medium-high heat. Add hash brown mixture; cook about 10 minutes, stirring and turning occasionally, or until mixture begins to brown. Reduce heat; cook 10 minutes or until browned.

3. Heat remaining 1½ teaspoons oil in 12-inch nonstick skillet over medium-high heat until hot. Add chicken tenders. Sprinkle with thyme and pepper. Cook about 5 minutes, turning once, or until no longer pink in center. Remove from skillet; keep warm.

4. Add spinach and water to same skillet. Cover; cook about 3 minutes, stirring once.

5. To serve, divide spinach and hash brown mixture evenly among 4 plates. Top each with 3 chicken tenders.

*Makes 4 servings*

**chicken with spinach and celery hash**

# side dishes

## nutrients per serving:

3 tomato slices with 2½ tablespoons red pepper mixture
Calories: 80
Carbohydrate: 9 g
Dietary Fiber: 1 g
Total Fat: 2 g
Calories From Fat: 30%
Saturated Fat: 1 g
Cholesterol: 3 mg
Sodium: 342 mg
Protein: 3 g

**Exchanges:** 2 Vegetable, ½ Fat

## roasted red pepper & tomato casserole

1 jar (12 ounces) roasted red peppers, drained
1½ teaspoons red wine vinegar
1 teaspoon olive oil
1 clove garlic, minced
¼ teaspoon salt
¼ teaspoon black pepper
⅓ cup grated Parmesan cheese, divided
3 medium fresh tomatoes (about 1½ pounds), sliced
½ cup (about 1 ounce) herb-flavored croutons, crushed

**Microwave Directions**

1. Combine red peppers, vinegar, oil, garlic, salt and black pepper in food processor. Cover; process, using on/off pulsing action, 1 minute or until slightly chunky. Reserve 2 tablespoons cheese for garnish. Stir remaining cheese into red pepper mixture.

2. Arrange tomato slices in 8-inch round microwavable baking dish; microwave at HIGH 1 minute. Spoon red pepper mixture on top; microwave at HIGH 2 to 3 minutes or until tomatoes are slightly softened.

3. Sprinkle with reserved 2 tablespoons cheese and croutons. Garnish, if desired.

*Makes 6 servings*

## nutrients per serving:

½ cup salad
Calories: 65
Carbohydrate: 8 g
Dietary Fiber: 3 g
Total Fat: 3 g
Calories From Fat: 36%
Saturated Fat: 1 g
Cholesterol: 3 mg
Sodium: 238 mg
Protein: 2 g

**Exchanges:** 1½ Vegetable, ½ Fat

## cool and creamy pea salad with cucumbers and red onion

2 tablespoons finely chopped red onion
1 tablespoon reduced-fat mayonnaise
⅛ teaspoon salt
⅛ teaspoon black pepper
½ cup frozen green peas, thawed
¼ cup diced red bell pepper
¼ cup diced cucumber

1. Combine onion, mayonnaise, salt and black pepper in medium bowl; stir until well blended.

2. Add remaining ingredients; toss gently to coat.

*Makes 2 servings*

**roasted red pepper & tomato casserole**

# zucchini delight

**nutrients per serving:**

⅙ of total recipe
Calories: 92
Carbohydrate: 18 g
Dietary Fiber: 3 g
Total Fat: 2 g
Calories From Fat: 14%
Saturated Fat: <1 g
Cholesterol: 1 mg
Sodium: 426 mg
Protein: 4 g

**Exchanges:** 3½ Vegetable

1 can (10¾ ounces) reduced-fat condensed tomato soup, undiluted
1 tablespoon lemon juice
1 teaspoon sugar
2 cloves garlic, minced
½ teaspoon salt
6 cups ½-inch zucchini slices
1 cup thinly sliced onion
1 cup coarsely chopped green bell pepper
1 cup sliced mushrooms
2 tablespoons grated Parmesan cheese

Combine soup, lemon juice, sugar, garlic and salt in large saucepan; mix well. Add zucchini, onion, bell pepper and mushrooms; mix well. Bring to a boil; reduce heat. Cover; cook 20 to 25 minutes or until vegetables are crisp-tender, stirring occasionally. Sprinkle with cheese before serving. *Makes 6 servings*

# jalapeño coleslaw

**nutrients per serving:**

about 1 cup coleslaw
Calories: 47
Carbohydrate: 12 g
Dietary Fiber: 2 g
Total Fat: <1 g
Calories From Fat: 4%
Saturated Fat: <1 g
Cholesterol: 0 mg
Sodium: 304 mg
Protein: 1 g

**Exchanges:** ½ Starch, 1 Vegetable

6 cups shredded cabbage or coleslaw mix
2 medium fresh tomatoes, seeded and chopped
6 green onions, coarsely chopped
2 jalapeño peppers,* finely chopped
¼ cup cider vinegar
3 tablespoons honey
1 teaspoon salt

*Jalapeño peppers can sting and irritate the skin. Wear rubber gloves when handling peppers and do not touch eyes. Wash hands after handling peppers.*

1. Combine cabbage, tomatoes, green onions, jalapeño peppers, vinegar, honey and salt in serving bowl; mix well. Cover; chill at least 2 hours before serving.

2. Stir well immediately before serving. *Makes 8 servings*

**Tip:** For a milder coleslaw, discard the seeds and veins when chopping the jalapeños, since this is where much of the heat of the peppers is stored.

**zucchini delight**

# polenta triangles

**½ cup uncooked yellow corn grits**
**1½ cups fat-free reduced-sodium chicken broth, divided**
**2 cloves garlic, minced**
**½ cup (2 ounces) crumbled feta cheese**
**1 red bell pepper, roasted,\* peeled and finely chopped**

*\*Place pepper on foil-lined broiler pan; broil 15 minutes or until blackened on all sides, turning every 5 minutes. Place pepper in paper bag. Cose bag; let stand 15 minutes before peeling.*

1. Combine grits and ½ cup chicken broth in small bowl; mix well. Set aside. Pour remaining 1 cup broth into large heavy saucepan; bring to a boil. Add garlic and moistened grits; mix well. Return to a boil. Reduce heat to low. Cover; cook 20 minutes. Remove from heat; add feta cheese. Stir until cheese is completely melted. Add roasted bell pepper; mix well.

2. Spray 8-inch square pan with nonstick cooking spray. Spoon grits mixture into prepared pan. With wet fingertips, press grits evenly into pan. Refrigerate until cold.

3. Spray grid with nonstick cooking spray. Prepare grill for direct cooking. Turn polenta out onto cutting board; cut into 4 (2-inch) squares. Cut each square diagonally into 2 triangles.

4. Place polenta triangles on grid. Grill over medium-high heat 1 minute or until bottoms are lightly browned. Turn triangles over; grill until browned and crisp. Serve warm or at room temperature. *Makes 8 servings*

# collard greens

**4 bunches collard greens, stemmed, washed and torn into bite-size pieces**
**2 cups water**
**½ medium red bell pepper, cored, seeded and cut into strips**
**⅓ medium green bell pepper, cored, seeded and cut into strips**
**¼ cup olive oil**
**¼ teaspoon salt**
**¼ teaspoon black pepper**

Place all ingredients in large saucepan; bring to a boil. Reduce heat; simmer 1 to 1½ hours or until tender. *Makes 10 servings*

**polenta triangles**

# roasted butternut squash

Nonstick cooking spray
1 pound butternut squash, peeled and cut into 1-inch cubes (about 4 cups)
2 medium onions, coarsely chopped
8 ounces carrots, peeled and cut into ½-inch diagonal slices (about 2 cups)
1 tablespoon dark brown sugar
¼ teaspoon salt
Black pepper to taste (optional)
1 tablespoon butter or margarine, melted

1. Preheat oven to 400°F. Line large baking sheet with foil and coat with cooking spray. Arrange vegetables in single layer on foil; coat lightly with cooking spray. Sprinkle vegetables with brown sugar, salt and pepper, if desired.

2. Bake 30 minutes. Stir gently; bake 10 to 15 minutes more or until vegetables are tender. Remove from oven. Drizzle with butter; toss to coat.          *Makes 5 servings*

**nutrients per serving:**

1 cup squash
Calories: 143
Carbohydrate: 30 g
Dietary Fiber: 8 g
Total Fat: 3 g
Calories From Fat: 16%
Saturated Fat: 2 g
Cholesterol: 7 mg
Sodium: 167 mg
Protein: 3 g

**Exchanges:** 1½ Starch, 1½ Vegetable, ½ Fat

# maple-glazed carrots & shallots

1 package (16 ounces) baby carrots
1 tablespoon margarine or butter
½ cup thinly sliced shallots
2 tablespoons reduced-fat maple-flavored pancake syrup
¼ teaspoon salt
⅛ teaspoon white pepper

1. Place carrots in medium saucepan. Add enough water to cover carrots. Bring to a boil over high heat. Reduce heat; simmer carrots over low heat 8 to 10 minutes or until carrots are tender. Drain; set aside.

2. In same saucepan, melt margarine over medium-high heat. Add shallots; cook and stir 3 to 4 minutes or until shallots are tender and beginning to brown. Add drained carrots, syrup, salt and pepper; cook and stir 1 to 2 minutes or until carrots are coated and heated through.          *Makes 4 servings*

**nutrients per serving:**

¼ of total recipe
Calories: 80
Carbohydrate: 14 g
Dietary Fiber: 3 g
Total Fat: 3 g
Calories From Fat: 31%
Saturated Fat: 1 g
Cholesterol: 0 mg
Sodium: 279 mg
Protein: <1 g

**Exchanges:** 2½ Vegetable, ½ Fat

**roasted butternut squash**

# pepper and squash gratin

nutrients per serving:

⅛ of total recipe
Calories: 106
Carbohydrate: 15 g
Dietary Fiber: 2 g
Total Fat: 3 g
Calories From Fat: 26%
Saturated Fat: 2 g
Cholesterol: 8 mg
Sodium: 267 mg
Protein: 4 g

**Exchanges:** 1 Starch, ½ Fat

> **12 ounces russet potato, unpeeled**
> **8 ounces yellow summer squash, thinly sliced**
> **8 ounces zucchini, thinly sliced**
> **2 cups frozen pepper stir-fry blend, thawed**
> **1 teaspoon dried oregano leaves**
> **½ teaspoon salt**
> **Black pepper**
> **½ cup grated Parmesan cheese or shredded reduced-fat sharp Cheddar cheese**
> **1 tablespoon butter or margarine, cut into 8 pieces**

1. Preheat oven to 375°F. Spray 12×8-inch glass baking dish with nonstick cooking spray. Pierce potato several times with fork. Microwave at HIGH 3 minutes. Cut potato into thin slices.

2. Layer half of potato slices, yellow squash, zucchini, pepper stir-fry blend, oregano, salt, black pepper and cheese in prepared baking dish. Repeat layers. Top with butter. Cover tightly with foil; bake 25 minutes or until vegetables are just tender. Remove foil; bake 10 minutes more or until lightly browned. *Makes 8 servings*

# black-eyed peas

nutrients per serving:

¹⁄₁₀ of total recipe
Calories: 86
Carbohydrate: 14 g
Dietary Fiber: 1 g
Total Fat: 2 g
Calories From Fat: 21%
Saturated Fat: <1 g
Cholesterol: 18 mg
Sodium: 259 mg
Protein: 3 g

**Exchanges:** ½ Starch, 1 Vegetable, ½ Fat

> **1 bag (1 pound) dried black-eyed peas, soaked overnight, drained**
> **1½ cups diced onion**
> **2 shallots, finely chopped**
> **⅓ medium green bell pepper, cored, seeded and chopped**
> **¼ cup vegetable oil**
> **1 teaspoon *each* salt and black pepper**
> **3 to 4 cups water**

1. Place soaked black-eyed peas in large stockpot or Dutch oven. Add onion, shallots and bell pepper. Cover; let stand 20 minutes. Add oil, salt and black pepper; stir. Cover; let stand 10 to 15 minutes. Add enough water to cover peas by 1 inch. Bring to a boil. Lower heat; simmer, covered, 50 to 60 minutes or until tender.

2. Before serving, remove ½ cup cooked peas; mash. Return mashed peas to stockpot; stir until slightly thickened. *Makes 10 servings*

**pepper and squash gratin**

# light lemon cauliflower

nutrients per serving:

about ⅔ cup cauliflower with 1½ tablespoons sauce and 2 teaspoons cheese

Calories: 53
Carbohydrate: 6 g
Dietary Fiber: 3 g
Total Fat: 2 g
Calories From Fat: 33%
Saturated Fat: 1 g
Cholesterol: 3 mg
Sodium: 116 mg
Protein: 4 g

**Exchanges:** 1 Vegetable, ½ Fat

**¼ cup chopped fresh parsley, divided**
**½ teaspoon grated lemon peel**
**6 cups (about 1½ pounds) cauliflower florets**
**1 tablespoon reduced-fat margarine**
**3 cloves garlic, minced**
**2 tablespoons fresh lemon juice**
**¼ cup shredded Parmesan cheese**

1. Place 1 tablespoon parsley, lemon peel and about 1 inch water in large saucepan. Place cauliflower in steamer basket; place in saucepan. Bring water to a boil over medium heat. Cover; steam 14 to 16 minutes or until cauliflower is crisp-tender. Remove to large bowl; keep warm. Reserve ½ cup hot liquid.

2. Heat margarine in small saucepan over medium heat. Add garlic; cook and stir 2 to 3 minutes or until soft. Stir in lemon juice and reserved liquid.

3. Spoon lemon sauce over cauliflower. Sprinkle with remaining 3 tablespoons parsley and cheese before serving. Garnish with lemon slices, if desired.

*Makes 6 servings*

# vegetable confetti rice

nutrients per serving:

½ cup vegetable confetti rice

Calories: 90
Carbohydrate: 14 g
Dietary Fiber: 2 g
Total Fat: 2 g
Calories From Fat: 22%
Saturated Fat: <1 g
Cholesterol: 5 mg
Sodium: 103 mg
Protein: 4 g

**Exchanges:** ½ Starch, 1 Vegetable, ½ Lean Meat

**1 tablespoon vegetable oil**
**1 cup finely chopped celery**
**½ cup uncooked long-grain white rice**
**½ cup bottled roasted sweet red peppers, diced**
**1 can (14½ ounces) fat-free reduced-sodium chicken broth**
**2 packages (10 ounces each) mixed broccoli-cauliflower florets, cut into equal-size pieces**

1. Heat oil in large nonstick skillet over medium heat. Add celery; cook, stirring occasionally, about 5 to 6 minutes or until crisp-tender. Add rice; cook and stir about 3 to 4 minutes or until rice is opaque. Add diced red peppers; stir to combine. Add broth. Cover; simmer about 12 minutes or until rice is just cooked through.

2. Add broccoli-cauliflower florets. Cover; cook about 10 minutes or until vegetables are tender. Add water, if necessary, to prevent burning. Combine vegetables and rice before serving.

*Makes 8 servings*

**light lemon cauliflower**

# mashed sweet potatoes & parsnips

nutrients per serving:

½ cup
Calories: 142
Carbohydrate: 27 g
Dietary Fiber: 4 g
Total Fat: 3 g
Calories From Fat: 19%
Saturated Fat: 1 g
Cholesterol: <1 mg
Sodium: 251 mg
Protein: 3 g

**Exchanges:** 1½ Starch, ½ Vegetable, ½ Fat

**2 large sweet potatoes (about 1¼ pounds), peeled and cut into 1-inch pieces**
**2 medium parsnips (about ½ pound), peeled and cut into ½-inch slices**
**¼ cup evaporated skimmed milk**
**1½ tablespoons margarine or butter**
**½ teaspoon salt**
**⅛ teaspoon ground nutmeg**
**¼ cup chopped chives or green onion tops**

1. Combine sweet potatoes and parsnips in large saucepan. Cover with cold water; bring to a boil over high heat. Reduce heat; simmer, uncovered, 15 minutes or until vegetables are tender.

2. Drain vegetables; return to pan. Add milk, margarine, salt and nutmeg. Mash potato mixture over low heat to desired consistency. Stir in chives.

*Makes 6 servings*

# brussels sprouts with lemon-dill glaze

nutrients per serving:

¼ of total recipe
Calories: 58
Carbohydrate: 13 g
Dietary Fiber: 5 g
Total Fat: 1 g
Calories From Fat: 9%
Saturated Fat: <1 g
Cholesterol: 0 mg
Sodium: 31 mg
Protein: 3 g

**Exchanges:** 2 Vegetable

**1 pound brussels sprouts***
**2 teaspoons cornstarch**
**½ teaspoon dried dill weed**
**½ cup fat-free reduced-sodium chicken broth**
**3 tablespoons lemon juice**
**½ teaspoon grated lemon peel**

*\*Or, substitute 1 package (10 ounces) frozen brussels sprouts for fresh brussels sprouts. Cook according to package directions; drain.*

1. Trim brussels sprouts. Cut an "X" in stem ends. Bring 1 cup water to a boil in large saucepan over high heat. Add brussels sprouts; return to a boil. Reduce heat to medium-low. Simmer, covered, 10 minutes or just until tender. Drain well; return to pan. Set aside.

2. Meanwhile, combine cornstarch and dill weed in small saucepan. Blend in chicken broth and lemon juice until smooth. Stir in lemon peel. Cook and stir over medium heat 5 minutes or until mixture boils and thickens. Cook and stir 1 minute more. Pour glaze over brussels sprouts; toss gently to coat. Serve hot.

*Makes 4 servings*

**mashed sweet potatoes & parsnips**

nutrients per serving:

1/6 of total recipe
Calories: 82
Carbohydrate: 13 g
Dietary Fiber: 1 g
Total Fat: 3 g
Calories From Fat: 30%
Saturated Fat: <1 g
Cholesterol: 3 mg
Sodium: 101 mg
Protein: 3 g

**Exchanges:** 1/2 Starch, 1 Vegetable, 1/2 Fat

# vegetables with spinach fettuccine

**6 solid-pack sun-dried tomatoes**
**3 ounces uncooked spinach fettuccine**
**1 tablespoon olive oil**
**1/4 cup chopped onion**
**1/4 cup sliced red bell pepper**
**1 clove garlic, minced**
**1/2 cup sliced mushrooms**
**1/2 cup coarsely chopped fresh spinach**
**1/4 teaspoon salt**
**1/4 teaspoon ground nutmeg**
**1/8 teaspoon black pepper**

1. Place sun-dried tomatoes in small bowl; pour boiling water over tomatoes to cover. Let stand 10 to 15 minutes or until tomatoes are tender. Drain tomatoes; discard liquid. Cut tomatoes into strips.

2. Cook pasta according to package directions, omitting salt. Drain.

3. Heat oil in large nonstick skillet over medium heat until hot. Add onion, bell pepper and garlic; cook and stir 3 minutes or until vegetables are crisp-tender. Add mushrooms and spinach; cook and stir 1 minute. Add sun-dried tomatoes, pasta, salt, nutmeg and black pepper; cook and stir 1 to 2 minutes or until heated through. Garnish as desired.                    *Makes 6 servings*

**vegetables with spinach fettuccine**

# curried rice & green beans

**2 teaspoons vegetable oil**
**2 cups sliced mushrooms**
**1 clove garlic, minced**
**½ teaspoon curry powder**
**¼ teaspoon cumin seed (optional)**
**1 cup fat-free reduced-sodium chicken broth**
**1 cup fresh sliced green beans or frozen cut green beans**
**½ cup uncooked long-grain white rice**
**4 slices Canadian bacon, cut into short thin strips**
**¼ teaspoon black pepper**

1. Heat oil in small saucepan. Add mushrooms and garlic; cook and stir over medium-low heat about 5 minutes. Add curry powder and cumin seed, if desired; cook and stir 30 seconds.

2. Add chicken broth; bring to a boil. Stir in green beans and rice. Reduce heat to low. Cover; simmer about 18 minutes or until rice is tender and liquid is absorbed. Stir in Canadian bacon and pepper. Heat just until bacon is hot.          *Makes 6 servings*

# sweet potato puffs

**2 pounds sweet potatoes**
**⅓ cup orange juice**
**1 egg, beaten**
**1 tablespoon grated orange peel**
**½ teaspoon ground nutmeg**
**¼ cup chopped pecans**

1. Peel sweet potatoes; cut into 1-inch pieces. Place potatoes in medium saucepan; add enough water to cover. Bring to a boil over medium-high heat. Cook 10 to 15 minutes or until tender. Drain potatoes; place in large bowl. Mash until smooth. Add orange juice, egg, orange peel and nutmeg; mix well.

2. Preheat oven to 375°F. Spray baking sheet with nonstick cooking spray. Spoon potato mixture into 10 mounds on prepared baking sheet. Sprinkle pecans over tops of mounds. Bake 30 minutes or until centers are hot.          *Makes 10 servings*

**curried rice & green beans**

nutrients per serving:

about 1 cup

Calories: 91
Carbohydrate: 10 g
Dietary Fiber: 4 g
Total Fat: 3 g
Calories From Fat: 30%
Saturated Fat: 1 g
Cholesterol: 3 mg
Sodium: 188 mg
Protein: 7 g

**Exchanges:** ½ Starch, 1 Vegetable, ½ Fat

# creamed spinach

**3 cups water**
**2 bags (10 ounces each) washed, stemmed and chopped fresh spinach**
**2 teaspoons margarine**
**2 tablespoons all-purpose flour**
**1 cup fat-free (skim) milk**
**2 tablespoons grated Parmesan cheese**
**⅛ teaspoon white pepper**
**Ground nutmeg**

1. Bring water to a boil. Add spinach. Reduce heat; simmer, covered, about 5 minutes or until spinach is wilted. Drain well; set aside.

2. Melt margarine in small saucepan over medium-low heat. Stir in flour; cook over medium-low heat 1 minute, stirring constantly. Using wire whisk, stir in milk. Bring to a boil. Cook, whisking constantly, 1 to 2 minutes or until mixture thickens. Stir in cheese and pepper.

3. Stir spinach into sauce; heat thoroughly. Spoon into serving bowl; sprinkle lightly with nutmeg. Garnish as desired. *Makes 4 servings*

## tip

Stem fresh spinach by first folding each leaf lengthwise in half along the stem. (The underside of the leaf should be facing you.) Pull the stem off by bringing it up towards the leaf tip.

**creamed spinach**

# potatoes au gratin

**1 pound baking potatoes**
**1 tablespoon plus 1 teaspoon reduced-fat margarine**
**1 tablespoon plus 1 teaspoon all-purpose flour**
**1¼ cups fat-free (skim) milk**
**¼ teaspoon ground nutmeg**
**¼ teaspoon paprika**
**Pinch white pepper**
**½ cup thinly sliced red onion, divided**
**⅓ cup whole wheat bread crumbs**
**1 tablespoon finely chopped red onion**
**1 tablespoon grated Parmesan cheese**

1. Spray 4- or 6-cup casserole with nonstick cooking spray; set aside.

2. Place potatoes in large saucepan; add water to cover. Bring to a boil over high heat; boil 12 minutes or until potatoes are tender. Drain. Let potatoes stand 10 minutes or until cool enough to handle.

3. Meanwhile, melt margarine in small saucepan over medium heat. Add flour; cook and stir 3 minutes or until small clumps form. Gradually whisk in milk. Cook 8 minutes or until sauce thickens, stirring constantly. Remove saucepan from heat. Stir in nutmeg, paprika and pepper.

4. Preheat oven to 350°F. Cut potatoes into thin slices. Arrange half of potato slices in prepared casserole. Sprinkle with half of onion slices. Repeat layers. Spoon sauce over potato mixture. Combine bread crumbs, finely chopped red onion and cheese in small bowl; sprinkle evenly over sauce.

5. Bake 20 minutes. Let stand 5 minutes before serving. Garnish as desired.

*Makes 4 servings*

**potatoes au gratin**

# desserts & sweets

## cherry bottom pie

nutrients per serving:

1 pie slice
(¹⁄₁₀ of total recipe)
Calories: 192
Carbohydrate: 25 g
Dietary Fiber: 1 g
Total Fat: 8 g
Calories From Fat: 38%
Saturated Fat: 3 g
Cholesterol: 16 mg
Sodium: 217 mg
Protein: 3 g

**Exchanges:** 2 Starch

**12 sheets low-fat graham crackers, crumbled**
 **4 tablespoons margarine, melted**
 **3 tablespoons sucralose-sugar blend, divided**
 **1 can (20 ounces) light cherry pie filling, divided**
 **1 envelope (¼ ounce) unflavored gelatin**
**¼ cup cold water**
**¾ cup boiling water**
 **1 package (8 ounces) reduced-fat cream cheese, softened**
 **1 teaspoon vanilla**
**½ (8-ounce) container thawed fat-free whipped topping**
  **Chocolate shavings (optional)**

1. Preheat oven to 350°F. Combine graham cracker crumbs, margarine and 1 tablespoon sucralose-sugar blend in medium bowl. Press crumb mixture evenly on bottom and up side of 9-inch deep-dish pie plate. Bake 8 to 10 minutes. Remove to wire rack; cool completely.

2. Spread two thirds of pie filling over crust. Cover remaining filling; refrigerate until ready to serve.

3. Combine gelatin and cold water in small bowl; let stand 5 minutes to soften. Add boiling water; stir until gelatin is completely dissolved. Cool gelatin mixture 5 to 10 minutes.

4. Beat cream cheese, remaining 2 tablespoons sucralose-sugar blend and vanilla in large bowl with electric mixer at medium speed until smooth. Slowly add ¾ cup gelatin mixture *(discard remaining ¼ cup gelatin mixture)*. Beat at low speed until blended. Stir in whipped topping; mix until smooth. Pour cream cheese mixture over cherry filling in pie crust. Cover and refrigerate at least 3 hours or until firm.

5. Top with remaining pie filling. Sprinkle with chocolate shavings, if desired. Cover and refrigerate any remaining pie.

*Makes 10 servings*

**cherry bottom pie**

nutrients per
serving:

1 cake slice
(1/10 of total recipe)
Calories: 190
Carbohydrate: 26 g
Dietary Fiber: 1 g
Total Fat: 8 g
Calories From Fat: 38%
Saturated Fat: 3 g
Cholesterol: 85 mg
Sodium: 240 mg
Protein: 4 g

**Exchanges:** 1½ Starch,
1 Fat

# flourless chocolate cake

**3 squares (1 ounce each) semisweet chocolate, chopped**
**3 tablespoons margarine**
**1 tablespoon espresso powder or instant coffee granules**
**2 tablespoons hot water**
**4 eggs, separated**
**2 egg whites**
**⅔ cup sugar, divided**
**3 tablespoons unsweetened cocoa powder, sifted**
**1 teaspoon vanilla**
**½ teaspoon salt**
   **Thawed fat-free whipped topping (optional)**
   **Fresh raspberries (optional)**
   **Fresh mint leaves (optional)**

1. Preheat oven to 300°F. Grease 9-inch springform pan; line bottom of pan with parchment paper.

2. Melt chocolate and margarine in small heavy saucepan over low heat, stirring frequently; cool. Dissolve espresso powder in hot water in small bowl.

3. Place 6 egg whites in large bowl; set aside. Beat egg yolks in medium bowl with electric mixer at high speed about 5 minutes or until pale yellow in color. Add ⅓ cup sugar; beat about 4 minutes or until mixture falls in ribbons from beaters. Slowly beat in melted chocolate mixture and espresso mixture at low speed just until blended. Beat in cocoa and vanilla just until blended.

4. Add salt to egg whites; beat at high speed 2 minutes or until soft peaks form. Beat in remaining ⅓ cup sugar until stiff peaks form. Stir large spoonful of egg whites into chocolate mixture. Fold chocolate mixture into egg whites until almost blended. Spoon batter into prepared pan.

5. Bake 1 hour or until cake begins to pull away from side of pan. Cool on wire rack 10 minutes; run thin spatula around edge of cake. Carefully remove side of pan; cool completely. Invert cake; remove bottom of pan and paper from cake. Cover and refrigerate at least 4 hours. Serve chilled with whipped topping, raspberries and mint, if desired.

*Makes 10 servings*

**flourless chocolate cake**

# chocolate chip-cherry oatmeal cookies

⅔ **cup sugar**
⅓ **cup canola oil**
¼ **cup cholesterol-free egg substitute**
  1 **teaspoon vanilla**
¾ **cup all-purpose flour**
½ **teaspoon baking soda**
½ **teaspoon ground cinnamon**
⅛ **teaspoon salt**
1½ **cups quick oats**
¼ **cup mini semisweet chocolate chips**
¼ **cup dried cherries**

1. Preheat oven to 325°F. Spray cookie sheets with nonstick cooking spray.

2. Beat sugar, oil, egg substitute and vanilla in large bowl with electric mixer at medium speed until well blended. Add flour, baking soda, cinnamon and salt; beat until smooth. Stir in oats, chocolate chips and cherries.

3. Drop slightly rounded teaspoonfuls of dough about 2 inches apart on prepared cookie sheets.

4. Bake 7 minutes (cookies will not brown). Cool cookies 2 minutes on cookie sheets. Remove to wire rack; cool completely.                *Makes about 4 dozen cookies*

**Tip:** You can substitute dried cranberries or raisins for the dried cherries.

**chocolate chip-cherry oatmeal cookies**

# berries with banana cream

⅓ **cup reduced-fat sour cream**
½ **small ripe banana, cut into chunks**
1 **tablespoon frozen orange juice concentrate**
2 **cups sliced strawberries, blueberries, raspberries or a combination**
   **Ground cinnamon or nutmeg**

1. Combine sour cream, banana and juice concentrate in blender. Cover; blend until smooth.

2. Place berries in 2 serving dishes. Top with sour cream mixture. Sprinkle with cinnamon.

*Makes 2 servings*

**nutrients per serving:**

1 cup berries with about 3 tablespoons sour cream mixture

Calories: 135
Carbohydrate: 23 g
Dietary Fiber: 4 g
Total Fat: 4 g
Calories From Fat: 25%
Saturated Fat: 3 g
Cholesterol: 13 mg
Sodium: 29 mg
Protein: 4 g

**Exchanges:** 1½ Fruit, 1 Fat

# butterscotch bars

¾ **cup all-purpose flour**
½ **cup packed brown sugar**
½ **cup fat-free butterscotch ice cream topping**
¼ **cup cholesterol-free egg substitute**
3 **tablespoons margarine or butter, melted**
1 **teaspoon vanilla**
¼ **teaspoon salt**
½ **cup toasted chopped pecans (optional)**

1. Preheat oven to 350°F. Lightly spray 8-inch square baking pan with nonstick cooking spray; set aside.

2. Combine flour, brown sugar, butterscotch topping, egg substitute, margarine, vanilla, salt and pecans, if desired, in medium bowl; stir until blended. Spread into prepared pan.

2. Bake 15 to 18 minutes or until firm to the touch. Cool completely in pan on wire rack. Cut into 16 bars.

*Makes 16 servings*

**nutrients per serving:**

1 bar

Calories: 103
Carbohydrate: 19 g
Dietary Fiber: <1 g
Total Fat: 2 g
Calories From Fat: 21%
Saturated Fat: <1 g
Cholesterol: 6 mg
Sodium: 90 mg
Protein: 1 g

**Exchanges:** 1 Starch, ½ Fat

**berries with banana cream**

nutrients per serving:

1 apricot biscotti
Calories: 86
Carbohydrate: 16 g
Dietary Fiber: 1 g
Total Fat: 1 g
Calories From Fat: 10%
Saturated Fat: <1 g
Cholesterol: 21 mg
Sodium: 108 mg
Protein: 2 g
**Exchanges:** 1 Starch

# apricot biscotti

**3 cups all-purpose flour**
**1½ teaspoons baking soda**
**½ teaspoon salt**
**⅔ cup sugar**
**3 eggs**
**1 teaspoon vanilla**
**½ cup chopped dried apricots***
**⅓ cup sliced almonds, chopped**
**1 tablespoon reduced-fat (2%) milk**

**Other chopped dried fruits, such as dried cherries, cranberries or blueberries, can be substituted.*

1. Preheat oven to 350°F. Lightly coat cookie sheet with nonstick cooking spray; set aside.

2. Combine flour, baking soda and salt in medium bowl; set aside.

3. Beat sugar, eggs and vanilla in large bowl with electric mixer at medium speed until blended. Add flour mixture; beat until well blended.

4. Stir in apricots and almonds. Turn dough out onto lightly floured work surface. Knead 4 to 6 times. Shape dough into 20-inch log; place on prepared cookie sheet. Brush dough with milk.

5. Bake 30 minutes or until firm. Remove from oven to wire rack; cool 10 minutes. Slice diagonally into 30 biscotti. Place slices on cookie sheet. Bake 10 minutes; turn and bake additional 10 minutes. Cool on wire rack. Store in airtight container.

*Makes 30 servings*

**apricot biscotti**

# pear-ginger upside-down cake

2 unpeeled Bosc or Anjou pears, cored and sliced into ¼-inch-thick pieces
3 tablespoons fresh lemon juice
1 to 2 tablespoons melted butter
1 to 2 tablespoons packed brown sugar
1 cup all-purpose flour
1 teaspoon baking powder
1 teaspoon ground cinnamon
¼ teaspoon baking soda
⅛ teaspoon salt
⅓ cup fat-free (skim) milk
3 tablespoons no-sugar-added apricot fruit spread
1 egg
1 tablespoon vegetable oil
1 tablespoon minced fresh ginger

1. Preheat oven to 375°F. Spray 10-inch deep-dish pie pan with nonstick cooking spray; set aside.

2. Toss pears in lemon juice; drain. Brush butter evenly onto bottom of prepared pan; sprinkle sugar over butter. Arrange pears in pan; bake 10 minutes.

3. Meanwhile, combine flour, baking powder, cinnamon, baking soda and salt in small bowl; set aside. Combine milk, apricot spread, egg, oil and ginger in medium bowl; mix well. Add flour mixture; stir until well mixed. (Batter will be very thick.) Carefully spread batter evenly over pears to edge of pan.

4. Bake 20 to 25 minutes or until golden brown and toothpick inserted into center comes out clean.

5. Remove pan to wire rack; cool 5 minutes. Use knife to loosen cake from side of pan. Place 10-inch plate over top of pan; quickly turn over to transfer cake to plate. Place any pears left in pan on top of cake. Serve warm. *Makes 8 servings*

**pear-ginger upside-down cake**

# rice pudding mexicana

> **1 package (4-serving size) fat-free rice pudding**
> **1 tablespoon vanilla**
> **¼ teaspoon ground cinnamon**
> **Dash ground cloves**
> **¼ cup slivered almonds**
> **Additional ground cinnamon**

1. Prepare rice pudding according to package directions.

2. Remove pudding from heat; stir in vanilla, ¼ teaspoon cinnamon and cloves. Divide evenly among 6 individual dessert dishes.

3. Top evenly with almonds and additional cinnamon. Serve warm.

*Makes 6 servings*

**nutrients per serving:**

1 dessert dish rice pudding (⅙ of total recipe)
Calories: 146
Carbohydrate: 22 g
Dietary Fiber: 1 g
Total Fat: 4 g
Calories From Fat: 27%
Saturated Fat: 1 g
Cholesterol: 6 mg
Sodium: 106 mg
Protein: 4 g
**Exchanges:** 1 Starch, ½ Milk, ½ Fat

# banana pistachio pie

> **¾ cup cinnamon graham cracker crumbs**
> **2 tablespoons reduced-fat margarine, melted**
> **2 packages (4-serving size each) fat-free sugar-free instant pistachio pudding and pie filling mix**
> **2½ cups fat-free (skim) milk**
> **1 large ripe banana, sliced**
> **¼ teaspoon ground cinnamon**
> **1 cup thawed frozen reduced-fat nondairy whipped topping**
> **Additional thawed frozen reduced-fat nondairy whipped topping (optional)**

1. Combine graham cracker crumbs and margarine in small bowl; stir with fork until crumbly. Press crumb mixture onto bottom of 9-inch pie plate.

2. Prepare pudding mix according to manufacturer's pie directions, using 2½ cups milk. Gently stir in banana and cinnamon; fold in 1 cup whipped topping. Pour into prepared crust. Refrigerate at least 1 hour. Top with additional whipped topping before serving, if desired.

*Makes 8 servings*

**nutrients per serving:**

1 pie slice (⅛ of total recipe)
Calories: 143
Carbohydrate: 22 g
Dietary Fiber: 1 g
Total Fat: 4 g
Calories From Fat: 24%
Saturated Fat: 1 g
Cholesterol: 2 mg
Sodium: 450 mg
Protein: 3 g
**Exchanges:** 1½ Starch, 1 Fat

**rice pudding mexicana**

# tropical fruit coconut tart

**1 cup cornflakes, crushed**
**1 can (3½ ounces) sweetened flaked coconut**
**2 egg whites**
**1 can (15¼ ounces) pineapple chunks in juice, undrained**
**2 teaspoons cornstarch**
**2 packets sugar substitute *or* equivalent of 4 teaspoons sugar**
**1 teaspoon coconut extract (optional)**
**1 mango, peeled and thinly sliced**
**1 medium banana, thinly sliced**

1. Preheat oven to 425°F. Coat 9-inch springform pan with nonstick cooking spray; set aside.

2. Combine cornflakes, coconut and egg whites in medium bowl; toss gently to blend. Place mixture in prepared pan; press firmly to cover bottom and ½ inch up side of pan. Bake 8 minutes or until edge begins to brown. Cool completely on wire rack.

3. Drain pineapple, reserving juice. Combine pineapple juice and cornstarch in small saucepan; stir until cornstarch is dissolved. Bring to a boil over high heat. Continue boiling 1 minute, stirring constantly. Remove from heat; cool completely. Stir in sugar substitute and coconut extract, if desired.

4. Combine pineapple, mango slices and banana slices in medium bowl. Spoon over baked crust; drizzle with pineapple juice mixture. Cover with plastic wrap; refrigerate 2 hours. Garnish with pineapple leaves, if desired.          *Makes 8 servings*

**Note:** The crust may be made 24 hours in advance, if desired.

**tropical fruit coconut tart**

# triple citrus cheesecake

**28 reduced-fat vanilla wafers, finely crushed**
**2 tablespoons margarine, melted and cooled**
**2 packages (8 ounces each) reduced-fat cream cheese, softened**
**1 package (8 ounces) fat-free cream cheeese, softened**
**½ cup sugar**
**2 tablespoons all-purpose flour**
**2 eggs**
**2 egg whites**
**2 tablespoons lemon juice**
**1 tablespoon lime juice**
**1 teaspoon vanilla**
**2 teaspoons grated lemon peel**
**1 teaspoon grated orange peel**
**1 teaspoon grated lime peel**
**Lemon slices (optional)**

1. Preheat oven to 350°F. Spray 9-inch springform pan with nonstick cooking spray.

2. Combine vanilla wafer crumbs and margarine in medium bowl until well blended. Press mixture onto bottom of prepared pan. Bake 10 minutes. Cool on wire rack. *Reduce oven temperature to 325°F.*

3. Beat cream cheeses, sugar and flour in large bowl with electric mixer at medium speed 1 minute or until fluffy. Beat in eggs, one at a time. Beat in egg whites, lemon juice, lime juice, and vanilla until just blended. Stir in lemon, orange and lime peels.

4. Pour mixture into prepared crust. Bake 30 to 35 minutes or until cheesecake is firm. Run knife around outside edge. Cool completely in pan on wire rack.

5. Cover and refrigerate at at least 4 hours. Remove edge of pan. Garnish with lemon slices.

*Makes 12 servings*

# recipe index

# general index

# METRIC CONVERSION CHART

## VOLUME MEASUREMENTS (dry)

1/8 teaspoon = 0.5 mL
1/4 teaspoon = 1 mL
1/2 teaspoon = 2 mL
3/4 teaspoon = 4 mL
1 teaspoon = 5 mL
1 tablespoon = 15 mL
2 tablespoons = 30 mL
1/4 cup = 60 mL
1/3 cup = 75 mL
1/2 cup = 125 mL
2/3 cup = 150 mL
3/4 cup = 175 mL
1 cup = 250 mL
2 cups = 1 pint = 500 mL
3 cups = 750 mL
4 cups = 1 quart = 1 L

## VOLUME MEASUREMENTS (fluid)

1 fluid ounce (2 tablespoons) = 30 mL
4 fluid ounces (1/2 cup) = 125 mL
8 fluid ounces (1 cup) = 250 mL
12 fluid ounces (1 1/2 cups) = 375 mL
16 fluid ounces (2 cups) = 500 mL

## WEIGHTS (mass)

1/2 ounce = 15 g
1 ounce = 30 g
3 ounces = 90 g
4 ounces = 120 g
8 ounces = 225 g
10 ounces = 285 g
12 ounces = 360 g
16 ounces = 1 pound = 450 g

## DIMENSIONS

1/16 inch = 2 mm
1/8 inch = 3 mm
1/4 inch = 6 mm
1/2 inch = 1.5 cm
3/4 inch = 2 cm
1 inch = 2.5 cm

## OVEN TEMPERATURES

250°F = 120°C
275°F = 140°C
300°F = 150°C
325°F = 160°C
350°F = 180°C
375°F = 190°C
400°F = 200°C
425°F = 220°C
450°F = 230°C

## BAKING PAN SIZES

| Utensil | Size in Inches/Quarts | Metric Volume | Size in Centimeters |
|---|---|---|---|
| Baking or Cake Pan (square or rectangular) | 8 × 8 × 2 | 2 L | 20 × 20 × 5 |
| | 9 × 9 × 2 | 2.5 L | 23 × 23 × 5 |
| | 12 × 8 × 2 | 3 L | 30 × 20 × 5 |
| | 13 × 9 × 2 | 3.5 L | 33 × 23 × 5 |
| Loaf Pan | 8 × 4 × 3 | 1.5 L | 20 × 10 × 7 |
| | 9 × 5 × 3 | 2 L | 23 × 13 × 7 |
| Round Layer Cake Pan | 8 × 1½ | 1.2 L | 20 × 4 |
| | 9 × 1½ | 1.5 L | 23 × 4 |
| Pie Plate | 8 × 1¼ | 750 mL | 20 × 3 |
| | 9 × 1¼ | 1 L | 23 × 3 |
| Baking Dish or Casserole | 1 quart | 1 L | — |
| | 1½ quart | 1.5 L | — |
| | 2 quart | 2 L | — |